D1593724

PRISONERS OF CONGRESS

Having thus remarked on your Proposal protesting our Innocence, We again repeat our pressing demand to be informed of the Cause of our Commitment, & to have a Hearing in the Face of our Country, before whom we shall either stand acquitted or condemned.

Mason's Lodge

Philad.ᵃ Sept.ʳ 8ᵗʰ 1777

Detail, Israel Pemberton et al., [Protest], "To the President and Council of Pennsylvania," September 8, 1777. After previous oral and written protests had gone unanswered, the twenty-two men irregularly arrested and then held in the Freemason's Lodge protested their "innocence," demanding to know the charges against them and to have a hearing "in the face of our Country before whom we shall either stand acquitted or condemned." Final page of manuscript petition with signatures of petitioners in MC 950–153, Quaker and Special Collections from Haverford College. Reproduced with permission from Haverford College.

PRISONERS OF CONGRESS

PHILADELPHIA'S QUAKERS

IN EXILE, 1777–1778

NORMAN E. DONOGHUE II

THE PENNSYLVANIA STATE UNIVERSITY PRESS
UNIVERSITY PARK, PENNSYLVANIA

Library of Congress Cataloging-in-Publication
Data

Names: Donoghue, Norman E., II, author.
Title: Prisoners of Congress : Philadelphia's
    Quakers in exile, 1777–1778 / Norman E.
    Donoghue II.
Description: University Park, Pennsylvania :
    The Pennsylvania State University Press,
    [2023] | Includes bibliographical references
    and index.
Summary: "Examines how and why the
    Continental Congress and Pennsylvania's
    newly elected leaders detained Quaker
    pacifists and exiled them to Virginia in
    1777–78"—Provided by publisher.
Identifiers: LCCN 2022061221 |
    ISBN 9780271095073 (cloth)
Subjects: LCSH: Society of Friends—
    Pennsylvania—Philadelphia—
    History—18th century. | Society of
    Friends—Virginia—Winchester—History—
    18th century. | Exiles—Pennsylvania—
    Philadelphia—History—18th century. |
    Exiles—Virginia—Winchester—History—
    18th century. | United States—History—
    Revolution, 1775–1783—Religious
    aspects—Society of Friends. | United
    States—History—Revolution, 1775–1783—
    Conscientious objectors. | Philadelphia
    (Pa.)—History—Revolution, 1775–1783. |
    Winchester (Va.)—History—18th century.
Classification: LCC E269.F8 D66 2023 |
    DDC 973.3088/2896—dc23/eng/20230118
LC record available at https://lccn.loc.gov
    /2022061221

Published by The Pennsylvania State University
Press,
University Park, PA 16802–1003

10 9 8 7 6 5 4 3 2 1

The Pennsylvania State University Press is
a member of the Association of University
Presses.

It is the policy of The Pennsylvania State
University Press to use acid-free paper.
Publications on uncoated stock satisfy
the minimum requirements of American
National Standard for Information Sciences—
Permanence of Paper for Printed Library
Material, ANSI Z39.48–1992.

Frontispiece. Israel Pemberton et al.,
[Protest] "To the President and Council of
Pennsylvania," September 8, 1777, detail,
manuscript document, QSC.

For my dearest Peggy O,
the light of my life

The most Dangerous Enemies America knows & such as have it
in their power to Distress the Country more than
all the Collected Force of Britain.
—Major-General John Sullivan, writing of the Quakers
to the Continental Congress, August 25, 1777

This day we were told that tomorrow was appointed for
sending us forward to Virginia & that notwithstanding
we had procured Writs of Habeas Corpus for the twenty
prisoners brought here, by which our Jailers are commanded
forthwith to bring us before [Chief Justice] Thomas McKean
for an examination into the grounds of our commitment,
yet they say they have positive Orders from the President &
Council to disregard the said Writs & that they shall Execute
their Orders, which are to convey us as soon as conveniently
may be to Winchester in Virginia. . . . We behold the daily
strides made over the Rights & Liberties of Men & the swift
advances towards absolute & Despotic Tyranny as the sure &
certain presages of the Downfall of such lawless Oppression.
—Henry Drinker to Elizabeth Drinker, September 18, 1777

Humanity pleads strongly in their behalf.
—George Washington to
President Thomas Wharton Jr., April 6, 1778

Treason . . . is of a most malignant nature;
it is of a crimson color, and of a scarlet dye.
—Pennsylvania Chief Justice Thomas McKean, 1778

CONTENTS

ILLUSTRATIONS

FIGURES

ACKNOWLEDGMENTS

As a novice author who had discovered an incredibly interesting and yet understudied story of the American Revolution, I considered myself quite lucky. As I progressed through the early research, I felt even more fortunate. At first, I needed confirmation that what I was finding was real, that my understanding of it was correct, and, most importantly, that my research and writing would bring new and better insights to the subject. Then, I needed suggestions for how best to organize the material and later help in recognizing and discarding distractions from the real story, sharpening the arguments, and allowing the inherent drama to show through. Thus, the need for nine years of work to bring it to fruition.

I am grateful to the many scholars who gave me encouragement as they volunteered to read and comment on my manuscript. They include Scott Paul Gordon, Lehigh University, my first reader and mentor; J. William Frost, Swarthmore College emeritus, my first expert on Quakers; Gary B. Nash, UCLA, a grand master of the profession who had already written thirty-two titles, many of them on the American Revolution (and particularly about Quakers); Richard Godbeer, Kansas University, author of a half dozen books about the seventeenth and eighteenth centuries, who coached me in the art of the crossover book; Patrick Spero, author as well as librarian and director at Benjamin Franklin's American Philosophical Society in the heart of the city where this all took place; Sarah Crabtree, San Francisco State University, author of *Holy Nation*; Richard C. Wiggin, author of a detailed study of revolutionary war soldiers from one town; Darrell W. Gunter, author and interviewer; and Timothy J. Boyce, a former law partner of mine and editor of a key Holocaust diary kept by Odd Nansen, *From Day to Day: One Man's Diary of Survival in Nazi Concentration Camps.*

I also reached out with success to other scholars: S. Spencer Wells (Southern Utah University), Mary V. Thompson (George Washington's Mount Vernon), Robert A. Selig, Professor Cassandra Good (Marymount University), Judge Stephanos Bibas (US Court of Appeals for the 3rd Circuit), Juliana Bibas, Judge Ronald P. Wertheim (Superior Court of the District of Columbia), Professor Philip Hamburger (Columbia University Law School), Professor Jane E. Calvert (University of Kentucky), Professor Emily M. Teipe (California State University, Fullerton), Kim Burdick (Hale-Byrnes House), and Sandra Hewlett, Certified Genealogist. I am deeply grateful to them all for the wisdom and professional guidance I received. I am also very grateful to the two anonymous peer reviewers who read my manuscript and saw in it what I saw (and more) and especially to the Pennsylvania State University Press acquisitions editor, Kathryn B. Yahner, who recognized in my work something valuable and led me so gracefully through the peer review process. Thanks to George W. Boudreau (University of Pennsylvania) for introducing me to Kathryn a second time.

Even before I met these substantial scholars, I excitedly recounted the story to my former law partners, Robert A. Cohen and Robert L. Freedman. Both listened attentively, questioned me intelligently, and gave me the constant encouragement I needed. Lifelong friend and scholar Jack Martens's work inspired me, as did the work of my late brother Bill Donoghue, an author of popular investment books (one of which made it on the *New York Times* Best Seller list). My nephew Jackson O'Donnell (then a fresh high school graduate, now a PhD student in physics) and my new friend Raquel Guzman, Esq., a busy general counsel, gave history a priority and read my work and picked through issues. I received early encouragement from literary agent Richard Morris of Janklow & Nesbit, for which I was and remain very grateful. I thank friend and noted collector John Connors (Penn Treaty Museum) for letting me tag along on his trip to Haverford College Library where I first saw, touched, and read the Henry Drinker–Elizabeth Drinker letters of 1777–78.

I give the most respectful bow to the institutions that kept this story alive in their archives: Quaker and Special Collections, Haverford College; Friends Historical Library at Swarthmore College; Historical Society of Pennsylvania; Chester County Historical Society; American Philosophical Society (with its integrated David Library of the American Revolution) and the Library Company of Philadelphia, both progeny of Benjamin Franklin; and the Handley Regional Library of Winchester, Virginia. Early in my research I attended the insightful 2014 Conference of Quaker Historians and Archivists, which met at Westtown School. There I learned of sources, soaked in the Quaker atmosphere, and met Thomas Hamm and Spencer Wells, who graciously encouraged me on occasion.

I owe a particular debt to my editorial consultant, Christina Larocco, PhD, whose firm hand steered me away from pitfalls and guided me on the proper path with her unerring historical and editorial judgment. She is a gifted scholar and a joy to work with.

For whatever is wrong or inaccurate about my book, I take full responsibility. Many other people, and you know who you are, contributed editing stints along the way or were at least willing to read or hear me ramble on about my obsession.

For constant support and a high tolerance for the habits of an aspiring author, and the love that makes it all worthwhile, I thank my dear, smart, and wise wife, Peggy O'Donnell, and my loving and smart children, Maya O'Donnell-Shah and Maggie Donoghue. I credit my parents, Norm and Betty Brumbaugh Donoghue, and my grandmother, Margaret Valentine Brumbaugh, with giving me the original inspiration for embracing American history as a major preoccupation, and my cousin David C. Sinding with sustaining it in recent pandemic years.

Thank you all for helping me be the one to tell this remarkable story of how a committed religious minority, through great suffering, struggled to define American values in the early republic and how the other Patriots struggled in opposition to save that same, hard-won republic from an early oblivion.

ABBREVIATIONS

AP	John Adams. *The Adams Papers, Diary and Autobiography of John Adams.* Edited by L. H. Butterfield. 4 vols. Cambridge, MA: The Belknap Press of Harvard University Press, 1963.
APS	American Philosophical Society
CRP	Samuel Hazard, ed. *Colonial Records of Pennsylvania.* 16 vols. Harrisburg, PA: Theo. Fenn, 1838–53.
DED	Elizabeth Sandwith Drinker. *The Diary of Elizabeth Drinker.* Edited by Elaine Foreman Crane et al. 3 vols. Boston: Northeastern University Press, 1991.
DTO	Sarah Logan Fisher. "'A Diary of Trifling Occurrences': Philadelphia, 1776–1778." Edited by Nicholas B. Wainwright. *PMHB* 82, no.4 (Oct. 1958): 411–65.
EV	Thomas Gilpin [Jr.], ed. and comp. *Exiles in Virginia, with Observations on the Conduct of the Society of Friends During the Revolutionary War, Comprising the Official Papers of the Government Relating to That Period, 1777–1778.* Philadelphia: privately published, 1848.
FHL	Friends Historical Library of Swarthmore College
FO	Founders Online. "Correspondence and Other Writings of Seven Major Shapers of the United States." National Archives. https://founders.archives.gov/.
HSP	Historical Society of Pennsylvania
JCC	Continental Congress. *Journals of the Continental Congress, 1774–1789.* Edited by Worthington C. Ford et al. 34 vols. Washington, DC: US Government Printing Press, 1904–37.
JHMM	Henry Melchior Muhlenberg. *The Journals of Henry Melchior Muhlenberg.* Edited and translated by Theodore G. Tappert and John W. Doberstein. 3 vols. Philadelphia: Evangelical Ministerium of Pennsylvania and Adjacent States, and the Muhlenberg Press, 1942–58.

KJV	The Holy Bible, Authorized (King James) Version
LDC	Paul H. Smith et al., eds. *Letters of Delegates to Congress, 1774–1789.* 25 vols. Washington, DC: Library of Congress, 1976–2000.
PA	Samuel Hazard et al., eds. *Pennsylvania Archives.* 118 vols. Harrisburg, PA: Theo. Fenn & Co., 1852–1935.
PGW	George Washington. *The Papers of George Washington.* Revolutionary War Series. Edited by Philander D. Chase et al. 23 vols. Charlottesville: University of Virginia Press, 1983–2016.
PMHB	*Pennsylvania Magazine of History and Biography*
PNG	Nathanael Greene. *The Papers of General Nathanael Greene.* Edited by Richard K. Showman. 13 vols. Chapel Hill: University of North Carolina Press, 1976–2015.
PYM	Philadelphia Yearly Meeting
QSC	Quaker & Special Collections, Haverford College
SEC	Supreme Executive Council of Pennsylvania
SLP	James T. Mitchell and Henry Flanders, comps. *The Statutes At Large of Pennsylvania from 1682 to 1809.* 14 vols. Harrisburg: State Printer of Pennsylvania, 1896–1915.
TCD	The Colonial Dames of America

The Quaker Exiles of 1777–1778, Their Nemeses, and the Women's Mission

THE QUAKER EXILES

Israel Pemberton, 62, merchant, former legislator, and Quaker activist, derisively
    called "King of the Quakers" and "King Wampum"
James Pemberton, 54, merchant, former legislator, and Quaker activist
John Pemberton, 50, merchant and minister
Samuel Pleasants, 41, merchant, married to Molly, daughter of Israel Pemberton
    Above: three brothers and a son-in-law
Thomas Fisher, 36, merchant, husband of diarist Sarah Logan Fisher
Samuel Rowland Fisher, 32, merchant
Miers Fisher, 29, merchant and lawyer
Thomas Gilpin Sr., 50, merchant and scientist, married to Lydia, sister of the
    Fisher brothers (Gilpin and the three Fishers were partners of Joshua Fisher
    and Sons; Joshua, elderly, took house-arrest parole to avoid exile, sent
    youngest son Jabez Maud Fisher to England to avoid harsh treatment.)
    Above: three brothers and a brother-in-law
Henry Drinker, 43, merchant, iron master, and husband of diarist Elizabeth
    Drinker
Thomas Wharton Sr., 46, merchant, first cousin to younger namesake president
    (see below) of Supreme Executive Council (SEC) of Pennsylvania
Edward Penington, 56, sugar merchant, brother-in-law of Samuel Shoemaker, who
    took house-arrest parole yet later served as a city magistrate under British
    General Sir William Howe
John Hunt, 65, British-born merchant and minister who moved to Philadelphia
    from London in 1760s
    Above are the twelve most prominent exiles, many of whom held leadership
        positions in the Philadelphia Yearly Meeting (PYM) of the Society of
        Friends in America. Wealthy and elite merchants, most owned carriages
        and had second homes in the countryside.

OTHER EXILED QUAKERS

Owen Jones Jr., 33, merchant, who was substituted by act of Timothy Matlack for
    his namesake elderly, ailing father, the last treasurer of the colony
Thomas Affleck, 37, Scottish-born cabinetmaker
William Smith, broker, 30s, merchant
Charles Jervis, 46, hatmaker, first cousin of Elizabeth Drinker
Charles Eddy, 23, ironmonger

DISOWNED FORMER QUAKERS AMONG THE EXILES

Elijah Brown, 37, aspiring merchant and debtor
William Drewet Smith, 27, apothecary

NON-QUAKER EXILE

Thomas Pike, 40s (estimated), British-born dancing master, equestrian, and
    instructor in the small sword

NEMESES OF THE QUAKER EXILES

John Adams, 42, Massachusetts delegate to Continental Congress, congressional
    committeeman, head of board of war, diplomat to France
Thomas Paine, 40, British-born author of *Common Sense* and *American Crisis*, his
    father a Quaker
Thomas Wharton Jr., 42, president of SEC, disowned former Quaker
George Bryan, 46, vice president of SEC
Colonel Timothy Matlack, 41, secretary of SEC, disowned former Quaker
Richard Henry Lee, 45, Virginia delegate to Continental Congress
Major-General John Sullivan, 37, Continental Army, former New Hampshire
    delegate to First Continental Congress
Colonel William Bradford, 56, Pennsylvania militia, printer, proprietor of London
    Tavern (Patriot haunt), highest-ranking officer in exiles' arresting party, lessee
    of exile John Pemberton
Chief Justice Thomas McKean, 43, first chief justice of Pennsylvania, 1777–1799

THE WOMEN'S MISSION MEMBERS

Susanna "Suky" Evans Jones, 57, mother of exile Owen Jr., wife of Owen Sr.
Mary "Molly" Pemberton Pleasants, 57, wife of exile Samuel, daughter of Israel,
    niece of James and John Pemberton, draftsperson with her stepmother Mary
    of the women's petition

Elizabeth Sandwith Drinker, 41, diarist, wife of exile Henry, first cousin of exile
   Charles Jervis, and former school classmate of Timothy Matlack
Phoebe Lewis Morton Pemberton, 39, third wife of James, mother of teenage
   diarist Robert Morton

INTRODUCTION

The last days of February 1778 brought rain, snow, hail, and ice to the frontier town of Winchester, Virginia, where a group of Quaker men had been held since their banishment from Philadelphia six months earlier. Forcibly torn from their families, friends, and useful lives, the eighteen remaining exiles—a dozen of whom were leaders in the Philadelphia Yearly Meeting (PYM) of the Religious Society of Friends and members of an elite cadre of transatlantic merchants—found comfort only by trudging several miles from their separate places of confinement (see map 2) through ugly winter weather to join together in worship. Illness proliferated, and relief was unlikely to arrive in time even for those exiles who, like Henry Drinker, suffered such relatively minor afflictions as "the Fever upon me, my head disordered with it, and a pain pretty constant a little above my left Groin."[1] Even if the presence of two armies between Winchester and Philadelphia had not prevented the free movement of individuals and goods, Henry noted that "the roads are likely to remain so deep & bad for a considerable time to come that we are discouraged from sending for many necessaries we are in want of."[2] On March 2, Thomas Gilpin, a fifty-year-old husband, father, milling entrepreneur, merchant, and scientist, whose invention of a hydraulic pump had delighted Benjamin Franklin, became the first of the Quaker exiles to die.

Days later, a second exile, sixty-two-year-old Quaker minister John Hunt, experienced a mortification of one leg. It had suddenly lost all utility. Doctors concluded that amputation was the only way to save Hunt's life. When it came time to perform the operation, the only surgeon available had a curious history of inebriation, and, unlike the pacifist Hunt, had served—as a general—in George Washington's army. Hunt survived the operation without anesthetic, and his condition briefly seemed to improve. He, too, however, would die before the month was out.

March 1778 represented the absolute nadir of the Quaker sect's ninety-six years of political life in Pennsylvania. After nearly a century as the pre-dominant cultural force in the colony and state, its members were out of office, out of influence, and out of business. Some struggled to survive out of their native state, where they were out of supplies and nearly out of luck. They were at the lowest ebb of their powers. Although in some senses they had never felt so helpless, the Quakers remained stalwart in their faith and strict in their religious principles. John Hunt, a pious man, had prepared himself for martyrdom. Still, he must have wondered as he lay dying how he and his coreligionists, who had not been accused of any crimes by either the Continental Congress or the Supreme Executive Council (SEC) of Pennsylvania, had ended up in this situation—and how it would end.

Politics and religion are a volatile combination—whether in 2023 or in 1777. The same is particularly true when individual civil liberties come into conflict with a perceived threat to national security. These conflicts are at the core of the narrative here. Long the preeminent power in Pennsylvania, in 1776 the Quakers found themselves out of step with revolutionary sentiments. Though the general population was well aware of their refusal to bear arms, to Patriot leaders, this minority religious sect now constituted a serious, persistent, and perhaps existential security threat to the new republic and the state in which they lived.

After Congress, in mid-August 1777, ordered Pennsylvania and Delaware to apprehend their disaffected Quakers, Major-General John Sullivan of the Continental Army sent a letter to Congress asserting strongly that if what he suspected was true, Quakers were "the most Dangerous Enemies America knows . . . Covered with that Hypocritical Cloak of Religion under which they have with Impunity So Long Acted the part of Inveterate Enemies to their Country."[3] With that letter full of dire accusations, he enclosed some papers—what came to be called the Spanktown Papers—confiscated from a suspected deserter. On the surface, the papers appeared to confirm his fears that Quakers were feeding military intelligence to the British. The timing, virulence, and look (with supposed tangible evidence) of Sullivan's accusations suggest strongly that these factors played a major role in Congress's unprecedentedly harsh actions against the Quaker leaders arrested in their wake.

In response, on September 11, 1777, the Second Continental Congress and the government of the newly organized state of Pennsylvania exiled twenty men. Seventeen of the exiles were Quakers. Their objections to the revolution and the war were sincere, religiously rooted, and courageous. Though they were never formally accused or convicted of any crime, the exiles were arrested and summarily banished—with no chance to be heard in their own defense—for over seven months to a frontier village in Virginia where prisoners of war were held in barracks (though the exiles would be housed separately). They were also stripped of traditional rights held sacred for centuries—particularly that bundle of rights embodied by habeas corpus, the right to be heard by an impartial judge and released if he found them to be illegally arrested (which the Quakers—Israel Pemberton and Miers Fisher, very knowledgeable in such matters—strongly believed was the case). In dealing with a perceived threat, Patriots seemingly betrayed the principles underlying their own rebellion against the British.

The Quaker exile was common knowledge in the years during and after the revolution. A significant swath of the populace avidly followed the exile and thought the banishment of the Quaker leaders appropriate. Today, however, few—even among scholars—have ever heard of it, and still fewer know fully why or how it happened. After two hundred and forty some years, no previous historian has ever written a comprehensive story of the Quaker exile. This book does that and thereby restores the Quaker exile to its unique and proper place within the literature of the American Revolution, deepening our understanding of the British Army's Philadelphia Campaign and the surprising strategies Patriots used to deal with the well-organized, contrarian Quakers. The book also addresses a comparatively understudied phenomenon that has received relatively little attention in the annals of Quaker history in America: What happened to the relatively small Quaker sect between their colonial dominance in Pennsylvania for nearly all of its first century and their later reemergence as nationally prominent leaders in nineteenth- and twentieth-century education, reform, abolition, and peace movements?

As *Prisoners of Congress* reveals, nascent ideas about the relationship between political dissent and national security determined the fate of the Quaker leaders in 1777. The exile represented one of the first times that Congress called for the arrest of a group of citizens of one religion who seemed to some to pose an existential national security threat yet had not been accused of committing any chargeable crime. Suspected Loyalists, sympathetic to the Crown and grateful for the support of the British Empire in their business ventures, the Quaker exiles endured a more than seven-month preventive detention in which they were held as political prisoners (likely the first in the new republic), though it took two centuries before someone applied that term to them.[4] Political prisoners are not an entirely unheard-of phenomenon in the American experience. For example, some woman suffragists in 1917 were arrested, convicted, and imprisoned more for their views than for actual misdeeds. Few, however, are aware that socially and commercially prominent, pacifist merchants in the former colonial capital could become the targets of the supposedly enlightened founding fathers during the American Revolution—and for their thoughts and speech, not for acts they committed. With this treatment, Congress adhered at first to a template established for removing out of harm's way former Crown officials who had committed no crime but were straddlers, neither Patriots nor overt, active Loyalists. Congress placed these men in states remote from their usual residence, away from the coast and post towns, making it harder for them to escape or communicate with outside forces. But Pennsylvania upped the ante. When the Quaker leaders protested their exile, Patriots also stripped them of their English common law and Pennsylvania constitutional rights, accomplished by a rare suspension of the privilege of habeas corpus, which protects individuals against an arbitrary government's overzealous confinement. Parliament had in earlier times passed such laws for the protection of autocratic, divine-right kings; during the revolution, it suspended habeas corpus for Americans captured on the high seas.[5] Such a suspension could even happen today: the United States Constitution allows it "when in Cases of Rebellion or Invasion the public Safety may require it." Far from a niche story, the Quaker exile is relevant to conflicts occurring today.

Led by John Adams, who had developed a strong bias against Philadelphia Quakers, the Second Continental Congress recommended scrutiny of the sect. Then, using as a pretext the Spanktown Papers, faked evidence of Quaker collusion with the British, Congress instigated the arrest and exile of men solely because they were Quaker leaders, arresting a few ordinary Quakers as a further act of intimidation. Equating Quakerism with suspected loyalty to the British Crown, Patriots determined the Quaker leaders constituted a serious threat to national security, though they claimed only that the Quaker leaders had an unspecified "correspondence and connection highly prejudicial to the public safety."[6] Pennsylvania's government had already placed the Quaker leaders on its own secretive hostiles list of men deemed "inimical to the cause of America."[7]

Once Congress acted, Pennsylvania rounded up the Quaker leaders and other suspected British sympathizers. At this point in time, between September 2 and 11, 1777, Philadelphia Quakers were situated at the virtual epicenter of the American Revolution, though historians have consistently portrayed them as quaint or curious but decidedly peripheral players in the revolutionary drama. On September 8, the Quaker leaders delivered a dramatic protest letter to Pennsylvania's executive requesting a hearing in their defense, a right usually afforded almost any defendant under English colonial law (see frontispiece, app. B). Pennsylvania refused, after which Congress reiterated its earlier refusal. On September 9, after spending nine hours debating the fate of the Quakers while the British Army marched toward the city from barely forty miles away, Congress denied the Quakers any hearing and ordered Pennsylvania to send them into exile. The congressional board of war, which would supervise their confinement, chose the location. The exiles were held in loose confinement on the frontier for over seven months.

Quakers had previously refused to bear arms during the French and Indian War (1754–63) two decades earlier. Not content with refusing to bear arms or swear oaths in the mid-1770s, most Quakers adamantly refused to participate in the common defense in more than a dozen documented ways, to the exasperation of military leaders. Quakers would not voluntarily pay any of the cost of the common defense of their city and state. They even refused, and this may have been a tipping point, the government's request that they donate blankets (for which compensation was offered) to comfort the soldiers who were sleeping in nearby camps. Quakers also continued to sing the praises of their history of prosperity within the British Empire, never evincing any interest in changing the colonies' status, certainly not in a violent way—all to the increasing anger and resentment of fellow citizens. In the run-up to the Revolutionary War, Quaker leaders self-righteously proclaimed that their entire body of some twenty-five thousand coreligionists in southeastern Pennsylvania were strictly neutral religious pacifists, yet as time passed, their neighbors found confusing the numerous instances where some Quakers acted to the contrary. During the British Army's sweep through the area, many civilians, including some Quakers and former Quakers, became active Loyalists, while others fought for the Continental Army or were elected or appointed to offices at the highest levels in the wartime Pennsylvania government. This book focuses on the treatment of people who rejected the government's admonitions to swear or affirm an oath of allegiance to the new republic. Despite claims of neutrality, Philadelphia Quakers leaned toward Loyalism, and between 1778 and 1781, nearly thirty Quakers were among the approximately five hundred people accused of high treason by the new state government. Generally, the legislature or the SEC (also referred to as the Council) of Pennsylvania issued these accusations through the ancient shortcut method of bills of attainder, a legal technique of proclaiming traitors by legislative fiat with names advertised in the newspaper. As a result of this visible Loyalism, many contemporaries cried hypocrisy and came to deeply mistrust all Quakers.

Politics and religion thus became entangled at the birth of the new republic, even in a state known as a haven for religious toleration. It happened even against a supposedly peaceable minority whose loyalties came under intense question, for quite understandable reasons, and never quite recovered. The great difficulty of staying true to founding principles while attempting to ensure the safety and security of civil society is a lesson from the eighteenth century that—amid questions of the global war on terror and cries of religious profiling—remains intensely relevant to the twenty-first century.

This book situates the exile amid the British Army's Philadelphia Campaign, a military exercise lasting from August 26, 1777, to June 18, 1778. Since June 1776, when the British fleet took New York Harbor, Philadelphia's residents had assiduously prepared for a similar incursion into their own territory. The Council of Safety, the SEC, and thousands of civilians collaborated to hide important documents, including the journals of the Continental Congress, and anything that the British could make into ammunition, such as the giant bell at the State House (Independence Hall). Quaker architect Robert Smith designed a clever series of chevaux-de-frise, submerged wooden beams with iron spikes sticking out, which blocked the mouth of the Delaware River. Smith, however, was an outlier. Quaker leaders urged Friends not to cooperate with what they saw as an illegitimate government, including in its preparations to defend the city and state from a powerful invader. Still, despite a defeat at the Battle of Brandywine and a subsequent eight-month occupation of its capital city (September 25, 1777–June 18, 1778), these careful preparations helped the American cause survive the Philadelphia Campaign. Holding Philadelphia also cost the British forces dearly elsewhere: by being there, General Sir William Howe placed his army beyond the reach of his subordinate General John Burgoyne, who was forced to surrender fifty-eight hundred troops at the Battle of Saratoga in upstate New York. Most importantly, despite his more experienced and better equipped troops, Howe was never able to deal a decisive blow to Washington and the Continental Army. As Benjamin Franklin reportedly observed from France, Howe had not captured Philadelphia; Philadelphia had captured him.[8]

Patriot leaders, of course, could not predict this outcome to the Philadelphia Campaign. This book demonstrates that the Quaker exile was a joint Pennsylvania state and congressional defensive strategy for dealing with the British Army's invasion of the Philadelphia area. Both bodies perceived the exile of Quaker leaders as a vitally necessary strategy against an *existential* threat. The narrative demonstrates what historian Gary B. Nash has called "the glorious messiness" of the American Revolution—something its participants knew well but that earlier historians preferred to sanitize. Even the founding fathers "experienced Revolution . . . as a seismic eruption from the hands of an internally divided people, two decades of problems that sometimes seemed insoluble, a gnawing fear that the course of the Revolution was contradicting its bedrock principles, and firsthand knowledge of shameful behavior that was interlaced with heroic self-sacrifice."[9]

The research for this book benefited from the many Quakers and others in Philadelphia who kept intimate records in diaries and correspondence, much of which survives today. In fact, the vast Quaker archive may be one of the finest bodies of resources available today to explore the experiences of men and women on the home front during the revolution. Archives at Haverford and Swarthmore Colleges, meccas for Quaker research, as well as the extensive resources at the Historical Society of Pennsylvania, the Library Company of Philadelphia, the Free Library of Philadelphia, and the American Philosophical Society, which now includes the David Library of the American Revolution, opened for me the world of turmoil amid the nation's founding.

Within this story of political and literal warfare is a personal narrative, consisting of the stories of several of the individual exiles and their families. This narrative is focused principally on four families—the Drinkers, Fishers, Pembertons, and Gilpins—representative of twenty families whose primary breadwinner was confined on the frontier, two hundred miles from home. The most central to the story are spouses Elizabeth Sandwith Drinker, forty-two, and exile Henry Drinker, a merchant, forty-three. A significant portion of the narrative relies on the more than sixty-five unpublished letters exchanged by Henry and Elizabeth Drinker during the exile and her now famous diary, *The Diary of Elizabeth Drinker*, a three-volume publication of enormous value for the wealth of detail it reveals of everyday life before, during, and after a shooting war on their doorsteps.[10]

Elizabeth Drinker also played a crucial role in one phase of the story (see chaps. 12 and 13), the women's mission, that especially deserves to be better known. Toward the end of the exile, when the exiled men were ill and out of medicine, two had died, letters from loved ones were scarce, and there was little hope, Elizabeth Drinker and other women relatives of the Quaker men began to plan their own efforts to get the men released. Though the men of Congress and Pennsylvania state government had agreed to it in correspondence, they were dragging their feet. The Quaker women wrote their own petition, and four of them, at great risk, left their families and homes and traveled with no weapon of defense, no pass, and no guard to see General George Washington at Valley Forge and to Lancaster to see the Pennsylvania authorities (in their own self-exile from the capital city, then occupied by the British Army). At no point did they allow men to speak for them. Though the politicians—all men—resisted and avoided them, the Quaker women held their own, engaging in multiple negotiations with elected officials, and were amply rewarded. In particular, the women's visit with the commander in chief and his wife benefited from previously unknown aspects of George Washington's relationship to the exile. While many Patriots—Washington included—disparaged Quakers generally, he also raised his voice for the release of the exiled men.

The story also highlights the tensions over protections for civil liberties of Americans in wartime. Patriots who had fought for American rights against the oppressive British government (and who thought the privilege of habeas corpus essential for a free society) became for this minority religious sect the tyrannical oppressors, equal—at least three Quakers intimately involved with the exile claimed hyperbolically—to those of the Spanish Inquisition. This was the only time since Pennsylvania's founding as a colony in 1682 that the government suspended the right of habeas corpus, part of English law since the Magna Carta of 1215.[11]

When Pennsylvania suspended habeas corpus in 1777, English law held that it was legally appropriate to suspend these civil rights in times of invasion or rebellion but only for a limited time. In what I call the "darker strain" of English law, Patriots tested this royal prerogative in the American environment. Would it matter that this test led to the deaths of two Quaker leaders? Only in 1784, when the Pennsylvania Council of Censors found the suspension of habeas corpus to be a violation of the state constitution, did government authorities seem to fully think so.

Lastly, the book highlights two key eighteenth-century social networks. In the early stages of the war, 1774–76, the network of the radical Patriots of Pennsylvania prevailed. As the colonial administrative apparatus faced declining respect, quasi-governmental revolutionary committees pushed Quakers and others to comply with defensive requisitions, bullying and shaming them publicly throughout the war when they did not. In 1777–78, the extensive network of the PYM came to the fore. Though Patriots had first painted that network as a singular threat, its entire mid-Atlantic apparatus of meetings and sectarian reports supported the men in exile and eventually was instrumental in enabling the Quaker leaders to gain release. Hundreds of supporters served as couriers of letters and supplies, as lobbyists protesting to Congress and Pennsylvania, and as sources of news and general comfort.

While the Quaker social network carried a unified message, it harkened backward to the glorious, pioneering political framework of empire-aided Pennsylvania prosperity, whereas the Patriot message looked forward to the promise of self-government and to the developing sense of being American. It is no small miracle that, though not constituting a majority of the American population, the Patriots developed a political message that seized public imagination and won the day. But this effective narrative produced collateral damage.

Only two previously published books are devoted solely to the Quaker exile. Historians of the revolution have tended to see the episode as a Quaker story: quaintly curious but without broader interest or import. Other accounts have downplayed the cruelty of the exile, almost to the point of apologism. In 1976, amid bicentennial celebrations of American patriots, a joint publication by the American Philosophical Society, Historical Society in Pennsylvania, and Library Company of Philadelphia claimed that the exiles "were not ill-treated. . . . They were not confined, were adequately housed and fed, and were allowed to send and receive letters and have visitors. . . . In April 1778, without having been tried on any charge, the 'exiles' were allowed to return home to Philadelphia."[12] Nothing in this summary is factually inaccurate: the exiles were not physically abused, and they received far better treatment than "ordinary" prisoners. Yet this description fails entirely to capture the emotional tenor and political significance of the exile for either the Patriots who enacted it or the men who endured it. Today, as a much-changed America prepares to observe over the next few years the 250th anniversary of the nation's founding events, the time is right for a franker as well as a fuller, more nuanced look at this complex episode full of such legal, religious, and political significance and redolent of so many aspects of the revolution as a whole.

Quaker historians have also paid scant attention to the exile, conversely because it shines a harsh light on their sect's leaders at a crucial moment in the nation's history, when many others were critical of and distrusted the sect. It is thus unsurprising that the only two books to focus entirely on the exile are a collection of primary documents and a novel. The first to appear was *Exiles in Virginia, with Observations on the Conduct of the Society of Friends During the Revolutionary War, Comprising the Official Papers of the Government Relating to That Period, 1777–1778* [. . .]. This privately printed and distributed volume was published for subscribers in 1848, compiled and edited by Thomas Gilpin Jr., the namesake son of one of the Quaker exiles who died during the exile. *Exiles in Virginia* presents government documents related to the exile alongside excerpts from the diary entries of the Quaker leaders. Thomas Jr. sought to demonstrate that the Quaker leaders had not committed any treacherous acts but rather were religiously pacifist, nonpolitical men on whom a grave injustice had been perpetrated. Gilpin's book glorifies the principled stand of most of the Quakers, attributes no political motives to them, and ignores the broader context and legitimate criticisms Patriots leveled against Quakers. *The Virginia Exiles*, a novel published in 1955 by Elizabeth Gray Vining, a convinced (converted) Quaker, sticks very close to the narrow facts of the exile, ignoring the larger context of the war, while adding a new character and a youthful romance. The exile also appears in books dedicated to the Quaker experience in colonial and/or revolutionary America, and it has been the focus of several journal articles, none ever attempting to plumb its depths.[13]

No previous historian has treated the Quaker exile of 1777–78 holistically in a monograph. This first book-length, nonfiction treatment of the exile since 1848—and the very first monograph—corrects this oversight. None of the existing literature, moreover, answered my questions about the exile. For these reasons, I felt it necessary to bring to the reader a broad range of Quaker-Patriot interactions in the greater Philadelphia area during the two years in question. I found that, simply put, the Continental Army and the Pennsylvania state government had what they considered, justly or not, to be a second adversary: a small but significant portion of the highly organized, tightly disciplined Quaker populace. Their knowledge of Philadelphia affairs and well-known antipathy toward the new government seemingly threatened to undermine efforts of elected leaders during a critical time. If they were wooed or tortured by the British, would members of this group divulge precious secrets or wittingly or unwittingly aid them in other ways?

In the face of an impending invasion, Quakers and other dissenters seemed to pose a real threat. The exile responded to this threat in several ways: it kept the Quakers away from both the Americans and the British, reducing contacts that could produce plots to impede the defense of the city. As a form of intimidation, it dissuaded others among their cohort from activities that could harm the American cause but without doing any intentional violence or incurring significant public expense. The exile was also a tactic intended to humiliate the Quaker leaders and perhaps intimidate other, particularly younger, Quakers into questioning their leaders. These men were political conservatives who valued established good order, and they were commercial titans and civic stalwarts accustomed to respect and privilege. By depriving them of this stature, the exile was perfectly aligned with the many shaming exercises of the earlier years of committee rule, which were characterized by frightening vigilantism that seemed to yield no deaths but sent a chilling message to pacifist dissenters.

Most importantly, the exile was a forced confinement that flagrantly disregarded traditional due process. Kings through the centuries had deployed this tactic in times of rebellion or invasion. Ironically, in their fight against parliamentary and monarchical oppression, Patriots adopted legal tactics that had previously buttressed autocratic rule.

Laden with questions about the relationships among religion, the citizen's duties to government, and civil liberties during wartime, the exile appears in hindsight as both a cautionary tale and an unfortunate precedent for future generations of Americans. This episode was not the only time when the government held members of a minority group in an internal exile (the internment of Americans of Japanese ancestry during World War II provides an imperfect analogy), arrested them in violation of their free speech rights (woman suffragists starting in 1917), accused them of being threats to national security (the Second Red Scare of the late 1940s and early 1950s), suspended habeas corpus (the Civil War), or simply seemed to take arbitrary and unnecessary action (examples abound). History suggests that the exile will continue to hold relevance, and now with an enhanced understanding of its many landmarks, join other examples of the complicated messiness and near miraculous success of the American Revolution.

The writing of this book emerged organically from my life. I grew up in rural Edge's Mill, in Caln Township, and West Chester, both in Chester County, and in Philadelphia, Pennsylvania, in all of which I was surrounded by the remnants of Quaker cultural dominance, their meetinghouses, and their excellent schools. Christian reformers persecuted in England since the sect's founding in 1647, Quakers have deeply influenced Pennsylvania since William Penn's arrival in 1681. For my first six years, in idyllic Edge's Mill, I lived in an eighteenth-century stone house. Quakers lived nearby. I napped on the hard benches at the Downingtown Friends Meeting preschool in 1950. Later, in West Chester, a sign was posted at the entrance to our small town, "West Chester Welcomes Thee." The town boasted two Quaker meetinghouses (one Orthodox and one Hicksite, from an 1820s schism), each within a block of my home. Classmates included both Quakers and those descended from Quaker families. I also attended summer tennis camp held at the nearby Westtown School, a Quaker mainstay.[14] The edge of our town bordered the bucolic landscape where the Battle of Brandywine took place in 1777 in the fields surrounding Birmingham Friends Meetinghouse, in whose cemetery soldiers of both sides were buried. Later, as a lawyer at the Dechert LLP firm in Philadelphia, I had several Quaker clients. In addition, my law partners included among them some men descended from as many as ten generations of Quakers. One of our daughters attended Friends Select School, and the second attended The Shipley School, originally founded by three Quaker sisters. Recently, I discovered that a former legal colleague is directly descended from one of the exiles, and a former high school classmate is descended from two Quaker exiles, Israel Pemberton and his son-in-law Samuel Pleasants.

The real key to my finding the Quaker exile, however, was my maternal fourth great-grandfather, Jacob Brumbaugh (1726–1799). He was a successful German immigrant farmer and member of the pacifist German Baptist Brethren sect in Hagerstown, Maryland. He introduced me (metaphorically) to the Quaker exile by buying land tracts in rural Pennsylvania in the years from 1786 to 1799 from Philadelphia Quaker merchant Henry Drinker and his wife, Elizabeth. On August 23, 1803, Brumbaugh's son showed up at the Drinker home in Philadelphia to pay off the remainder of the mortgage and was invited in for breakfast, thus meriting a mention in both Henry's account books and Elizabeth's diary.[15] These connections led me to learn more about the Drinkers, central figures in this story, by and about whom much has been written recently.[16]

Despite being an avid reader of history with a lifelong interest in Quakers, the story of the Quaker exile never came to my attention until, when I turned fifty, I first read of it in Catherine Drinker Bowen's memoir, *Family Portrait*. She related that her father, also Henry Drinker (1850–1937), a brilliant lawyer and engineer, president of Lehigh University, and an Episcopalian, was descended from an eighteenth-century namesake Quaker, Henry Drinker (1734–1809). To Bowen's father's great chagrin, this earlier Henry Drinker had been exiled from Philadelphia to Virginia, Bowen wrote, "for refusing to bear arms in the Revolution."[17] This statement took my breath away. I knew immediately that her explanation was seriously incomplete. The contemporaries of eighteenth-century Quakers knew and accepted that sect members refused to bear arms; they were not naïve about Friends' more complex motives. And why to Virginia? This offhand mention piqued intense curiosity, which I stored away. Fifteen years later, now retired from law and fundraising, I went with a friend to visit the Quaker collections at Haverford College's Magee Library, where I first held in my hands the letters that Henry and Elizabeth Drinker had exchanged in 1777–78. I was hooked. As I read further, I realized that my background as a lawyer would facilitate a new—and necessary—resurrection and reappraisal of these seminal events. For the last nine years, I have been determined to tell this unique and important story, so rich with revelations of the country's founding years and the nascent values, on both sides, taking hold in the new republic.

The times covered by this book, roughly 1774 to 1778, were full of turmoil, violence, and partisan clashes, while the Quakers sought calm, quiet spaces in which to contemplate their inward light and recall their prosperous past governing the colony. They had forged William Penn's "holy experiment" as the rare religious sect whose members actively governed a populous, diverse civil society, but now their political power was in free fall, its end in sight.[18]

The way forward for pacifists during a war is never easy. In 1777, the static vision of the Quaker leaders was resisted by articulate men like John Adams and Thomas Paine seeking to throw off the yoke of royalty and colonial masters and create a new way of governing. In this setting, the democratic republic created by the revolution called for a vigilant, active, and well-informed citizenry. At the same time, Quaker leaders called for their coreligionists to cease participation in this process because of a biblical prohibition against tearing down and setting up governments, but they, too, promoted lasting American values, enshrining healthy skepticism and respectful protest against governmental overreach in the fabric of the new nation. Eighteenth-century efforts of the founding fathers and thousands of others to establish the foundations of liberty and freedom and the necessary norms of democratic and republican behavior seem not unlike the efforts required today to sustain the nation's governmental framework in support of cherished institutions, values, and freedoms.

Chapter 1

QUAKER REBELLION

In November 1776, four short months after the Continental Congress approved the Declaration of Independence, Philadelphia's Council of Safety ordered its agents to collect from "the Housekeepers of this City . . . as many Blankets and woolen Stockings as each Family can spare, for the Use of the American Army, and if any person shall be *so Insensible to the distresses of our Countrymen now in the* [military] *service, and to the dictates of Humanity*, as to refuse, or anywise withhold them, you are to make use of proper force. You are to pay a reasonable price for the Blankets and stockings so taken."[1] Soldiers employed in the common defense were in dire need of blankets and woolen stockings so they could sleep in warmth, all the better to fight harder the next day.

This seemingly simple request earned the ire of a once powerful force in the city: the Religious Society of Friends, or Quakers. A wealthy Philadelphia Quaker in her mid-twenties and pregnant, Sarah Logan Fisher turned down eight government agents who came to her door requesting blankets in November 1776. "They took two [blankets] by force," she bitterly recorded in her self-described "diary of trifling occurrences."[2] Sarah's thirty-six-year-old merchant husband, Thomas; two of his brothers, thirty-two-year-old Samuel Rowland Fisher and twenty-nine-year-old Miers Fisher; and their brother-in-law, Thomas Gilpin—all prominent transatlantic merchants—were among the Quakers exiled from the city the following year. The Fisher brothers were a study in contrasts: Thomas was cool, efficient, and resourceful; Samuel was curmudgeonly, obstinate, and stubborn; and Miers was studious and active. Gilpin was an earnest and observant tinkerer, constantly devouring new knowledge. Sarah's friend Elizabeth Drinker, whose worka-holic, pious, and brilliant husband, Henry, was also exiled, recorded in her diary that she, too, refused an attempted requisition on June 5, 1777, when "an officer and 2 constables called on us for Blankets, went away without any—as others had done 3 or 4 times before."[3]

Quaker opposition to war requisitioning came from above: the PYM had made clear its opposition to "ordinances compelling them to participate in the war effort" applied even to the collection of blankets from its mem-bers' homes.[4] The executive or policy-making committee of the Religious Society of Friends, called the Meeting for Sufferings, reported to the mem-bership on the damages that their members had suffered so far in the war, including "by having blankets taken from them on account of their non-compliance with a requisition that was made for a number of blankets."[5] But though Quaker policy came from its Meeting for Sufferings, its mani-festations depended on the day-to-day decisions of such individuals as Sarah Logan Fisher, Elizabeth Drinker, and thousands of their coreligionists, who were forced to stake out a position rebelling against local government amid a larger rebellion of the thirteen colonies against British rule.

On May 17, 1777, General Philip Schuyler sent to the prominent Quaker minister and future exile John Pemberton a polite, respectful, and even gen-erous letter. Schuyler freely acknowledged the Quakers' pacifism. Yet he noted that the Society of Friends had "on many Occasions exercised their Benevolence to Soldiers by making Contributions of Clothing & provision to them & by affording them medical Relief when in Sickness, [and] I can-not entertain a Doubt but that the same Humane principle continues to influence their conduct." Schuyler requested "an immediate Supply of one thousand Blankets . . . for the purpose of covering Soldiers, who are braving the Rigours of a Campaign & hazarding their Lives." Soldiers did so, Schuy-ler emphasized, so that all Americans, Quakers included, could enjoy their inherited civil and religious rights, and the government offered compensa-tion for this service. Schuyler "entertain[ed] the fullest Confidence that a Request so reasonable in Its Nature and affording to the Friends an Oppor-tunity of evincing their Humanity and Patriotism would meet with a cheer-ful Compliance."[6]

When Schuyler learned that John Pemberton was out of town, he sent a copy of the letter to John's elder brother, Israel, whom non-Quaker Patriots referred to as "King of the Quakers" or "King Wampum" for his closeness to and profitable trade with Native Americans (figure 1).[7] The tall, hawk-nosed,

FIG. 1 | Detail of a 1764 political cartoon ridiculing Quaker government and hypocrisy by depicting Israel Pemberton (1715–1779)—dubbed "King Wampum" for trading with Native Americans—with a supposed moral flaw (i.e., carnal desire for Native American women). Delegates from several states picked up on the general disdain for Pemberton, a vocal and organizational mainstay of the PYM for decades. "An Indian Squaw King Wampum spies. [. . .]" cartoon [Bc 612 D32a], Historical Society of Pennsylvania. Reproduced with permission from the Historical Society of Pennsylvania.

meddling, and quarrelsome Israel would not have made a more receptive audience to this request than did his reserved, pious, and righteous brother. The third Pemberton brother, James, was no less self-assured, though his talent for language may have lent itself to a more artful or diplomatic response. Israel replied to Schuyler that the members of the meeting had refused to cooperate. Schuyler made one more attempt, averring in a second letter to Israel Pemberton that he respected the society's religious liberties but insisting that the very survival of the new nation was at stake. Again, Quakers bluntly refused to comply.[8] Schuyler promptly related to General Washington the Quakers' refusal, insisting to the commander in chief that he was "determined if they do not voluntarily afford us a thousand [blankets], to make Use of coercive Measures."[9] There is no indication he ever did so, but "coercive Measures" quickly became an understatement.

To the American soldiers collecting blankets, these refusals might have seemed like a petty and silly irritation. And maybe their consequent thefts of blankets in retaliation were equally petty. It could also have expressed a wider phenomenon, though—the growing disdain that the radical Whigs, who in the summer of 1776 had taken control of the Patriot government in Pennsylvania, felt for the once venerated and quietly powerful Quakers. Though the Patriots in Philadelphia understood and tolerated the pacifist Quakers' refusal to bear arms, such refusals would no longer be tolerated without serious consequences. For the Quakers, it had been a steep fall from political hegemony to persecuted dissent.

Pennsylvania had a very strong and deep Quaker influence dating back to the colony's founding in 1682. Self-professed Christian reformers, members of the Religious Society of Friends believed that all human beings, including Native Americans and enslaved Africans, possessed an inward light: a sign that God spoke to them and offered all individuals the possibility of salvation for their sins. "Quakers" was an epithet given them by an English judge to whom founder George Fox had explained that, when they heard the words of their Lord read aloud, they "trembled and quaked."[10] The name caught on quickly, and though derisive in origin and tone, members of the sect have long accepted it in common parlance, though they much prefer to be called "Friends."

Pacifism and nonviolence played a central role in the religious faith of Quakers. In 1660, in the first corporate statement of the Quaker peace testimony, Fox taught that "Wars and Fightings proceed from the Lusts of men (as James 4:1–3 [KJV]), out of which Lusts the Lord hath redeemed us. . . .

We . . . do utterly deny, with all outward Wars, and Strife, and Fightings with outward Weapons, for any end, or under any pretense whatsoever . . . the spirit of Christ which leads us into all Truth will never move us to fight and war against any man with outward Weapons. . . . We cannot learn War anymore."[11]

In the second half of the seventeenth century, the English government imprisoned and tortured hundreds of Quakers and even executed a few hundred.[12] When King Charles II of England transferred to Society of Friends member William Penn, in payment of a debt to Penn's father, a proprietary interest in a large swath of heavily timbered land in North America, many Quakers chose to follow Penn. Penn intended the colony to be a holy experiment of official religious toleration and individual freedom, concepts his fellow Quakers—but not everyone—embraced. He and his followers hoped to show others that a government following Quaker principles could produce peace and prosperity on a large scale.[13] Penn's 1701 constitution, or Charter of Privileges, codified the principle of freedom of conscience in the colony and guaranteed it *forever*, a promise to which the Quakers alone clung tightly. Once refugees from British injustice, during the American Revolution many Quakers nevertheless retained their faith in the British government.

Recalling their sect's treatment in England, Quakers in Philadelphia never uncritically accepted the authority of the British government—or any government.[14] Anticipating American colonists' rejection of parliamentary authority, as early as the 1690s, Quakers disputed English taxes on the colony.[15] As Jane E. Calvert maintains, "Quakers had cultivated a culture of dissent and resistance to what they perceived to be arbitrary authority."[16] Yet by the 1740s, Quakers' commitment to pacifism put them at odds with prevailing colonial sentiments. Starting in that decade, in an effort to purify the membership, the Religious Society of Friends in America disowned those among them who violated the central tenet of pacifism, among others. Disownment was an involuntary termination of membership in the meeting; thereafter, the former member could no longer attend business meetings but could, and often did, continue to attend meetings for worship and could remain eligible to be buried in Quaker burial grounds. Pacifism also caused the majority of Quakers in the Pennsylvania Assembly (the colonial legislature) to resign during the French and Indian War rather than taint their public service with preparations for war.

Quaker views on nonviolence were not entirely consistent. Quakers criticized men on the frontier for killing peaceable Native Americans, but when in 1764 the Paxton Boys threatened Philadelphia, dozens of Quakers with muskets, including future exile Edward Penington, joined in defense of the city. Some Presbyterians accused the Quakers of hypocrisy or at least of having limits to their commitment to nonviolence, as these men were never disciplined for violating the sect's own general refusal to bear arms.[17] This leniency, however, was an aberration. Since the sect's beginnings, Friends' duties to their God were always on a higher plane than, and so often in conflict with, their duties to temporal governments. This aspect of their religious practice intensified as they disowned lax members, leaving behind only the strictest of their own adherents.

Although they had not arrived in Pennsylvania wealthy, the Quakers prospered in their first century there. The area quickly became a hub of commercial farming and transatlantic exchange.[18] Prominent merchants—many of them Quakers—converted molasses and sugar to rum, and flour and wheat to bread, all to be transported abroad by ships they owned and operated. With profits from the foregoing, Quaker merchants bought from their coreligionists and others English-manufactured goods of all kinds for sale throughout the colonies. Nearly all the most prominent Quaker merchants owned carriages, which signified wealth: as of 1772, there were only eighty-four carriages in the city, 43 percent of which were owned by Quakers.[19]

Prosperous Quaker merchants, trading in large, wholesale businesses in far-flung international trade, often employing dozens if not hundreds of persons, had been among the leaders in the colonial opposition to Parliament over the Stamp Act in 1765 and even later protested vigorously in response to the partial repeal of the Townshend Acts.[20] Of the seventeen Quakers who would be exiled, eight or nine had endorsed the Philadelphia traders and merchants' nonimportation agreement protesting the 1765 Stamp Act. Israel Pemberton, James Pemberton, Samuel Pleasants, and Thomas Wharton, along with intended exile Owen Jones Sr., each signed. Abel James signed for James and Drinker, his firm with Henry Drinker, and Joshua Fisher signed for the firm he ran with Thomas, Samuel, and Miers Fisher. But when these men saw the conflict move away from economics and trend toward war and a violent break with England in 1774, they began to step back from further political involvement, or leadership, just as they had at the outbreak of the French and Indian War in 1756.[21]

Over the previous two decades, a sea change had taken place in the political control of Pennsylvania's Assembly, and religious and ethnic rivalries were central to it. Quakers and Anglicans had immigrated to the area first and acquired wealth and power. The Scots Irish and Germans arrived later. Since 1756, when Quakers stepped back from government, they had allied themselves with Anglicans to control about 75 percent of the seats in the legislature over the ensuing years. By 1776, however, the number of Presbyterians—mostly Scots-Irish—in the legislature had risen to 68 percent. Allying themselves with Lutherans and Reformed representatives to hold a combined 90 percent of seats, Presbyterians effected a stunning reversal of power in the state. Quaker Speaker of the House John Jacobs, berated by coreligionists for tainting himself through proximity to war, resigned and was replaced by John B. Bayard, a Presbyterian.[22] According to historians Wayne L. Bockelman and Owen S. Ireland, English and Welsh Quakers lost almost all influence.[23] The trend continued in 1778 and thereafter as the Scots-Irish Presbyterians consolidated power.[24]

Until 1775, the Quakers, though only 15 percent of the population in Pennsylvania, still constituted nearly 50 percent of the Assembly.[25] The sect remained especially influential in Philadelphia, and by the time of the revolution the sect's regional governing body, the PYM, boasted more members and held more influence than any other Quaker institution on the continent. Despite their minority status, by nearly all measures, Quakers were still a dominant factor in the culture of Pennsylvania.[26]

Pennsylvania was unique among the states of the new republic in that it had numerous pacifist religious sects that operated within its borders. Quakers were by far the largest group of religious pacifists in Pennsylvania. The sect comprised about twenty-five thousand individuals in southeastern Pennsylvania, while members of all the other pacifist sects in the state totaled only approximately ten thousand individuals.[27] Moreover, while many Quakers were wealthy and urban, the other sects were mostly rural agrarians, though Mennonites counted many wealthy farmers among their numbers, especially in Lancaster County. Not all were rural: Christopher Saur II of Germantown, who owned a German-language printing and publishing dynasty, was one exception. An urban intellectual and political neutral who served as a German Baptist Brethren bishop, Saur, fifty-five in 1776, was just handing over his business to his twenty-two-year-old namesake son, an active Loyalist who joined and strategized for the British Army in 1777–78 and after.[28]

All of Pennsylvania's religious sectarians were opposed, in varying degrees, to participation by their members in war, to bearing arms or joining the militia, and to the taking of oaths of allegiance. Mennonites, however, agreed to pay "commutation money" to the government and, following the biblical prescription to render unto Caesar what was Caesar's, to pay taxes, all the while considering themselves nonviolent. They had petitioned the Pennsylvania Assembly in November 1775, promising to feed the hungry and give drink to the thirsty and pray for both sides. In practice, they also loaned their horses and wagons to the army as well. Moravians, a highly structured and organized German sect, allowed their members to hire substitutes or pay taxes to buy freedom from military service. They also agreed under some duress to allow the government to use their facilities as hospitals (at Bethlehem and at Lititz) for the wounded, and several of their members died from diseases contracted from soldiers to whom they had to render medical care. The Moravians had a good relationship with Henry Laurens, the president of Congress, who valued John Ettwein, their erstwhile leader. Often the church itself paid fines for its members to avoid military service on the ground that it was a "common concern."[29]

The tiny Schwenkfelder sect, which originated in the German province of Silesia, also refused to bear arms. It did not penalize members who paid a substitute or loaned a wagon or a team of horses to the army. It paid militia fines from a common fund. In the end, one of its members could write to his friends back in Germany that the Schwenkfelders "got through [the Revolutionary War] easier than others that also did not resort to the use of arms."[30]

The Church of the Brethren, also called German Baptist Brethren, or more popularly, Dunkers, originated in Schwarzenau, Germany. Its members were mostly rural farmers whose home churches kept few if any records, numbered a few hundred, and held as denominational principles that they would neither bear arms nor swear or affirm any oath of allegiance. The Brethren would, however, follow the Mennonite example, joining in their petition in 1775 and sharing their position in paying the substitute tax and regular taxes and feeding the hungry and offering drink to the thirsty.[31] An offshoot of the Dunkers, the German Seventh-Day Baptists at Ephrata Cloister in Lancaster County, a small, monastery-like community, were required by the Continental Army to care for about five hundred wounded American soldiers from the Battle of Brandywine in September 1777. Many of the religious caregivers died of disease in that service.[32] Patriots closely watched printers Christopher Saur II and III, Dunkers who were potentially the most harmful to their cause.

This group of pacifists—Mennonites (which include Amish), Moravians, Schwenkfelders, and Dunkers—had coordinated a policy of resistance to military measures with the Quaker leaders periodically since at least 1748. During the revolution, this alliance was held together by the Saurs and their press. When Quakers published a testimony or manifesto during the revolution, they simultaneously printed hundreds of copies in the German language.[33]

In the early years of the war, the government monitored these groups' compliance or noncompliance with the Militia Act, the Test Act, and other requisitions, separating them out and targeting them for special scrutiny. Patriots occasionally engaged in ad hoc public jeering or shaming of the pacifists, but there were no concerted or widespread efforts to intimidate or punish them at this time. The Quakers of the PYM, by contrast, were considerably less compromising in their approach to war than were the German sectarians. Combined with their greater numbers, their wealth and prominence, and their long history of wielding political power, this intransigence would expose Quakers to especially harsh punishment.

Revolutionary War violence first broke out in New England in 1775, but it quickly spread to the mid-Atlantic. By the fall of 1776, the British occupied New York City, which they held until 1783. British sorties into New Jersey late in 1776 ignited fears of an imminent invasion of Philadelphia. Congress even moved to Baltimore, Maryland, from December 1776 to February 1777. As a precaution, General Washington cooperated with the Council of Safety, a temporary governmental authority composed of local Patriots, to place General Israel Putnam (a veteran of the Battle of Bunker Hill in 1775) in charge of Philadelphia until the risk of invasion temporarily subsided. The Council of Safety, headed by a disowned Quaker and middling merchant, Thomas Wharton Jr., was in charge of preparations for resistance to British authorities. While New York emerged as a safe haven for Tories behind British lines, Philadelphia in mid-1777 anxiously anticipated invasion as part of the next British campaign.

In 1776–77, most Philadelphians worked feverishly to prepare their defenses against a coming British invasion, which arrived in September 1777. Quaker leaders in Philadelphia, however, urged their coreligionists not to participate in these preparations, angering prominent Patriots. On July 16, 1776, not quite two weeks after and at a place only two blocks from the first public reading of the Declaration of Independence, Maryland troops marching to New York through Philadelphia forcibly broke into the Friends meetinghouse on Market Street and remained there for the night. The officer in charge of the soldiers did not deny Friends the right to use the building for Sunday worship, but the militia "retained possession of it."[34] This event confirmed a growing trend: between 1776 and 1778, both American and British military forces used more than a dozen Philadelphia-area Friends meeting-houses for quartering soldiers, as military hospitals, or for other purposes scores of times. On the American side, the Council of Safety mandated this intrusive use. (Other houses of worship were not so used, or, if they were, parishioners less grudgingly offered their premises.) In the plain Quaker meetinghouse, where silent worship was a staple and pacifism a fundamental principle, soldiers put down their weapons and other military gear for the night. No Quaker would have willingly allowed soldiers to camp in a meetinghouse. Refusing to be intimidated, Quaker worshippers insisted on having their First Day (Sunday) service at the meetinghouse anyway.

As the dispute with England erupted into violence, Quakers boldly proclaimed their disaffection toward the Patriot cause. Forty-three-year-old future exile Henry Drinker privately condemned the "arbitrary proceedings . . . [by] those that now exercise power," a phrase that he and other leading Quakers used often to imply the illegitimacy of the newly elected state government. A shipping and dry goods merchant and weighty Quaker committee member and activist, Drinker had long courted Patriot ire. In 1773, a fifty-man committee for tarring and feathering had pressured Drinker, business partner Abel James, and fellow exile Thomas Wharton Sr. to renounce their exclusive, lucrative commission to sell tea under the hated Parliamentary Tea Act. In addition to his participation in transatlantic trade, the self-conscious, needy, and vain Thomas Sr. was the cousin of Thomas Wharton Jr., who as president of Pennsylvania's SEC became one of the Quaker exiles' principal nemeses.[35]

In part because of statements like Drinker's that leaked to the public, contemporary non-Quakers thought the city was full of Tories or Loyalists. John Lansing Jr., an aide to assistant city administrator General Philip Schuyler, characterized Philadelphia in 1777 as "the asylum of the disaffected." He continued, "The very air is contagious and its Inhabitants breathe Toryism . . . Quakers in general are Wolves in Sheep's Clothing and while they shelter themselves under the pretext of conscientious Scruples [against bearing arms], they are the more dangerous."[36] Lansing's comments reflected a growing Patriot fatigue with the Quakers' official neutrality, which was tempered by sympathy toward Great Britain and obstruction of Patriots' defensive measures.[37]

Anger at the Quakers extended beyond the new government to include revolutionary intellectuals, most notably Thomas Paine. His revised edition of *Common Sense*, which added an "Epistle to the Quakers," borrowed the sect's own words to attack its commitment to the "happy connection we have

FIG. 2 | John Pemberton (1727–1795), a Quaker minister, merchant, landlord, and clerk of Quaker committees, was called a "traitor" by Thomas Paine in newspapers. He and John Hunt led the exiles' biweekly religious services, which the innkeeper and some of the public attended. Pemberton and Henry Drinker bonded during exile. Silhouette, David McNeely Stauffer Collection on Westcott's History of Philadelphia [#1095], Historical Society of Pennsylvania. Reproduced with permission from the Historical Society of Pennsylvania.

hitherto enjoyed with the kingdom of Great Britain." The same Quaker text quoted approvingly a 1696 directive "to pray for the king" and reaffirmed "our just and necessary subordination to the king." In the second and third installments of *The American Crisis*, Paine singled out the strict Quaker minister John Pemberton, the youngest of the three soon-to-be exiled brothers, as his particular target (figure 2). Though John was less openly political than his brothers, his role as clerk of the Philadelphia Quarterly Meeting (1755–77), the PYM's Meeting for Sufferings (1764–77), and the annual meeting of the ministers and elders (1766–82) conferred on him the responsibility to write and sign religious testimonies setting Quaker policy, even if the views expressed therein represented the consensus of his coreligionists. For example, Pemberton signed the December 1776 epistle to Quakers, which encouraged noncooperation with the war effort and condemned the Test Act. "If this be not treason," Paine wrote of the statement, "we know not what may properly be called by that name."[38]

Paine held Pemberton personally responsible for these statements, naming his nemesis four times in *Crisis*. The appropriate treatment of such individuals, Paine argued, was to "commit the signer [of the epistle] *together with such other persons as they can discover were concerned therein* into custody, until such time as some mode of trial shall ascertain the full degree of their guilt and punishment." By suggesting the committal of John Pemberton and the others, Paine either inspired or confirmed the plans local revolutionary leaders were already secretly devising.[39] Elsewhere, Paine invoked outrageous language—comparisons to "antiquated virgins"—designed to ridicule Quakers and make them a laughingstock. His writings were at their most popular in 1776 and 1777.[40]

In the eighty years in which they enjoyed virtual control of the colonial legislature, Quakers had never passed a militia law for the defense of the people (although some less direct accommodations had been made). By 1776, their political hegemony faced serious challenges. A newly elected Assembly, devoid of Quakers, demanded that members of the sect contribute equitably: those who did not serve in the militia were obligated to pay a substitute tax or a fine in proportion to their property.[41] This startling development shocked the Quakers clinging to Penn's 1701 Charter of Privileges, which had guaranteed forever their freedom of conscience, for which no payment was ever required.

The Council of Safety stated that "no excuse ought to be admitted or deemed sufficient against marching [as part] of the Militia at this time, except sickness, infirmity of Body, age, [or] Religious Scruples [etc.]."[42] Thus, it was clear that the Council of Safety and the populace at large fully recognized the Quaker peace testimony as a valid reason not to bear arms. In fact, Quakers' right not to bear arms was never seriously challenged, but the Patriots in Philadelphia determined for the first time in Pennsylvania history that pacifists should have to pay for that privilege. The Militia Act of March 17, 1777, required men either to serve or provide a substitute, or the money to pay a substitute, neither of which the Quakers could in good conscience do.[43] This was a controversy "at least as much about paying as about fighting."[44] The relative wealth of Quakers combined with their refusal to pay fines for not bearing arms exacerbated Patriot resentments.[45]

Patriots also decided that men in Pennsylvania should have to pledge their loyalty publicly. The Test Act of June 1777 required all white men over age eighteen to take a formal oath of allegiance, pledging fidelity to the newly organized state of Pennsylvania and also disavowing the authority of the king and Parliament.[46] Failure to comply with that law, though not in and of itself a crime, often resulted in the deprivation of such important civil rights as voting, buying and selling property, holding public office, and bringing lawsuits, though *never* by exile from the state. The aim of the radical Patriots who had gained governmental power in the state following the ratification of the constitution of 1776 "was to secure the overthrow of the Quaker government and block any dissent to the new rule." They disenfranchised those who would not subscribe to the test oath, which they well knew would be the case with the Quakers.[47] The sect had lost the right to vote in a political system its members had controlled for nearly a century.[48]

Quakers and Patriots also butted heads over the issue of slavery. While some Patriots painted the revolution as a movement "to free our countrymen in America from a compleat system of slavery," as one non-Quaker farmer's polemic put it, many Quakers were more concerned with literal slavery.[49] An excellent example is Quaker Daniel Byrnes, owner of a mill on White Clay Creek in Delaware (until 1776 part of Pennsylvania). In a published broadside of 1775, he boldly retorted to Patriot cries of freedom from British oppression: "What about those who are truly enslaved?"[50] This Quaker attitude toward the hypocrisy of Patriots' cries for freedom only intensified in 1776, when the Continental Congress averred in the Declaration of Independence that "all men are created equal and endowed with certain unalienable rights." Warner Mifflin, the premier Quaker abolitionist of the era, would later ask that Americans "live up to the inalienable rights clause of the Declaration of Independence by bringing slavery and the slave trade to an end."[51]

Quakers opposed slavery for the same reason that they opposed war: both involved violence by man against man. At its root, slavery, like war, violated the golden rule: do unto others as you would have them do unto you. The first Quaker petition against slavery—indeed, the first public document to protest slavery in North America—had been signed as early as 1688 in Germantown, just north of the city, sent by a preparative meeting of German American Quakers to the quarterly meeting. "We are against the traffick of men-body," its signers wrote.[52]

As the revolution approached, Quaker opposition to slavery grew. In 1774, the PYM resolved to disown any members who engaged in the slave trade.[53] The following year, Quakers formed what became the Pennsylvania Abolition Society, through which lawyers combatted slaveholders' overreach.[54] In 1776, the PYM resolved to disown members who continued to hold persons in bondage.[55] In Philadelphia, Quakers emancipated 343 enslaved persons between 1772 and 1790. In Delaware, Duck Creek Meeting (near Dover) members manumitted more than six hundred slaves, Warner Mifflin himself twenty-one and his father almost one hundred.[56]

Patriots took note of these actions. Broadside author Daniel Byrnes saw his home occupied and his crops seized by General Washington.[57] When Quaker Daniel Mifflin was fined for not serving in the military during the revolution, the sheriff secured the fine by other means: capturing and selling a boy whom Mifflin had previously enslaved.[58] Quakers were persecuted even for acts they did not intend as statements about the revolution. Mifflin complained, for example, of being persecuted simply for freeing his slaves: "Insinuations were also thrown out that my labor for the freedom of the blacks was in order to attach them to the British interest." The British governor of Virginia was offering freedom in exchange for service.[59]

By the summer of 1776, long-simmering tensions had collided with wartime exigencies. Council of Safety members began to sign warrants to arrest and secure those who were hostile to the new government without alleging the person had committed any crime. With no more than the charge of "being a Person strongly suspect[ed] of Practices Inimical to the States of America," they ordered commitment to the state prison.[60] The Council of Safety had also warned the disaffected, including Quakers, in a firm resolution of December 7, 1776, "that it is the opinion of this Board that every person who is so void of Honor, virtue and love of his Country, as to refuse assistance at this time of eminent public danger, may justly be suspected of designs Inimical to the Freedom of America . . . and such persons ought to be confined."[61] Patriots also began keeping a list of those persons not complying with their government's requisitions or other war measures, referred to herein as the hostiles list. The hostiles list eventually included hundreds of men.

Thomas Gilpin, another wealthy Quaker merchant, was among the first names on the hostiles list. Gilpin was a strict Quaker but of a cast different from many—from an early age he had an abiding interest in mathematics and science of all kinds. He was "a man of broad intellectual and scientific interests" who first surveyed the potential canal route between the Chesapeake and Delaware Bays in the 1760s, a feat of engineering that, with the aid of his son, reached fruition only in 1830.[62] He was at the same time involved in various economic activities, primarily milling, in Maryland and Delaware. A member of the elite American Philosophical Society, an organization founded by Benjamin Franklin in 1743 for the promotion of useful knowledge, he also prepared papers on insects, fish, and a hydraulic hand-pump for which Benjamin Franklin expressed delight. In 1764, Gilpin married Lydia Fisher, daughter of another hostiles lister, prominent merchant Joshua Fisher, and sister of the three later exiled Fisher brothers.[63] Patriot agents broke the locks on Gilpin's warehouse on May 10, 1777, and unsuccessfully searched his home and store for requisitioned goods hidden from Patriots.[64]

Quaker sufferings mounted through the summer of 1777. When the Patriots periodically declared a day of "fast," closing all places of business to celebrate the news of a victory in Boston or New Jersey, Quakers refused to participate.[65] As a matter of fact, they had never engaged in any such celebrations, even in colonial times.[66] On July 4, 1777, the first anniversary of independence, the city was illuminated, with Patriots everywhere placing lit candles in their windows. Quaker residents, however, believing since 1775 that the Patriots had illegally usurped the positions of the rightful British government, did not participate.[67] Sarah Logan Fisher's dark windows were conspicuous. That night, she and her husband had fifteen windows broken at their house; Quaker minister Nicholas Waln, fourteen; William Logan, also a Quaker, fifty panes or more.[68] Elizabeth Drinker recorded "a great number of Windows Broke" at her home.[69] As overzealous Patriots rioted outside his home, future exile Elijah Brown felt as if he were "in a *Jail*. . . . In an apartment in which my chambers were hourly woken by the clanking of chains and bolts & iron doors."[70] It was a scary night for this group of dissidents and their families.

On August 5, Henry Laurens, a delegate from South Carolina and soon to be president of the Congress, had written home about the Tories in Philadelphia. The "weak people" who had refused to illuminate their houses on July 4 would pay a price, he insisted. Laurens made clear even a month before the arrests that "some Steps have been taken by the Executive power to remove such Men from the Capital."[71] He undoubtedly referred to Pennsylvania's SEC (the Council of Safety's successor) and its members' growing plans to punish the men on the hostiles list by physically expelling them.

The exiled Quaker leaders—brothers Israel, James, and John Pemberton; the reserved Samuel Pleasants, Israel's son-in-law; brothers Thomas, Samuel Rowland, and Miers Fisher; the Fishers' brother-in-law, Thomas Gilpin; the punctilious, dignified sugar merchant Edward Penington; Henry Drinker; Thomas Wharton Sr.; and John Hunt—were prominent merchants and leading citizens from interconnected families who set the course for the PYM. They were all (except Hunt, who was a British immigrant) third-generation members of prominent, elite families. Five other exiles—Owen Jones Jr., young merchant; William Smith, broker (always referred to as "broker" to distinguish him from two other men of the same name); Charles Eddy, ironmonger; Charles Jervis, hatter; and Thomas Affleck, cabinetmaker—also belonged to the faith. Two others—Elijah Brown, failed merchant now deep in debt, and William Drewet Smith, pharmacist—had been disowned (the first for mismanaging debts, which reflected badly on the society, the second for marrying a non-Quaker). Only one exile, Thomas Pike, British immigrant, dancing master, and instructor in the use of the small sword, had never belonged to the Religious Society of Friends. None of the twenty exiles had been formally accused, let alone convicted, of any crime.[72]

Chapter 2

QUAKER REFUSALS

Historians and casual observers alike have often reduced the conflict between the Patriots and Quakers to the latter's refusal to bear arms. In fact, most contemporaries willingly, if not freely, granted the Quakers this well-known element of their religious beliefs. But most of the Philadelphia area's stricter Quakers in 1777, almost certainly including the exiled men, refused an ever-broader range of Patriot requests for cooperation far beyond militia service and displayed a stronger antipathy to the revolution than is usually appreciated.

Part of the conflict arose out of disagreements over what constituted political acts. For Quakers and other religious pacifists, temporal allegiances were inferior to their allegiance to the word of God. As heavily as the Quakers were invested in Pennsylvania, their primary loyalty was to their faith, to the king, and to the British Empire, under the aegis of which they and their ancestors had thrived in America. They maintained this loyalty despite the fact that, just scant generations prior, Quakers had been severely persecuted in Britain for their pacifism and their other reformist Christian beliefs and actions. The Quakers' clash with the Patriots was the result of a set of religious beliefs that, while on its face tolerant and humane, was politically dogmatic and conservative: it was biblically rooted and did not allow for people to change their government unless they saw that God did it for them.

Thus, the strictest Quaker leaders, including the exiles, refused to acknowledge the legitimacy of the new state government of Pennsylvania, often referring to it simply as "the present powers," "the Present Unsettled

Powers," or "an arbitrary power."[1] They hesitated even to acknowledge the war and generally avoided that word. Quakers maintained that only two sovereign nations could contest a war, and the province or colony of Pennsylvania was not, to their thinking (and certainly that of the British), a sovereign nation. They referred to the war as "commotions and tumult" or with other euphemisms. The Quakers insisted that their words and actions, such as decrying the legitimacy of the new government, not serving in the militia, and not paying the substitute tax, were religious duties, while Patriots and others saw them as political statements.[2]

Nowhere did the Quaker leadership reveal in testimonies or public statements all the governmental measures its members were exhorted to refuse on pain of disownment. The extent of their refusals grew with the circumstances of the war, and these details were communicated bit by bit and only among their members. Quakers considered whether each new revolutionary measure touched war to an extent that observant Quakers could not in good conscience comply with it. Quakers refused to accept employment in government positions of any kind or voluntary service on committees of safety, and after the Declaration of Independence many of them (such as those in southern Chester County) abandoned positions in local government to which they had previously been elected or appointed. They refused to contribute to the public collection of relief money for Boston residents, though they did send money of their own separately.[3] Quakers refused to comply with requisitions made by the local government for items necessary to aid resistance to the British, including lead from both the weights of tall case clocks and the gutters on their houses (used for shot and cannonballs). They refused offers of compensation when their crops, livestock, or wagons were seized by either the Continental Army or the British Army, reasoning that accepting payment, too, could taint them with involvement in the war. Quaker meetings admonished their members not even to give directions to soldiers of either army for fear that they could be charged with complicity.[4] And, of course, they refused to contribute blankets even when paid.

On September 1, 1777—just shy of two weeks after the British landed at Head of Elk, Maryland, and the day before the Quaker leaders were arrested—the PYM's Meeting for Sufferings sent a letter to Birmingham Friends Meeting in Chester County that serves as a useful distillation of this position. The main point was to remind Friends "not [to] join with the multitude in warlike exercise." The PYM also admonished members specifically to not pay the required fine in lieu of military service and to "withdraw from being active in Civil Government due to its founding in the Spirit of War and Fightings."[5] The committee also promised to study and provide further guidance on the matter of accepting Continental currency. Tellingly, the specific behaviors prohibited by this and other missives curtailed aid for the American side. Equally revealing, the PYM gave out no admonitions against cooperation with the British Army, who were camped nearby.

The warnings from Quaker leaders were serious—those who did not comply could be reported by fellow Quakers to the monthly Friends meeting and, after investigation by a small committee of fellow members, disowned by the entire meeting.[6] Indeed, hundreds of Philadelphia-area Quakers were disowned within a matter of months.[7] The exile of the Quaker leaders to Virginia was an outgrowth not of their refusal to bear arms or even to swear or affirm oaths but of their positions of power within the sect to influence others not to participate in their fellow citizens' struggle, supplemented by their oft-proclaimed loyalty to British rule.[8] The Patriots were justifiably led to anticipate from these "friends to [British] government" a disposition to aid the enemy.[9]

THE QUAKER REFUSAL OF CONTINENTAL CURRENCY

Of the more than a dozen types of Quaker refusals, none was more consequential than the refusal to accept Continental currency, the very foundation of Congress's power to wage war. It was also one of the most flagrant and public of refusals. Members of the Society of Friends rejected the new paper currency on the basis that it was "emitted for the purposes of war" and was unduly subject to inflation. Using the money, they also thought, would endorse an authority, the Continental Congress, whose legitimacy the Friends did not acknowledge.[10]

Refusal to accept Continental currency was a serious charge in the Patriots' calculus of offenses, and it often led to placement on the hostiles list. It was the primary reason for the arrest of several Quakers. Philadelphia revolutionary committees insisted that Quaker leaders who refused to accept Continental currency appear before them. Patriots accused Quakers of depreciating the Continental currency, causing it to decline in value. Four Quakers—Thomas, Miers, and Samuel Rowland Fisher and Owen Jones Sr., father of the exile of the same name—were originally summoned before the committees for refusing Continental currency. The same may have been true for four other Quaker merchants or shopkeepers also on the hostiles list.[11] The Pembertons—two of whom penned many of the Quaker disciplinary directives and encouraged the boycott of the money—very likely refused the currency. Henry Drinker's elder brother John had already been charged with doing so. As the two of them were fairly close in their views, it is likely that Henry Drinker, too, refused the Continental currency.

Quaker historian Arthur J. Mekeel characterized the refusal of Continental currency as an afterthought: "Another way of expressing one's disapproval of the war," he wrote, "was the refusal to accept the new Continental money."[12] But refusal of the currency was no trifling matter. It undergirded the entire rebel effort. When the Second Continental Congress first met in May 1775 to discuss the skirmishes at Concord and Lexington, it immediately raised an army, appointed a commander in chief and several generals, and placed orders for arms and munitions. But now its members had to develop a plan to pay for these measures. Their options for raising money were limited. There were basically three: taxation, capital markets (borrowing), or issuing paper money (the Continental currency)—a paper promise to pay at a later date.[13]

Taxation was an option but a difficult lift. It would require enormous effort to persuade the thirteen colonies to allow the Continental Congress to pass laws of taxation and administer them to a population that thought it was throwing off oppressors who taxed them from abroad. This option was highly unlikely to succeed in the short term. The second option, borrowing, was also challenging. Borrowing only works if an entity has an established tax base and a history of extracting taxes regularly from that base, which serves as a source from which the borrower can raise the funds to repay the lender in the future. These ingredients were not present. Another route was borrowing from nations that had a preexisting animus against Britain and a desire to see it defeated, like France or Spain. This was an option, but it could not be actuated before July 1776, as France would never loan money as long as the colonials were still legally part of Britain's empire. For this reason, the Patriots' later decision to declare publicly their independence in 1776 was fortuitous; as a sovereign nation, the new republic could borrow from France, Spain, and the Netherlands. The first two options, however, were off the table in 1775.

That left only one choice: issuing paper currency. Congress printed paper money and began issuing it on June 22, 1775.[14] This was more than a year prior to the Declaration of Independence. Prior to 1778, when other financing options were discovered, nearly 90 percent of the revenue generated for the new government came from currency issues.[15] This option also required the government to sustain the value of that currency so that people would continue to have faith in it. If anybody, especially important merchants, were to refuse this currency, it could have a ripple effect, undermining the value of the currency and in turn the entire war effort.[16]

Early in the war, local county committees punished offenders informally. For several months after July 4, 1776, extralegal committees carried out public functions to which the British colonial government had previously attended. They also published in newspapers the names of those seen as traitors, including individuals who refused Continental currency.[17] Fellow citizens would no longer do business with these individuals. In effect, such persons were ostracized commercially, meaning that they would have a hard time making a living until they accepted the Patriots' views.

Delegate to the Continental Congress Edward Rutledge of South Carolina, in a letter dated October 2, 1776, predicted that if the Quakers failed to respect the currency, the Patriots would have to "make a point of hanging them, which will bring on a storm that will take the wisest of all our wise men to direct."[18] Congress, in a shrewd move, even appointed a former member of the Religious Society of Friends, Israel Whelen, who also fought at the head of a company of militia, as a commissioner for signing Continental currency. His signature appeared prominently on paper money as early as February 1776. Perhaps congressional members hoped that seeing his name would endear Quakers to the new currency.[19]

On November 12, 1776, the Pennsylvania Council of Safety resolved that a committee comprising David Rittenhouse (Pennsylvania treasurer), Timothy Matlack (secretary of the SEC), and John Cannon (teacher at the Academy of Philadelphia), all radical revolutionaries, draw up recommendations to the Assembly for the "dangerous consequences" to be meted out for a refusal of the Continental currency.[20] In December, after General Howe and the British Army first threatened to invade Philadelphia, Washington appointed Major-General Israel Putnam to command the city. In his first general order to the citizenry, Putnam declared that, to his great astonishment, "several of the inhabitants of this city have refused to take the Continental Currency in payment for goods. In future, should any of the inhabitants be so lost to public virtue and the welfare of their country as to presume to refuse the currency of the American States in payment for any commodities they may have for sale, the goods shall be forfeited, and the person or persons so refusing committed to close confinement."[21] The language of righteous indignation became the standard way of expressing, in governmental minutes and proclamations, criticism of those persons daring to ignore Patriot rules.

The brilliant financier and merchant Robert Morris (1734–1806) described in a December 1776 letter to Benjamin Franklin and the other American commissioners in France a "gloomy picture . . . more distressing than all the rest, because it threatens instant and total ruin to the American cause. . . . Our internal enemies, who, alas! are numerous and rich, have always been undermining its value by various artifices, and now that our distresses are wrought to a pitch by the success and new approach of the enemy, they speak plainer and many peremptorily refuse to take it at any rate. . . . All this amounts to real depreciation of the money."[22] If Morris admitted these concerns to the commissioners in France, he surely communicated a similarly urgent message to his revolutionary colleagues in Philadelphia.

In the months leading up to the exile, Quakers and others in Philadelphia were warned. Penalties for depreciating the currency—including banishment—were published. On January 3, 1777, and again in early February, Congress and the Pennsylvania Council of Safety published a broadside posted throughout the city. Every person who refused the Continental money, it declared, should be liable "for the first offense to forfeit the goods & a sum of equal value, for the second offense to forfeit the same & to be banished [from] what they are pleased to call this state, to what place & in what manner they shall judge most proper." Sarah Logan Fisher (exile Thomas Fisher's wife) called the threat "unlike anything I have ever heard of, except the Spanish Inquisition. . . . A most extraordinary instance of arbitrary power & of the liberty we shall enjoy should their government ever be established, a tyrannical government it will prove from weak & wicked men."[23] Her husband, Thomas, his brothers, and their father, Joshua, spoke in a similar vein, as did many of the leading Quakers.

Punishments for refusing the Continental currency were meted out near and far. Joseph Fox was born in Pennsylvania and became a carpenter, among many other professions. When he married a Quaker in 1749, he became a Quaker too. He was elected to the Pennsylvania Assembly and twice served as its speaker, the highest elective office in the colony. In the 1770s, he was elected master of the Carpenters' Company, and as such could literally hang his hat at Carpenters' Hall, the humble yet stately building where the First Continental Congress held its meetings. At the same time, he was barrack master of Philadelphia. He subscribed to the oath of allegiance, and he had long served the colony of Pennsylvania and its inhabitants with distinction. Yet he was placed on the hostiles list to be arrested. Apparently, someone was aware that in 1775 he had refused Continental currency for repayment of a mortgage debt.[24]

Even leading Patriot figures could get caught on this serious charge. Pennsylvania delegate John Dickinson had advised his brother Philemon, a general in the army, not to accept Continental bills in payment from debtors.[25] In Virginia, delegate Richard Henry Lee faced charges that he had asked his tenants to convert their cash rent to tobacco and pay him in kind.[26]

This review of the importance of currency refusal closes with two examples from vernacular humor, both directed at Quakers. Joseph Stansbury, a non-Quaker Tory poet in Philadelphia, among other credits, crafted a "Petition of Philadelphia to Sir William Howe," which asserted that "many friends of government" in town

> Sold each half-joe for twelve pounds Congress trash,
> Which purchased six pounds of this legal cash;
> Whereby they have, if you will bar the bubble,
> Instead of losing, made their money double.[27]

Stansbury, who later became a go-between for General Benedict Arnold's contacts with the British Army, suggested that when a Quaker sold a half Johannes (a Portuguese gold coin and the unofficial standard for use in the colonies) for £12 of Continental currency (the equivalent of £6 of old Pennsylvania provincial currency), they doubled their money. It does not make as much sense as it does rhyme well and allow contemporaries to poke fun at allegedly money-grubbing Quakers, another part of the currency charge, fairly or unfairly, made against them.

The venerable Lutheran prelate Henry Melchior Muhlenberg, whose journal was always quick to dispense a proverb or commonsense illustration reflecting the tenor of the times, also weighed in on the currency controversy. He recorded a wry parable that he likely either created for his own amusement or picked up in conversation from local people in trade. In this tale, a Patriot butcher, incensed by a Quaker merchant who would not accept Continental currency, "paid" the man with lashes across his back. A Quaker quibbling about the currency became an excuse for ordinary Patriot neighbors to enact their own violent punishment.[28]

Beginning in June 1777, Pennsylvania authorities demanded that citizens swear oaths of allegiance to the state.[29] Unfortunately, oaths occupied a particular seat of dishonor in the Quaker hierarchy of detested sins of temporal governments. The Religious Society of Friends emerged in England during the English Civil War, when oaths were requested periodically from 1609 through the end of the century.[30] In its early years as a reformist Christian sect, Quakers had been imprisoned in England for their unwillingness to sign an oath of allegiance to the king. It took a half-century in England before authorities allowed Quakers to substitute their "affirmation" (e.g., I affirm the facts) for a sworn oath (I swear on the Holy Bible these facts) in court and elsewhere. The Quaker form of affirmation came from the biblical admonition in the New Testament to let your yea be yea and your nay be nay.[31]

Quakers did not necessarily oppose announcing their loyalty. Indeed, William Penn's 1701 Charter of Privileges had required that each officeholder and voter affirm loyalty to the king, to Penn as proprietor, and to the laws of Pennsylvania.[32] But Friends viewed the new state's oaths and affirmations very differently. In the end, refusing to take the oath to the State of Pennsylvania was also a refusal to acknowledge the legitimacy of the new state.

To Quakers, taking an oath implied dishonesty at other times, as if it were supposed that one only told the truth under oath. As William Penn put it, "The man who fears to tell untruth has no need to swear because he will not lie, while he that does not fear untruth, what is his oath worth?"[33] Indeed, events later in the revolution supported this argument: on May 30, 1778, Major-General Benedict Arnold swore an oath of allegiance crafted by the Continental Army. As if to prove the Quakers' point of the worthlessness of oaths, Arnold was exposed in September 1780 in the process of effecting the most brazen and potentially damaging act of treason committed during the entire war: attempting to turn over the American fortifications of West Point, New York, to the British Army.[34] Arnold's name became synonymous with treachery against one's own country.

Without the benefit of hindsight, Pennsylvania authorities barreled forward, passing the Test Act on June 13, 1777. This legislation required one to abjure the king, be true to the new state of Pennsylvania, and report any conspiracies against any of the thirteen states. Many Quakers, of course, refused to sign. It would be disingenuous, however, to attribute their treatment solely to a refusal to swear oaths. Every oath or parole offered to the Quakers included the option to affirm rather than swear.[35] The Quakers' protest in 1777 was really more about to whom they were asked to affirm loyalty, and they objected to the new Patriot government, which they thought had usurped the place of the British Empire.

Chapter 3

FRIENDS AS ENEMIES

In August 1777, the Continental Congress received a letter from Major-General John Sullivan of New Hampshire. Reporting from Hanover, New Jersey, Sullivan delivered troubling news about materials found in the baggage and possessions of an American officer on Staten Island whom Sullivan accused of defecting to the enemy. A search of these materials had allegedly yielded papers seeking the locations and strengths of various American military forces in the field.[1] Also found among the papers was a memorial dated August 19, 1777, supposedly emanating from the "Spanktown Yearly Meeting" in Rahway, New Jersey.[2] Several skirmishes and battles had been fought at Spanktown, which was located at the point where New Jersey is nearest to the southern tip of Manhattan.[3] If authentic, these papers strongly suggested that a Quaker meeting in Spanktown had committed treason by transmitting military intelligence to the British Army. Through guilt by association, the papers became the basis for an attack against all Quakers in America.[4]

In Philadelphia, it was a perilous time to receive bad news. In early April 1777, as the city stood on alert for a potential invasion by General Howe and the British Army, authorities sought to build up the region's defenses. In a broadside posted by the SEC of Pennsylvania, President Thomas Wharton Jr. called on "every Man among us [to] hold himself ready to march into the Field. . . . BE READY—for whenever the Time shall come wherein you must either tamely submit yourselves to the immediate Insults of haughty Tyrants, whose Lust and Avarice will make Prey of *every Thing* which human Beings . . . esteem worth possessing."[5] He instructed the state militia to be ready when needed to repulse the invaders.

After a long wait to see what General Howe would do, on July 23, 1777, the Continental Congress learned that over two hundred ships carrying British troops had left New York, but their exact destination was far from clear. Eyewitnesses saw the armada approach the mouth of the Delaware River, the quickest naval route to Philadelphia. The British learned, however, that the river was blocked by hundreds of submerged chevaux-de-frise, wooden beams with iron spikes sticking out and pointed downriver, cleverly designed by and placed in the river under the supervision of a volunteer for the Patriot government, Quaker architect Robert Smith.[6] At great cost in time, they sailed farther south to Norfolk, Virginia, and entered the mouth of the Chesapeake Bay. From there they sailed 180 miles to its northernmost landing point, disembarking on August 25 at Head of Elk, Maryland, within scant miles of Delaware and Pennsylvania state lines.

It is difficult to imagine how the timing could have been worse. Sullivan's message arrived in Congress just days after the British landing, when an invasion seemed imminent and the survival of the new nation threatened. The Spanktown Papers seemingly proved what Patriots had believed all along about the Quaker leaders and thus provided a pretext for their arrests.

SULLIVAN'S CHARGES

Accusing Quakers of giving intelligence to the enemy, Sullivan described a strikingly complete and alarming vision of betrayal by the Quakers: nothing short of a continental conspiracy to betray every American troop movement and military weakness to the British Army.[7] If his charges were true, obtaining military intelligence from the Quaker network would have given a huge tactical advantage to General Howe. Yet no historian has found any evidence of such a plan, concluding instead that the Spanktown Papers were clearly fabricated. Because the accusation was so alarming, however, the papers received a great deal of attention.

As soon as the Spanktown Papers were published in newspapers, at Congress's insistence, and the Philadelphia Quakers learned of the content, they disputed the papers' authenticity, but their rebuttal reached very few people.[8] Their defense was not printed in the newspapers until long after the incident, both because the Quakers were busy responding to the charges and arrests of their leaders and because they did not have a distribution network to circulate information to non-Quakers.[9] The Quakers' only official response in the moment was distributed to their own flock, not to the general public. Their handbill maintained that "Every Person who is acquainted with our Stile, may be convinced it [the Spanktown Papers] was never wrote at any of our Meetings, or by any of our Friends. Besides, there is no Meeting throughout our whole Society of that Name; nor was that Letter, or any one like it, ever wrote in any of our Meetings since we were a People. We therefore solemnly deny the said Letter and its Authors."[10] The Quakers firmly and consistently maintained several points: First, there was no "Spanktown Yearly Meeting." Second, Quakers never used in official minutes the names of months like August, which derived from pagan names, or days of the week like Sunday—rather, they used eighth month, first day, and so on, so that a date on a document typically read, for instance, "8th month 19th day 1777." Quaker meetings always had a named person who served as clerk and signed documents and meeting minutes: "John Jones, Clerk," rather than "Spanktown Yearly Meeting." Moreover, the letters lacked internal consistency: General Howe and his troops landed at the top of the Chesapeake Bay on August 25, 1777, and the paper stating that Howe had landed is dated August 19. It was impossible to know on the nineteenth that Howe would land six days later. Nonetheless, even if the materials were legitimate, there was nothing to connect the papers to the Philadelphia Quakers.

Quakers, had they been allowed to testify before an impartial judge or jury, could have established the Spanktown Papers to be fraudulent, but they were never given the chance. Only with time and in small groups, if at all, did their contemporaries in Philadelphia and elsewhere learn of the several critical defects that exposed the papers as fraudulent. Someone who called himself "a true Whig" republished the Spanktown Papers along with their Quaker rebuttals in the *Pennsylvania Packet* in August 1780, but that was nearly three years later.[11]

Determined to expose this supposed Quaker treachery, Congress ordered the publication in newspapers of the whole of the Spanktown Papers, along with several previously issued Quaker policy statements viewed as hostile to the American cause. These materials soon appeared together in three Philadelphia newspapers and also in newspapers in Rhode Island, New York, and elsewhere.[12] After the newspapers carried the items, General William Smallwood of Maryland interviewed Quakers in the Rahway area and determined that they had no relation to the Spanktown Papers. Like the Philadelphia Quakers' self-defense, this fact was only reported later, in 1780.[13]

The new national and state governments, as it turned out, were prepared to deal with such apparently treasonous behavior. As the Continental Congress moved toward independence in the spring and summer of 1776, its pro-independence members found that they lacked a way to punish conduct that undermined their cause. On May 15, 1776, Congress acted. Based on a resolution introduced by John Adams, all English statutory and common laws were suspended in the colonies. The reason for this action, Congress noted, was that the king had "excluded the inhabitants of these United Colonies from the protection of his crown" by sending army and naval forces to America, along with foreign mercenaries, to suppress the rebellion.[14] But according to Henry Young, who has traced the evolution of the legal systems in the nascent state of Pennsylvania, the impulse to revise colonial laws began with a keen interest in the crime of treason: state governments needed a way to punish those who actively fought against the new government on Britain's behalf. On June 24, 1776, only days before passage of the Declaration of Independence, the Continental Congress defined treason, declaring that "persons, members of, or owing allegiance to any of the United Colonies, . . . who shall levy war against any of the said colonies . . . , or be adherent to the king of Great Britain, . . . giving to him or them aid and comfort, are guilty of treason against such colony."[15] That same day, the Continental Congress recommended that the various state legislatures enact punishments for persons who rendered aid and comfort to the enemies of America.[16]

In Pennsylvania, the new legislative assembly passed a treason law on February 11, 1777. Under its terms, aiding and abetting an enemy of Pennsylvania constituted high treason. Acts such as discouraging enlistment in the militia and opposing revolutionary measures were defined as "misprision of treason," a lesser criminal charge for which the penalty was imprisonment for the duration of the war and forfeiture of one-half of one's estate.[17] Although the Quaker exiles were never charged or tried under these laws, the previous actions of several of them, if they could be proven in court, arguably could constitute misprision of treason.

With dissent already on its members' minds, the Continental Congress received Major-General Sullivan's letter on August 28 and that day appointed the committee on spies to consider his charges. The committee comprised Richard Henry Lee, well-known scion of one of the wealthiest, most respected

Virginia planter families; William Duer, a prosperous mill owner and anti-Tory zealot representing New York; and John Adams of Massachusetts. There is no direct indication here which of the committee members dominated, but circumstantial evidence would suggest it was Adams.[18]

Adams was the delegate most experienced at congressional committees and of the strongest opinions about matters under discussion. Unlike Pennsylvania, Massachusetts Bay Colony featured a virulent strain of anti-Quakerism dating back almost to the colony's founding. A seventeenth-century body of colonial legislation had resulted in the severe suppression of Quakers generally and in the public execution of four of them. Cotton Mather (1663–1728), a famous Puritan preacher from Boston, graphically described Quakerism as "*The Sink of all Heresies*, [in which] we see the *Vomit* cast out in the By-past Ages, by whole Kennels of Seducers, lick'd up again for a New Digestion, and once more exposed for the Poisoning of Mankind."[19] Traveling to Philadelphia—the American capital of Quakerdom—as a delegate to the Continental Congress a century later, John Adams could not escape this history.

On October 14, 1774, Adams arrived at Carpenter's Hall for a somewhat extracurricular evening meeting to find it "almost full of People, and a great number of Quakers seated at the long Table with their broad brimmed Beavers on their Heads." Led by Israel Pemberton—a man "of large Property and more intrigue," according to Adams—some fifty Friends had gathered to demand that Massachusetts respect religious liberty and repeal its anti-Quaker laws. Startled, Adams was "greatly surprised and somewhat indignant, . . . at seeing our State and her Delegates thus summoned before a self-created Trybunal, which was neither legal nor Constitutional. . . . A suspicion instantly arose in my mind . . . that this artful Jesuit [Pemberton] . . . was endeavoring to avail himself of this opportunity, to break up the Congress, or at least to withdraw the Quakers and the Governing part of Pennsylvania from Us."[20] The following year, Adams identified Pemberton as one of the three most important opponents of the movement toward independence.[21] It did not help, as Adams wrote the night of the meeting, that "Old Israel Pemberton was quite rude."[22] Decades later, Pemberton's criticism still rankled Adams, who attributed the rancor to the Quakers' pro-British sympathies. "The Quakers were not generally and heartily in our Cause," he recalled, "they were jealous of Independence."[23] In 1775, Adams claimed that the Patriots should have already "arrested every Friend to Government [i.e., Quaker Tory] on the Continent and held them as Hostages for the poor victims of Boston."[24]

Under Adams's leadership, and with this bias, three years later Congress's committee on spies embarked on an investigation of the Spanktown Papers and Major-General Sullivan's implication that all Quakers were treasonous Tories. However, this committee reported nothing at all about the Spanktown Papers themselves, the Quaker meeting in question, or the purported intelligence gathering and dissemination network that Sullivan had alleged. Rather, it hastily concluded to Congress later that same day that "the uniform tenor of the conduct and conversation of a number of persons of considerable wealth, who profess themselves to belong to the society of people commonly called Quakers render it certain and notorious, that those persons are, with much rancor and bitterness, disaffected to the American cause: that, as these persons will have it in their power, so there is no doubt it will be their inclination, to communicate intelligence to the enemy, and in various other ways to injure the councils and arms of America."[25] This report was striking in that it did not concern itself at all with the papers or other facts it was intended to analyze, but it made observations about certain men's circumstances and drew from their behavior conclusions about their allegiances. From that point, it jumped to the specific, malign actions those accused could be expected to take in the future. It was anything but a lawyerly report, but it was a uniquely effective, conclusory denunciation of those it attacked. Given his proven animus toward Quakers, Adams clearly led this effort.

The quickly assembled report went on to recommend that certain named Quaker men in Philadelphia be arrested and confined and their papers seized because these persons "maintained a correspondence and connection *highly prejudicial to the public safety*."[26] Translated into today's language, the committee identified these men as a serious threat to national security, though if the word "national" was a nascent term, the phrase "national security" would surely have been even more so. Yet this precise moment encapsulates the birth of a concept. Concerns about national security were baked into the founding of the nation itself. The charge above also represented one of the first times in the new republic that a congressional committee used the argument that national security alone justified confining a group of men without any criminal charges or any other explanation of the precise factual charge against them. The action Congress took that day could indeed set its own dangerous precedent for the new republic.

The report of the committee on spies focused almost entirely on the loyalties of Quaker men in general and eleven specific men in Philadelphia, none of whom was mentioned in any of the Spanktown Papers. Indeed, it is likely that many members of Congress had never met some of them. Three of the men singled out for arrest—James Pemberton, John Pemberton, and Henry Drinker—had signed controversial PYM testimonies, epistles, or minutes as a clerk of one meeting or another. In addition, the committee named for arrest Thomas Fisher, Samuel R. Fisher, Joshua Fisher, Abel James, John James, Israel Pemberton, Samuel Pleasants, and Thomas Wharton Sr.[27] These men, the committee asserted, "have uniformly manifested by their general conduct and conversation a disposition highly inimical to the cause of America." They were *all* Quakers. There was no proven link whatsoever between these men and the Spanktown Papers. Ultimately, Congress obliged: on August 27, it informed all nearby states that "all persons . . . notoriously disaffected, forthwith to be apprehended, disarmed, and secured, till such time as the State shall think they may be released without injury to the common cause."[28] The following day, Congress instructed the SEC of Pennsylvania to apprehend and secure the eleven men Adams's committee had named. In hindsight, the records suggest that the Spanktown Papers, though false on their face, reignited prejudices, or legitimate suspicions, built up over the prior several years against the leading Quakers in Philadelphia.

When one year earlier Major-General Sullivan had delivered up to Congress a message from Lord Richard Howe and his brother Sir William, Adams dismissed Sullivan as a mere "decoy duck." Joseph J. Ellis reports that Sullivan's reputation had gone into "deeper decline for having been duped by Howe."[29] But Sullivan's low reputation exposes all the more starkly the heightened general distrust of Quakers. Even men as discerning as Adams believed the decoy duck when his accusations confirmed long-held suspicions.

Chapter 4

QUAKER ARRESTS

When the Continental Congress's recommendation for arresting eleven local Quakers reached the SEC of Pennsylvania, it invited the Council to add to the list names of others whom it thought might sympathize with the British or resist the new government and round them up. The Council eventually decided to arrest forty-one men, but in none of the cases did it allege any specific act worthy of arrest. Indeed, no direct accusations of criminality were ever made, though the clear insinuation was there. Moreover, though Congress and the SEC had in many cases correctly identified disaffected Quakers, others "seemed picked out almost at random as object lessons to the Quaker community."[1]

Pennsylvania authorities had likely been preparing their hostiles list for over a year. Since May 1776, the Council of Safety and its staff had been in a constant frenzy of daily activity to prepare the city for war. On May 15, 1776, in this flood of emergency planning, the Council of Safety passed a resolution to collect war materiel. The announcement included a clear threat: "It is expected that every virtuous Citizen will immediately and cheerfully Comply with this requisition but if any Persons should be so lost to all senses of the public good as to refuse, a List of their names is directed to be returned to this Committee."[2]

On July 2, 1776, the SEC appointed a committee of secrecy and charged it with examining "all inimical and suspected persons that come to their knowledge."[3] This was very likely the beginning of the list of persons from which authorities chose those to be arrested and exiled in September 1777. On August 31, 1777, the same committee—consisting of David Rittenhouse (the new state treasurer), Colonel William Bradford, Colonel Sharp Delaney, and Captain Charles Willson Peale, among others—convened. Timothy Matlack, secretary of the SEC, was certainly involved. A versatile go-to man in the Patriot inner circle, Matlack was in on every key decision for many years, and he, Christopher Marshall (another disowned and disgruntled former Quaker in Patriot councils), Thomas Paine, and John Adams were known to have coffee or dinner together and talk through the night.[4] At this point, the Quaker leaders were conscious that "a report had for some weeks prevailed that lists of a great number of persons were made out, with an intent shortly to apprehend and confine them, but for what cause was a profound secret . . . it was understood that four or five hundred of the respectable inhabitants were to be secured and sent out of the city."[5] From this group, the committee of secrecy selected thirty names to add to the eleven men Congress had named, resulting in the forty-one men on the hostiles list. The SEC met with the arresting party, a specially assembled group of twenty-five militia members, on Monday, September 1, and instructed them to "treat Men of reputation with as much tenderness as the Security of their Persons & Papers will admit." The arrests began the following day, with general warrants signed by SEC Vice President George Bryan.[6]

The fact that the SEC chose the state militia instead of the sheriff to apprehend these Quakers hinted that these were very unusual arrests. Colonel William Bradford was the highest-ranking militia officer in the arresting party. He operated both a printing press and the London Coffee House and had been a leading figure of the committee for tarring and feathering in the Tea Act crisis of the fall of 1773. During that crisis, the Bradford firm printed three broadsides directed at the Delaware River pilots and the captain of the English tea ship *Polly* and one card directed specifically at the mercantile firm James and Drinker (Abel James and Henry Drinker). With intimidating rhetoric, the publications demanded particular actions and threatened specific physical punishment, such as tarring and feathering. Bradford's own Quaker forebears, who had printed for William Penn and other Quakers in Philadelphia, had long before been run out of the city by Quaker leaders and converted to Anglicanism in New York.

Along with Bradford, the Council sent Colonel Lewis Nicola, a veteran soldier, "town major," member of the American Philosophical Society, and author of a published manual of arms, and Charles Willson Peale, a part-time soldier who later would be in charge of throwing Loyalists out of their houses when the government passed laws requiring those who had worked for the British to forfeit their estates. Peale's true métier, however, was in an altogether different realm: formal oil portraits of revolutionary men on the rise. Peale later founded the first museum of art in Philadelphia. Despite Bradford's origins in a prominent family and Nicola's and Peale's rising fortunes, these men were in a station of life altogether different from those whom they set out to arrest. James Cannon, a schoolteacher, ardent revolutionary, secretary and spokesman for the committee of privates (which advocated for noncommissioned soldiers), and fellow member of the arresting party, had earlier warned that "an aristocratical junto"—precisely the sort of men he was charged with apprehending—was trying to make the middling merchants, mechanics, and artisans their "beasts of burden." In revolutionary Philadelphia, conflicts between Patriots and actual or suspected Loyalists often mapped themselves onto preexisting class tensions.[7]

Prior to the arrests, a whispering campaign produced extensive foreboding. "It was made known to us before we were apprehended that they would banish us," the exiles' journal later noted.[8] When the militiamen showed up at the arrestees' houses, then, it was not a complete surprise, though a great feeling of righteous indignation prevailed. The arresting party offered to many of its targets the first of several oaths, any one of which, had the Quakers been willing to sign them, would have allowed them to escape arrest. Only eight of the forty-one men on the hostiles list took the oath and accepted parole, the most notable of which was merchant and former mayor Samuel Shoemaker.[9] According to Israel Pemberton, most would not because "signing such a paper would be an acknowledgment of guilt, and would subject us to be removed at an hour's warning without knowing the charge against us . . . we refused to become voluntary prisoners for supposed offenses, because we knew ourselves innocent of any."[10]

Each detainee who refused the parole offer risked exile. Soldiers searched the prisoners' desks for political papers, sometimes smashing the desks. They seized some Quaker testimonies and minutes. They took the minute book of the PYM from Henry Drinker's desk as well as some additional public papers found on John Hunt and John Pemberton. Papers seized from the prisoners, including minutes of Quaker meetings, were referred to the committee that originally had been asked to look into the Spanktown Papers. The arresting party was also instructed to confiscate all "firearms, swords, and bayonets" discovered on the prisoners. No such weapons were found among any of the men to be arrested, and the reports of the arresting party did not cite finding any.[11]

Charles Willson Peale was the only member of the arresting party to leave a written account of the affair. He had been charged with the delicate task of dealing with ministers John Pemberton and Samuel Emlen. He offered Pemberton the parole, which the forty-nine-year-old minister rejected out of hand. After attempting to cajole Pemberton, Peale called for an armed force, and he had his soldiers parade up and down the street opposite Pemberton's home. Pemberton indicated he would not go without being forced. Peale once again tried to reason with Pemberton, raising the specter of attracting a mob. Still there was no movement. Peale then ordered the guard into the house and pointed to Pemberton, who "would not move until he was taken by the arm and partly raised on his feet." The experience clearly disquieted Peale. In ordinary times and with ordinary arrests, it is unlikely that Peale would have bothered to record his military duty in such minute detail.[12] But these were no ordinary times.

John Pemberton, too, recalled his arrest. "I told them, that as they had nothing justly to lay to my Charge, & my House was my Own & I a freeman, I could not Consent to comply with their Unreasonable demand." With no just cause, the arresting party would need to remove him by force, he insisted. One guard "took me by the arm & said he would force me to go, but I would not move from my seat. . . . So I was lifted by two of them off my seat & led to the Door."[13]

There are no reports that any of the others resisted as determinedly as John Pemberton, though Thomas Wharton Sr. had to be forced into a wagon. A neighbor commented, "One impudent Jack in an officer insulted our neighbor Wharton as they were forcing him into the wagon and called him a d__d Tory."[14] John Pemberton's brother Israel also resisted, refusing to move without first seeing a warrant. He remained at his home with minister John Hunt and son-in-law Samuel Pleasants, and the arresting party had to return the next day and forcibly arrest the men. From John Pemberton's, Peale next went to minister Samuel Emlen's home. Peale found the slight and elderly man bedridden. According to Peale's diary, Emlen began from his supine posture in bed to "preach on the occasion—that he [Peale] would have to answer at a future day etc." Peale insisted that he was only there to do his duty. Since Emlen was confined by sickness, Peale noted, "nothing personal was done." The soldiers searched for political papers, but "nothing of treasonable nature appearing, his papers were left, as they were found." Emlen took a parole and stayed behind.[15] When the arresting party arrived at Thomas Gilpin's home and offered him the parole, he told them that, while he "had not done anything contrary to the requests, [he] could not comply with it." He would rather plead his case before the SEC than sign the oath. He agreed to accompany the arresting party to the Freemason's Lodge, where he expected—incorrectly, it turned out—to find Thomas Wharton Jr. and the Council.[16]

When Reverend Thomas Coombe, assistant rector of the two main Anglican churches in Philadelphia (Christ Church and St. Peter's) was arrested, his rector and the wardens of those churches immediately petitioned the SEC, fearing that Coombe's "Civil & Religious Rights" had been violated.[17] Hastily replying by letter, the Council defensively insisted that Coombe's arrest was not for religious reasons; rather, "his case is wholly political."[18] Arrested not because of crimes committed but because of suspicion of intercourse with the enemy and for their attitudes, these men were very clearly made political prisoners and taken into preventive detention—both modern terms—presumably to keep them from taking actions that were only imagined by Patriots.[19] And although these religiously principled men of conscience were prisoners of Pennsylvania, they were also clearly prisoners of Congress.

The arresting party took its prisoners to the Freemason's Lodge, where they were confined as long as nine days pending exile. It stationed one or two guards outside and allowed friends to visit the prisoners, who were sometimes allowed to visit their homes. It was intended as a "gentle imprisonment."[20] Yet these peaceable men encountered unexpected confrontation, as "one of [the guards] presented his gun, cocked, and threatened to fire."[21] There seemed, moreover, to be no clear reason for them to face such danger, with neither Bradford, Peale, nor Nicola providing an adequate explanation. Like the SEC and Congress, the members of the arresting party tossed responsibility for the prisoners back and forth between themselves, continuing a sustained pattern of behavior on the Patriot side.

The detainees quickly sought recourse for their inexplicable treatment. On September 2, the prisoners, aided by two Quaker attorneys—William Lewis and another—and SEC secretary Timothy Matlack (as a dragooned liaison), asked to be heard before the Council. The Council answered: "The arrest has been made by order of Congress & that at present the Council decline hearing them."[22] The next day, Bradford told the detainees that a hearing was likely, though SEC Vice President George Bryan quickly dashed that hope when he informed the prisoners through Philadelphia magistrate Benjamin Paschall that they were to be sent to Virginia without a hearing.

"Conscious of their innocence," the prisoners demanded a copy of the arrest warrant from Bradford.[23] Noting only that the men had "evidenced a disposition inimical to the cause of America," the warrant specified no crimes. Under the law, such a warrant would be insufficient, and the Quaker leaders knew it. The Quakers confined at the lodge protested to Congress the "arbitrary, unjust, and illegal proceeding against us, and demanded our undoubted right of being heard. . . . The proceedings you have chosen and prescribed [are ones] by which the liberty, property, and character of every freeman in America, is or may be endangered."[24]

The Pennsylvania Constitution of 1776, enacted one year prior to the arrests, provided that "without oaths or affirmations first made [i.e., testimony by a witness], affording a sufficient foundation for [the warrant], and whereby any officer or messenger may be commanded or required to search suspected places, or to seize any person or persons, his or their property, not particularly described, are contrary to that right, and [such a warrant] ought not to be granted."[25] This section of the constitution was designed to protect citizens against precisely the kind of warrant Bryan had signed, and the Quakers (particularly Israel Pemberton), though they resented the new constitution, knew it. In an impartial court of law, their objections to the arrest might have prevailed, and they would likely have been released. But for the Quaker prisoners, Anne M. Ousterhout noted, the new legal protections were merely a "cruel hoax."[26] The arrests were legally flawed.

Lawmakers made occasional, scattered attempts to mitigate the harshness of the proceedings. The SEC, with the permission of Congress, offered release contingent on signing a shorter oath of allegiance, though none of the prisoners agreed to do so.[27] On September 4, Congress directed the Council "to hear what Israel Pemberton & divers others . . . can alledge [*sic*] to remove the suspicion of their being disaffected or dangerous to the United States." Operating out of the same State House as Congress occupied, the Council replied that it lacked the time to do so, as it was in the midst of making final preparations to banish the prisoners and flee itself.[28] It asked Congress to handle the matter.[29] In nearly daily missives, the prisoners continued to protest their treatment, which they deemed "to be the highest act of tyranny that has been exercised in any age or country, where the shadow of liberty was left. . . . The charge against us of refusing 'to promise to *refrain* from corresponding with the enemy,' insinuates that we have already held such correspondence *which we utterly and solemnly deny*."[30] Others, too, mobilized on the arrestees' behalf. A group of over one hundred local men sent a remonstrance against this violation of civil and religious liberties to the SEC.[31] Many of the signers of this statement were fellow Quakers.

On September 8, the twenty-two men at the lodge pled one more time for a hearing at which they could defend themselves. In a petition headed "To the President and Council of Philadelphia," the men remonstrated strongly against the manner in which their previous two protests had gone unanswered. They emphasized the "illegal and unconstitutional" measures taken by the Council, including the general warrant issued earlier, and noted the executive council had now determined in writing to exile the men, seemingly crafting a new law to allow it without consulting the Assembly. The Quakers caught Patriot authorities in an obvious blunder of overreach. The Quaker leaders were good at deconstructing the SEC's intentions and criticizing it. They accused the executive branch of inappropriately and illegally taking over the job of the legislative branch, usurping powers it did not have. They ended this blast at the Council with the plea "to be informed of the cause of our commitment, and to have a hearing in the face of our country, before whom we shall either stand acquitted or condemned." The men boldly signed their names in a way reminiscent of the document signed by Congress itself on July 4, 1776 (frontispiece, app. B).[32] On receipt, Timothy Matlack responded curtly that same day to advise the men in the lodge that their protest had been read to the Council and that its members were referring it to Congress. Both bodies desperately wanted simultaneously to maintain face and rid the city of these Quakers before the British arrived.

The two Anglicans arrested also had colleagues who protested their seizures. By September 9, the rector and church wardens of Philadelphia's two Anglican churches had written their own protest of the detention of Reverend Thomas Coombe, their assistant minister.[33]

Time, however, quickly ran out for the detainees. Over the course of two days of debate (Friday, September 5, and Tuesday, September 9) in a five-day time span, Congress spent more than nine hours debating the ethics of exiling the men without a hearing—a "Silly point," according to Henry Laurens of South Carolina, a man soon to succeed John Hancock as president of Congress.[34] Laurens's two long letters to a correspondent at home are the only contemporaneous accounts of the debate, and they convey little specificity beyond Laurens's own views in favor of the exile. The only kind of hearing he seriously considered was one that would require the Quakers to prove to Congress that they were *not* dangerous *"Enemies to the Independence of the United States."*[35] After all, he reasoned, Congress and the

Council had merely asked of the Quakers that they behave inoffensively and not damage or undermine the state. By refusing to affirm their loyalty, Laurens wrote, the Quakers claimed protection of America's laws without granting the state any allegiance. The necessity of governmental self-preservation, he asserted, would justify Congress in confining these "notorious Enemies of the State."[36] One noteworthy delegate, John Adams, who only seven years before defended British soldiers charged with murder in the Boston Massacre, had famously argued that the perpetrators had rights and deserved a fair trial.

Several days later, Lutheran prelate Henry Melchior Muhlenberg privately illustrated this view of Quakers with a parable in his diary. In this tale, a family of nine embarks on a dangerous journey. Only six of its members contribute to the effort, while the remaining three refuse to cooperate and instead repeatedly thwart the family's labors. When faced with danger, however, the three stubborn outliers quickly demand protection from their better-prepared and more realistic relatives. Far from a neutral party that refused out of principle to engage in any war-related activity, Muhlenberg posited, the Quakers sought to benefit from others' preparations while simultaneously undermining these efforts.[37] Muhlenberg himself was not a neutral party either. Though an especially keen and insightful observer of the contemporary scene, he also carried his own special religious animus against the Quaker sect.

Lacking Muhlenberg's literary flair, Laurens likely was repeating many of the charges he heard in the debate that day, though he failed to include much from the other side. His own anti-Quaker views probably account for this oversight. But surely there were dissenters among the delegates. The issue would not otherwise have engendered more than nine hours of debate. Ultimately, Congress resolved only that it would be improper to give the men any hearing before Congress for the reason that they were residents of Pennsylvania, thus using a procedural point to rid itself of a divisive and irritating matter. On September 9, Congress ordered that the men be escorted by Pennsylvania militia guards to Virginia for an indefinite period of confinement.[38]

In doing so, Congress drew on a template it had developed in August 1776 for dealing with recalcitrant royal officers, many of whom who were seen as straddlers, neither wholly Patriot nor Loyalist. George Washington, in a letter to the governor of Connecticut, revealed that it was intended for men of "Rank & Education," often former Crown officers, who commanded some respect, were wealthy enough to pay their own expenses, and, importantly, had not been detained on criminal charges. Instead, their confinement depended "merely on Suspicion arising from a General Line of Conduct, unfriendly to the American Cause." To ensure public safety, persons in this category would be kept away from the coast, which offered escape routes, or from post towns, where they might have easy communication access. Those restrictions aside, they would be accorded "every Accommodation & Indulgence having a Respect to their Rank & Education which may be deemed consistent with Safety; and they are given to understand that your Humanity & Politeness will most effectually prevent their being liable to any unnecessary Hardships." Shielded from abuse by local Patriots by the governor, detainees would enjoy a protective custody designed for both their own good and the government's. Pennsylvania subjected its special straddlers (e.g., former governor John Penn and former colonial chief justice Benjamin Chew) to a similar "indulgent confinement," sending them to a private estate in New Jersey.[39] At least the twelve most prominent Quaker detainees were major employers and would be needed for the economic success of the new government.

On September 9, Congress directed the Council to carry out the banishment. The SEC obligingly ordered the removal of twenty-two "persons who have uniformly manifested by their general conduct and conversation a Disposition highly inimical to the cause of America . . . it appears they consider themselves as subjects of the king of Great Britain, the Enemy . . . in emergencies equal to the present, when the Enemy is at our Door, . . . such proceedings may be justified by the conduct of the freest nations & the authority of most judicious Citizens." Even then the prisoners protested their treatment, sending the Council a series of questions about the logistics of their banishment, including the number of wagons they would be granted and the expense of the journey. As before, the answers were either ambiguous or inadequate. In response to a question about financial support, for example, the SEC could only commit to covering travel expenses provided that Congress would later reimburse them.[40]

Quaker opponents cheered this series of developments. John Adams wrote to Abigail on the night of September 8: "You will see by the Papers inclosed, that We have been obliged to attempt to humble the Pride of some Jesuits who call themselves Quakers, but who love Money and Land better than Liberty or Religion. The Hypocrites are endeavoring to raise the Cry of Persecution, and to give this Matter a religious Turn, but they can't succeed. . . . American Independence has disappointed them, which makes them hate it. Yet the Dastards dare not avow their Hatred to it, it seems."[41] Adams had settled a score with the Quakers. A wide swath of congressional leaders expressed similar sentiments. Virginia delegate Richard Henry Lee accused the Quakers of having "a uniform, fixed enmity to American measures." Elbridge Gerry, delegate from Massachusetts, and John Hancock, president of the Congress, voiced similar sentiments.[42] Major-General Nathanael Greene, the suspended Quaker anchorsmith and self-taught military strategist from Rhode Island, commented that "the villainous Quakers are employed upon every quarter to serve the enemy. Some of them are confined and more deserve it."[43] James Lovell, delegate of Massachusetts, also believed that the exile was merited for the safety of the union. The exiles' refusal to assure their allegiance or comply with defensive requisitions was enough to satisfy him.[44]

Ironically, delegates to the Continental Congress had just spent two years demanding that the British respect the fundamental rights and liberties of free men in Boston and elsewhere. These were the same men who had loudly complained that the people of Boston had been punished by the British, "unheard." The First Continental Congress's "Address to the People of Great Britain" decried "men being condemned to suffer for imputed crimes, unheard, unquestioned, and without even the specious formality of a trial."[45]

Some prominent men revealed doubts about the legitimacy of the arrests and exile. James Allen, a leading Philadelphia lawyer, Anglican, and legislator, commented in his diary on the proceedings against the Quakers: "These proceedings bear the mark of the most wanton Tyranny ever exercised in any Country. Many people who disapprove Independence, have no other wish than to remain at peace, & secure their persons without influencing the minds of others. This some members of Congress have acknowledged to be the temper of most of the disaffected Gentlemen of Philadelphia & yet they are sent into banishment to a remote part of the country, exposed to the insult of the rabble wherever they go. . . . It is said, many of the warmest Whigs think this an instance of unjustifiable oppression."[46] Allen was a Loyalist, but he was not entirely alone in his assessments. An unnamed New Hampshire congressional delegate confessed: "I fear we shall fail of that proof that is Expected."[47] The Patriots' muzzling of these dissidents seemed to many a clear violation of the Quakers' legal rights and, in retrospect, seems a stunning betrayal of American revolutionary ideals, though there is no evidence either at the congressional or the state level that the

Patriots later regretted their actions. At the time, many considered Philadelphia Quaker leaders an existential threat.

The peril to Philadelphia in August and September of 1777 was real. The SEC noted on Howe's landing in Maryland that "the British Army . . . [has] a professed design of enslaving this free Country, & is now advancing towards this City, as a principal object of hostility."[48] By the time of the arrests, Howe's army was only forty miles away, in the southernmost townships of Chester County, Pennsylvania. As John Adams explained to Abigail, only one element stood between the British general and the city: "All the Apology that can be made, for this Part of the World is that Mr. Howes march from [Head of] Elke to Philadelphia, was thro the very Regions of Passive obedience. The whole Country thro which he passed is inhabited by Quakers. There is not such another Body of Quakers in all America, perhaps not in all the World."[49] Philadelphia's sole line of defense, that is, was a group that few trusted to act in the city's or nation's best interests. Adams must have felt then that Congress and the Council's actions were justified. On September 11, 1777, the same day that the exiles were ignominiously carted out of Philadelphia as disgraced Tories, British General Howe defeated Washington's troops at the Battle of Brandywine, thanks in part to help Howe received from the man who had voyaged with him from New York, his chief, native-born strategist, Joseph Galloway. Galloway, though not a Quaker, was closely identified with the sect. A former friend of Franklin, he had long led the Quaker party as speaker of the Pennsylvania Assembly, the leading elected official in the colony, and he served as a delegate at the First Continental Congress, where his proposal of a new form of union with Britain had been rejected. At the end of 1776, he slipped out of his grand home north of the city and headed on horseback to New York, where he joined the British Army, and by September 1777 he held a colonel's rank. A savvy attorney and strategic thinker with extensive contacts among Pennsylvania Quakers, Galloway provided Howe with crucial insider intelligence and attracted to his side Quakers and Loyalists for this purpose. As Adams wrote to his wife in late September, Howe was settling in for an indefinite occupation of the American capital.[50]

Chapter 5

PEACEABLE CARAVAN

_____

The September 11 banishment was a controversial public spectacle. Some of the prisoners headed into exile on their own horses or in their own horse-drawn carriages, but other Quaker men were evacuated by force into wagons.[1] John Pemberton even refused to lift his arms and legs, not wishing to show cooperation with what he deemed an illegal measure by an illegal government. He wrote in the margin of his *Poor Will's Pocket Almanack* that day that "I was deprived of my liberty, and taken into confinement by order of Congress, and . . . the Council of Penna. . . . Without any just cause."[2] In a prose poem he wrote in response, Robert Morton, sixteen-year-old stepson of James Pemberton, addressed this plaintive paean to his native city, lamenting the fate of those "dragged by a licentious mob from their near and dear connections, and by the hand of lawless power, banished from their country unheard, perhaps never more to return. . . . Thou hast denied them . . . in a manner more tyrannical and cruel than the Inquisition of Spain."[3] This young Quaker diarist rightly recognized this eleventh day of ninth month 1777 as a watershed date for threats to liberty in the city's first century.

The resulting caravan of some twenty-eight men was not inconspicuous. It included two carriages, six wagons carrying men and baggage, and three exiled men on horseback. Militia captains Alexander Nesbitt and Samuel Caldwell led, and six cavalrymen on light horse accompanied them.[4] Since the British Army threatened to approach Philadelphia from the south and west, the caravan went west to cross the bridge over the Schuylkill River, then northwest toward Potts Grove (now Pottstown), which later became the main western portal into the occupied city. The caravan also hoped to

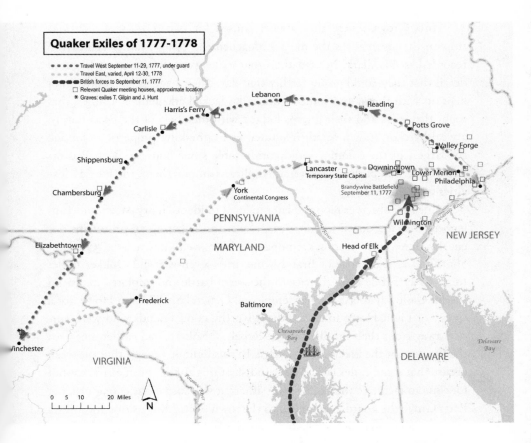

Lebanon

Reading

Harris's Ferry

Potts Grove

Carlisle

Valley Forge

Shippensburg

Lancaster
Temporary State Capital

Downingtown

Lower Merion

Philadelphia

Chambersburg

York
Continental Congress

Brandywine Battlefield
September 11, 1777

PENNSYLVANIA

Wilmington

NEW JERSEY

Elizabethtown

MARYLAND

Head of Elk

Frederick

Baltimore

Chesapeake
Bay

Delaware
Bay

Winchester

VIRGINIA

DELAWARE

0   5   10   20 Miles

N

MAP 1 | Map of the roundabout journey (designed to avoid two armies) under guard into exile from Philadelphia to Winchester, Virginia, in September 1777 and the return via Lancaster and Downingtown to Philadelphia in April 1778. Created by W. Paul Fritz, mapmaker. Chester County Planning Commission.

avoid the American forces, who were still skirmishing occasionally in the no-man's-land on the collar of the city in the aftermath of the Battle of Brandywine (map 1).

On the first night away from Philadelphia, the exiles and their guards were turned away from a crowded inn but found lodging in some private homes nearby. Despite their trying circumstances, at least some of the men were unbowed. Henry Drinker explained why: "Storms, Tempests, & raging Billows will not remove from the Rock of Ages, the sure Refuge [Christ] . . . my way seems clear & open . . . in as much as the blessed Testimony [the Quaker peace testimony] has been supported & not baulked by me a weakling."[5]

Potts Grove, where the caravan paused for two days, was a curious stop on the journey. As the men approached the village, James Pemberton recorded in his diary, he and the other exiles complained to their guard detail that they could go no farther that day. Their baggage wagon had not kept up with them, and some of the exiles lacked adequate clothing.[6] That night the exiles and their guards lodged with members of the Potts family, a wealthy clan known for their numerous ironmaking properties—among the largest in the colonies—and comfortable stone houses.[7] With Patriots and Tories, and both Quakers and Anglicans among them, the Pottses' loyalties were divided.

A nearby observer reported later to local resident Henry Melchior Muhlenberg that the dozen Quaker leaders were anticipating an imminent rescue by light horse troops accompanied by a well-known local Quaker.[8] Shortly after the Battle of Brandywine, fifty-seven-year-old Quaker miller John Roberts rode from the city to the site of battle and implored his friend Joseph Galloway to ask his new employer, General Sir William Howe, for a "party of Light Horse to rescue those worthy good Friends who were hurried away from their families by the Rebels."[9] Roberts had earlier met with the Quakers at the Freemason's Lodge. In this light, it appears that the weak excuse that some exiles lacked a second shirt might have been a ruse to stall for time to facilitate the rescue. The situation was suspicious enough that at Potts Grove the guards sent ahead to the town of Reading asking for militia reinforcements to come and help the guards make the caravan press forward.

On September 13, John Adams signed a letter from the congressional board of war to the county lieutenant in Winchester, Virginia, instructing him that rather than taking the exiled men to their original destination of Staunton in Augusta County, Virginia, the caravan should stop nearly a hundred miles short, in Winchester.[10] President Wharton had earlier informed Congress that although the SEC itself was indifferent to the place of their detention in Virginia, at least one individual had suggested to the board that Winchester would be a more comfortable and convenient location for the prisoners. This suggestion represented an unusual attentiveness to the comfort of prisoners, but these were special prisoners who had not been charged with any crime.[11]

At this point, the highest officials of the Pennsylvania government either perpetrated an act of grave injustice toward the Quaker exiles or made a canny cost-benefit calculation, depending on one's view. On about September 13, lawyers for the exiles applied for writs of habeas corpus before the first chief justice of Pennsylvania, Thomas McKean, installed only days earlier. McKean, then holding court outside the city, reviewed the general warrant letter from SEC Vice President George Bryan to Colonel Lewis Nicola, which stated that the Quakers had been arrested because they were suspected of being inimical to the cause of liberty and because Congress recommended it. In accordance with the law, the chief justice decided the Bryan letter was insufficient to constitute a proper warrant for the arrests. McKean found he had little choice but to scribble "allowed" over his signature on all the writs. The exiles were thus entitled by law to appear before a judge, who would examine impartially the charges against them and decide if they should be released.

The lawyers gave the writs to couriers Levi Hollingsworth and Benjamin Bryan, who happily rode out of Philadelphia at breakneck speed to catch up to the caravan, thinking they had saved the day. On September 14, they reached the caravan in Potts Grove and duly served the writs on the guards holding the exiles. The guards, however, refused to honor these legal orders from the chief judicial officer of Pennsylvania. They had orders, they explained, from the SEC to take the prisoners to the town of Reading. While the Quakers continued to wait at Potts Grove, the lawyers took applications for habeas from the remaining nine of the twenty exiles to the chief justice, returning that night with these last writs also allowed by McKean.[12]

On September 16, the Assembly of Pennsylvania met to pass a new law. Often referred to as the Banishing Law, this legislation was tailored specifically to deal with the exiled men. That fact is betrayed by an introductory clause in which the SEC had revealed that it had "at the recommendation of Congress, taken up [arrested] several persons who have refused to give to the State the common assurance of their fidelity and peaceable behavior . . . [and] who cannot at this juncture be safely trusted with their freedom." The law enabled the state to exile any person *suspected* of aiding and abetting the enemy and to confine or remove them to another place of safety, and it contained another key provision.[13]

The legal apparatus that facilitated the exile relied on a long-recognized exception under English law to the writ of habeas corpus. Since the Magna Carta of 1215, habeas corpus—the right to force the government to take an arrested person before a neutral judge to determine if the arrest was legal or if the person should be set free—had encompassed an important bundle of key individual rights for detainees. Habeas was therefore a special tool in contending with arbitrary state power. As legal historians have noted, however,

English law also recognized that in emergencies the Crown claimed the right, in order to preserve the government itself, to arrest persons who may be thought dangerous to the state, without having to follow procedural due process—a somewhat darker strain of law. Particularly during an invasion or a rebellion, the executive authority sought a lever "with which the political branches could balance the needs of national security against the liberty interests of those enjoying the protection of domestic law."[14] In Britain, this lever became the suspension of the right of habeas corpus. In Pennsylvania, the Banishing Law of September 16, 1777, which suspended habeas corpus for certain persons and enabled their exile, copied this ancient practice.[15]

The Banishing Law provided for the release of the putative offender if the person would swear or affirm the oath of allegiance to the state. No judge, however, was allowed under the new law to issue a writ of habeas corpus in the case of persons charged under this law. Thus, the law effectively suspended all further writs of habeas corpus in this case and ordered that the exiled prisoners be released and immediately rearrested with a new warrant dated September 16 and signed by SEC Vice President Bryan. In this way, the state could claim that the earlier, signed writs of habeas corpus were now irrelevant, as they only applied to the first arrest, not the second. The law now provided that the issuance of any new writ of habeas corpus was ineffective against the rearrests. Consequently, the exiles would continue to be confined and sent on their way to banishment in Virginia.[16] Though these machinations constituted extraordinary procedural chicanery, they also reflected the suspension of habeas from that darker strain of English law. Thus, the exiled men were to be three times silenced, shut out of the halls of government: unheard by Congress or by the Council and, additionally, unheard by any court in their defense. Instances of such extraordinary oppression against nonviolent men not charged with a crime are rare or nonexistent, but the stakes on the other side of the equation—invasion by a mighty army and navy such as Britain's—were high, and the entire American experiment could have been crushed.

The only lawyer among the exiles, Miers Fisher, wrote to Chief Justice McKean on September 18 from Reading. Thinking that McKean was, because of his earlier decision to allow habeas, a neutral judge, Fisher advised the jurist that the local authorities in Potts Grove had arrested one of the messengers who had brought them the signed writs. He asked McKean to grant a *supersedeas*, a legal order overriding the man's arrest.[17] Little did Miers

Fisher know what McKean's own correspondence with John Adams later that month would reveal.

McKean evidently worried that his decision to approve the first writs of habeas corpus would be unpopular in Congress and the SEC and that their members might even think him guilty of Loyalism. Indeed, there were those in Congress who were "disillusioned and outraged by his actions." Consequently, he felt compelled to justify himself in a letter to Adams. As McKean reminded his fellow lawyer, the governing habeas corpus law imposed an immense fee on a judge who improperly failed to grant a writ of habeas corpus where the facts and law required it. As he told it, McKean had granted the writs against his passionate political interest in order to avoid a huge fine.[18]

McKean also revealed to Adams that, in informing the SEC of Pennsylvania of his decision to issue the writs, McKean had inquired if the Council had yet done what other governments had: pass a law suspending the right of certain individuals to habeas corpus. This had been done in England, he wrote, "in almost every war since the making [of] the statute."[19] McKean had advised a coequal branch of the government of a way to skirt around and undermine his own lawful judicial order.[20]

When the exiles' lawyers returned to McKean again on September 18, however, McKean protested his helplessness, insisting that he disapproved of "the unprecedented measure" the Council and the Assembly had taken in passing the Banishing Law. He would grant the Friends a hearing were it in his power, he claimed, but the Council had prevented him from doing so. The young Philadelphia Quaker and poet Robert Morton, not cognizant of McKean's private communications, observed McKean's verbal exchange with the Friends and concluded, as Miers Fisher had earlier, that the chief justice's actions were "worthy of imitation."[21]

Days later, an irritated Henry Drinker complained about what he called "our persecutors." He railed that the new law, "if it is yet a Law, no Man or *Woman* is to spread false News, unless it is such as favors [the Patriots'] designs. For tho' a Man or *Woman* may hear intelligence of which they may have no cause to doubt the Truth, yet unless it has their [the Patriots'] mark, Banishment stares *him or her* in the Face." He fulminated at great length in his correspondence over "the Arbitrary & oppressive proceedings respecting us, & the Measures pursuing in Philadelphia to strengthen the hands of Evil Men, by framing Ordinances & Laws to suit their Iniquitous purposes

[and] the daily strides made over the Rights & Liberties of Men & the swift advances towards absolute & Despotic Tyranny."[22] In short, his words mirrored those of Congress in its complaints about Parliament. What Drinker and the others may or may not have noticed in the Banishing Law was a sunset provision mandating the law's expiration on the first day of the next session of the Assembly, which was due to occur on January 2, 1778. This provision was both a legacy of English law as well as a sign that some legislators were uncomfortable with the law and wanted it curtailed relatively soon.

Loyalist attorney James Allen viewed the Banishing Law similarly. In his diary, he leveled a charge that the Pennsylvania legislators "not only trample on the most express laws of their own Government, but those of natural Justice & humanity. The Chief Justice Mr. McKean having granted an Habeas corpus on their application, the Assembly prevented its execution by a law to suspend the Habeas corpus act, thereby making a law, ex post facto [after the fact] & pendente lite [during the litigation]; the very extreme of Tyranny."[23]

An ex post facto law, the Banishing Law was an illegal attempt to set the legal consequences for certain acts after the facts of the case had taken place. It aimed to render punishment while also suspending the fundamental writ of habeas corpus, for which the litigants had already successfully applied. Combined with the fact that the exiles were never charged with any specific acts or crimes, this over-the-top legal action further confirms that the Patriots were desperate to muzzle and remove Quaker leaders and that the Quaker exiles were true political prisoners.[24] It also explains why each level of government pointed to the other as the responsible party. Ousterhout concludes, "Laws such as [the Banishing Law] made a mockery of the state constitutional guarantees."[25]

The men in the caravan did not know of McKean's duplicity as they traveled from Potts Grove to Reading, sixty-five miles northwest of Philadelphia. The exiles noted "much enmity amongst the people, and some stones were thrown at us . . . the face of everything much changed. Our friends . . . were violently pulled away, struck and stoned." Quaker Isaac Zane Sr., accompanying the caravan as a supporter, was "considerably bruised and hurt."[26] The populace had heard that the alleged Tories had been stalling and that armed reinforcements had to be called up to move the caravan forward. Such treatment contrasted starkly with the men's relatively comfortable lodgings, the pleasure they took in one another's company, and the unwavering commitment with which they clung to their faith.[27] According to Captain Alexander

Graydon, a twenty-five-year-old non-Quaker and fellow lawyer friend of exile Miers Fisher, "The prisoners were not much dejected, probably looking upon themselves as martyrs to the cause of their country."[28]

After leaving Reading, the exiles and their guards continued through the towns of Lebanon, Harris's Ferry (today's Harrisburg), Carlisle, and Shippensburg. Along the way, they confronted misinformation and verbal and actual threats. At one stop, a man pointed a gun and hurled invective at the exiles.[29] On September 29, they reached the southern Pennsylvania border—the limit of the SEC's jurisdiction—protesting before reluctantly crossing the Maryland state, or Mason-Dixon, line with their guards. About six miles south, at Watkins Ferry, they crossed another border, the Potomac River, protesting again before entering the Commonwealth of Virginia.[30]

Each time the exiles passed from one state into another, they wondered under whose authority they traveled and to whom they should address their next protest. At this point, the Continental Congress's board of war, which John Adams chaired, was as much in charge of the prisoners as were the Pennsylvania authorities, particularly when it was convenient for their own purposes for the Pennsylvania officials to say so. The exiles were unaware of the shifts in jurisdiction between the two governments, and at times each governmental body pointed to the other as to ultimate responsibility. Seeking redress, or at least dialogue, the Quakers received from their oppressors only obfuscation and disdain. This scene had the look and smell of men seeking to avoid future blame for treating some nonviolent citizens in a manner likely not well founded in the law.

Chapter 6

VIRGINIA EXILES

The caravan of exiles arrived in Winchester on September 29, 1777. The entire journey had taken eighteen days, and as autumn arrived the weather began to cool. In Winchester, the caravan of Quakers received a hostile reception from about thirty skeptical locals concerned that there would be more Tories in the neighborhood, as there were already about three hundred Hessian and British troops held in purpose-built barracks nearby. Washington's troops had captured them at various battles, including those at Trenton and Princeton. In addition, the county lieutenant (a revolutionary and civic position of trust), who was in charge of the prisoners, believed that the local population was intensely irritated with the Quakers and would have to be restrained from committing violence against them.[1]

The month before the exiles arrived in Frederick County, Virginia, local Patriots and militiamen had tied muskets to a group of a dozen or more young pacifist Quaker men and forced them to march two hundred miles to where Washington was camping in Pennsylvania. The perpetrators hoped to force these young men to complete Virginia's military recruitment quota. By the time the Virginia pacifists and their guards arrived in early October, General Washington, aided by the disowned former Quaker Colonel Thomas Mifflin (Quartermaster General of the Continental Army), sympathetically ordered this practice to end. He released the worn-out young Quakers, allowing them to leave camp and return to their homes on their own.[2]

Winchester was a frontier village of about eight hundred people.[3] It was favorably placed at the head of a long, fertile valley into which many German immigrants had migrated. The town was laid out on a grid, six streets north-south and four east-west. West of town was North Mountain. There was a German church and a Methodist one. At the north end of town was a fort built in the 1750s, where George Washington, then in the Virginia militia, had once been the officer in charge. The fort's purpose was to defend against Native Americans to the west. The Hopewell Friends meetinghouse, built seventeen years earlier, was about six miles north of the fort, and its congregation came from the countryside many miles around.

The exiled Quaker prisoners stayed that autumn in Philip Bush's inn (three and four men to a room), nestled among the houses of the little town. Henry Drinker reported, "We are all accommodated in one House as commodious as this Town affords."[4] The prisoners had to pay for their own food and lodging, and while the twelve most prominent Quaker leaders and Owen Jones Jr. (a young merchant from a well-to-do family) could well afford their room and board, the rest of the exiles—the four other Quakers, Thomas Affleck (Scottish-born cabinetmaker), Charles Jervis (hatter), Charles Eddy (ironmonger), William Smith, broker (merchant); two disowned Quakers, Elijah Brown (heavily indebted merchant) and William Drewet Smith (pharmacist or doctor); and the Anglican, Thomas Pike (dancing master, instructor in the use of the small sword)—were hard-pressed to support themselves, and their families back home often became the recipients of such wartime community charity as existed. Though the exiles were commodiously accommodated in their place of exile, it was not an entirely pleasant situation. As a backcountry village, Winchester became a major center for prisoners of war, which meant that food and other necessaries might get scarce quickly. The exiles, however, were totally separated from the prisoners of war, who were housed in the newly built barracks.[5]

As soon as the Quakers arrived, they began, as Henry Drinker told the story, to formulate a protest "to lay our Case fully before the persons entrusted with & exercising power in this province" (figure 3). Province, he wrote, not state, since he did not recognize Virginia's new governmental order either. The SEC had referred the exiles to the governor of Virginia should they have any grievances while there. They did just that, preparing and sending a protest to Patrick Henry, governor of Virginia, setting forth the illegal way they had been arrested and, even though held by the Pennsylvania authorities, conveyed out of that state into Maryland and then Virginia, where they were beyond the legal jurisdiction of their home state. Exile Samuel Pleasants had also written to his family in his native Virginia, hoping they could influence Governor Henry to take an enlightened, or at

FIG. 3 | Henry Drinker (1734–1809), a merchant and clerk of PYM committees, was opinionated, judicious, and valued by his peers. He deeply resented being taken away from his family, was determined not to betray the peace testimony, and piously considered each decision he made. Silhouette, David McNeely Stauffer Collection on Westcott's History of Philadelphia [#1095], Historical Society of Pennsylvania. Reproduced with permission from the Historical Society of Pennsylvania.

least less hostile, view toward the Philadelphia Quaker exiles.[6] To complain to Virginia was to Henry Drinker "highly proper—and the Event will show whether they mean to pursue the true ends of all good government in dispensing Justice & Righteous Judgment throughout the Land, . . . [or to] adopt the example which of late has been too frequent, of talking much & making a show of promoting the cause of Liberty and Virtue, while they have nothing less in view, & merely prostitute those terms to serve their base & wicked purposes."[7]

Drinker remained confident that even many Patriots found the exile tyrannical.[8] Even if this assessment were correct, however, sympathy for the exiles did not extend to congressional delegate Richard Henry Lee of Virginia, a member of the committee that had recommended the banishment of the Quaker leaders. On September 8, Lee had written from Philadelphia to his cousin, Governor Patrick Henry. Sending his cousin a packet of Quaker testimony from newspaper reprints, which he called "inimical testimonies," Lee described "the arrest of old [Israel] Pemberton and several others, to prevent their mischievous interposition in favor of the enemy at this critical moment, when the enemy's army is on its way here, . . . I hope you will have them well secured there, for they are mischievous people."[9]

Even without Lee's enmity, Governor Henry was unlikely to be sympathetic to the exiles. He had already written on September 15 to the officials in four counties of Virginia where Quaker meetings operated, telling those authorities of the arrests and asking them to seize Friends meeting records in their counties and "arrest any Quaker found guilty of treason." The *Virginia Gazette* also published the names of Loyalists considered hostile to liberty. Perhaps unsurprisingly, nearly seven weeks after their protest was sent to the Virginia governor, the exiles had still received no response from Williamsburg. Henry Drinker quickly added Virginia authorities to his list of "parties in the injustice & oppression," and perhaps by this he meant to turn the tables and compile a Quakers' hostiles list. In any case, the Quakers prepared another protest to send to Congress from Virginia.[10]

If leaving Philadelphia marked the end of the first phase of the exiles' confinement as prisoners of the state and the three-week journey to Winchester the second, the rest of the calendar year marked the third phase of confinement, very different in character from the fourth phase to come in the following year. In this fairly optimistic phase, the exiles settled in, acclimated to their surroundings, bonded as members of a persecuted religious group, and practiced—indeed deepened—their strong and disciplined faith, improvising under straitened circumstances. They then worked assiduously, aided by numerous supportive visitors, to protest their persecution in hopes of gaining their release.

Israel Pemberton remained, as before, their most active protest author. His brother James was their most active diarist, keeping a close record of their daily lives, perhaps also serving as an informal political analyst when needed. John Pemberton and John Hunt became their group's ministers, arranging regular religious services to which the public was invited (and some did join in). Thomas Fisher was calm and resigned and kept to his own diary and correspondence, but during the winter he also sketched a map of the Winchester area, indicating the homes of fellow Quakers where, after they left the Philip Bush residence/inn, exiles boarded in the latter months (figure 4).[11] He also studied the group's finances, figuring how to

FIG. 4 | Thomas Fisher (1741–1810), a merchant and eldest of four brothers, was married to diarist Sarah Logan and kept his own diary. In his twenties, while on a voyage to Europe, he was kidnapped by pirates and eventually released in France. Later, he led the Fisher mercantile firm. Silhouette, David McNeely Stauffer Collection on Westcott's History of Philadelphia [#1095], Historical Society of Pennsylvania. Reproduced with permission from the Historical Society of Pennsylvania.

FIG. 5 | Miers Fisher (1748–1819), was a merchant and lawyer. In 1774, he and his wife, Sarah, hosted a dinner for delegates to the Continental Congress, including John Adams and Thomas McKean; during the exile, he occupied himself with habeas corpus and wrote a last will for his brother-in-law, Thomas Gilpin. After the revolution, he advised Quakers making British Loyalist claims for compensation for damages. Pastel portrait by James Sharples, ca. 1794, Friends Historical Library of Swarthmore College.

FIG. 6 | Samuel Pleasants (1737–1807) was exiled with his father-in-law and uncles of his wife, Mary "Molly" Pemberton. In 1774, they hosted a dinner for delegates to the Continental Congress, including George Washington. Samuel's Virginia family visited at Winchester. Silhouette, Quaker and Special Collections, Haverford College [MC 850, Portraits and Miscellaneous Photographs].

divide up the later £20 lawyer's bill according to relative wealth, likely based on each member's property tax bills back home. Samuel Rowland Fisher rarely attracted public attention. Miers Fisher handled the habeas corpus legal activity, met with the group's lawyer, and months later prepared a will for his dying brother-in-law, Thomas Gilpin (figure 5). Henry Drinker was often sickly but maintained a vigorous correspondence with his wife and family and likely was an energetic participant in all key decisions, as he was opinionated, widely connected in Quaker circles, and a spirited writer. Edward Penington continued to nurse his strong aversion to the new government. Thomas Wharton Sr. was particularly incensed, as it was his own cousin (Thomas Jr.), the president of the SEC, who—if nothing else—had let the exile happen. Wharton loaned some money to two local men and bought two black horses during his time in exile. Samuel Pleasants, a native Virginian, kept in correspondence with his relatives, who also visited him (figure 6).[12]

Among the exiles about whom less evidence survives, there are unsubstantiated claims that Thomas Affleck, the high-end furniture maker, practiced his trade while in Winchester, as he needed an income to support his expenses there and his family back home. William Smith, broker, Charles

Jervis, and Charles Eddy seldom appear in the historical record. Elijah Brown had a great burden to bear, as he was perhaps deepest in debt and kept quiet. The final two exiles, William Drewet Smith and Thomas Pike, were outsiders among the men. They spent much time at the POW barracks, where Drewet Smith, an apothecary, administered medical treatment to Hessian and British prisoners while Pike assisted. Both later escaped, separately and months apart, on horseback to Philadelphia and joined the British Army.

THE QUAKER SUPPORT AND INFORMATIONAL NETWORK

While in exile, the Quakers relied on their extensive network of friends, coreligionists, and acquaintances to convey information and support to family in Philadelphia. The prisoners could send and receive letters, but they had to find someone who might volunteer (or perhaps be paid) to carry the letter to a distant town, where the messenger could entrust it to another Quaker traveling toward the letter's destination, and so on. Surprisingly, this network of couriers extended beyond expected sympathizers. On October 12, for example, Henry Drinker sent a letter via John Harvie, a newly elected delegate to the Continental Congress from central Virginia to the south. Harvie was soon to be a member of the very body responsible for the exile.[13] Obtaining a courier of such distinction was a curious circumstance. Cautiously sympathetic, Harvie had been passing through and visited socially with the Quakers. He was to take Drinker's letter to York, Pennsylvania, where Congress was then assembled, and hand it off to someone else who might be headed for Philadelphia. If the delegate could not hand the letters off to another messenger, he should send them "to Gen. Washington & ask him to forward them to our Wives," Drinker informed his wife.[14] Some of Drinker's letters, including this one, never reached their destination.

Once the British occupation of Philadelphia began on September 26, all letters passing through the collar of picket guards surrounding the city of Philadelphia were subject to being read by both armies' censors. Accordingly, writers were generally careful not to discuss certain subjects (war, troops, etc.). Whenever he sat down to write, Henry Drinker was "conscious of the difficulties . . . which forbid a free & unrestrained communication of Sentiments." That a censor may find his words "offensive or improper"— or, worse yet, unpatriotic—was not an unfounded fear.[15] In December, the congressional board of war complained to the exiles, based on "intercepted letters . . . from several of the Quakers," that they had not sent their corre-spondence first to the American Commissary of Prisoners for censorship as required.[16]

Under these circumstances, members of the close-knit Quaker commu-nity shared information any way they could. Henry Drinker, for example, sent to his family the love of fellow exile John Pemberton, and he asked Eliz-abeth to remember him affectionately to Hannah Zane Pemberton, John's wife.[17] He was pleased by the visits of some Quaker women, Rachel Hol-lingsworth and Elizabeth Joliffe, who had returned to Winchester from their attendance at the sessions of the PYM, where they had recently seen and talked with Henry's family and friends in Philadelphia.[18] Henry and the other Quaker exiles were happy to know that their "Afflicted & destitute Families . . . [had been] preserved through the several commotions & tryals which have happened."[19] The close-knit Quaker network made such com-munication possible, and the exile, in turn, brought members of the network closer together. Even such hard-nosed businessmen as Henry Drinker found solace and bonded in fellowship with their religious family.

The exiles thus valued their visitors not only for the information they brought but also for the moral support they gave and the correspondence they carried. In the fall of 1777, they welcomed an eclectic mix of core-ligionists, family members, and—perhaps surprisingly—curious, friendly Patriots. Friends John Parrish (figure 7) and John James left Philadelphia on November 7 to visit the exiles in Winchester, undertaking the dangerous two-hundred-mile journey.[20] Parrish was a brush manufacturer and minis-ter and one of the members of the Meeting for Sufferings. Parrish was par-ticularly useful in that, unlike many, he had taken the oath of allegiance in July 1777, which enabled him to travel freely. James, a businessman, was a relative newcomer to the circle of Quaker leaders but had gained their confidence. "So strong an Instance of Love affected our Minds," Drinker rejoiced when the exiles received the news of the impending visit.[21]

Parrish and James arrived around November 23.[22] They attended Hope-well Monthly Meeting during their visit and also traveled to the quarterly meeting at Fairfax, Virginia, some forty miles away. Congress had targeted John James for arrest in August, but the arresting party could not then find him. Now that he had left Philadelphia, the SEC distributed a bulletin some days later that John James, described in considerable visual detail, be arrested. Council members charged he had been sent out of the city "by the Enemy, upon Designs which are inimical to these United States."[23]

FIG. 7 | John Parrish (1728–1807), a brush manufacturer and Quaker minister, risked life and liberty to spend six weeks with the exiles and lobbied on their behalf. He and John James were jailed for a time. Silhouette, David McNeely Stauffer Collection on Westcott's History of Philadelphia [#1095], Historical Society of Pennsylvania. Reproduced with permission from the Historical Society of Pennsylvania.

The exiles also benefited from the visits of Isaac Zane Sr. of Philadelphia and Isaac Zane Jr. of Marlboro Iron Works in nearby Virginia (figure 8). In September, Isaac Sr., the seventy-year-old father-in-law of exile John Pemberton, visited his son-in-law and friends at their Reading, Pennsylvania, inn. While there he was "bruised and hurt" by onlookers who gathered to taunt the pacifist prisoners.[24] Thereafter his son Isaac Jr., an unusually bold Quaker who styled himself a "Quaker for the Times," felt compelled to act.[25] At the risk of being arrested himself, Isaac Jr. used his connections to improve the situation of the exiles. The details are unknown, but his position as a major iron contractor to the board of war of the Continental Congress likely provided opportunities. The exiles soon learned that their final destination had been changed from Staunton, Augusta County, Virginia (three hundred miles from home) to Winchester, Frederick County, Virginia (only two hundred miles from home), where there was an active Quaker congregation, Hopewell Friends Meeting, and a relatively new meetinghouse. Isaac Jr. had an added inducement to help the exiles: his sister Hannah was married to John Pemberton, who was also among those who held the mortgage on his Marlboro Iron Works plantation.[26]

Isaac Jr.'s intervention may have made a great deal of difference in the exiles' quality of life. He also helped them with other arrangements locally in Winchester. On Christmas day, Isaac Sr. arrived from Philadelphia with fresh news for the exiles from their families. He remained with the exiles or traveled elsewhere working on their behalf for forty-four days, partially concurrent with Parrish and James's even longer stay.[27] He lobbied Congress and the Council more than once.

The Zanes, Parrish and James, and certain other key Quaker supporters provided extraordinarily courageous support to their exiled colleagues, risking their lives and their freedom to do so. Parrish and James stayed with the exiles in Winchester the longest and had the riskiest profile, while also

FIG. 8 | Isaac Zane Sr. (1711–1794), a master builder, visited and lobbied on behalf of the exiles. Son Isaac Jr. (1743–1795), an ironmaster and major contractor to the congressional board of war, was a disowned Quaker who styled himself a "Quaker for the Times" (willing to be flexible about pacifism). Isaac Jr. used his influence to help the exiles. John Pemberton held the mortgage on his iron plantation. Silhouette of Isaac Zane Sr., Shippen Family Collection of Prints and Portraits [#3127], Historical Society of Pennsylvania. Reproduced with permission from the Historical Society of Pennsylvania.

making lobbying trips to York (Congress) and Lancaster (the SEC) and attending a nearby Friends quarterly meeting. Friend Thomas Lightfoot, a surveyor and strict Quaker, carried cash from Elizabeth for Henry Drinker and stayed in Winchester for a time in support of his friends. The five men mentioned here represent only a fraction of the support that the exiles received from their families and coreligionists. More than a hundred named Quakers brought mail, provisions, fresh news, and fellowship, and many took trips to lobby Congress or the Council.[28] The Quaker social network, reinforced by the framework of Friends' annual, quarterly, and monthly meetings, proved a uniquely fertile source of support to the Quaker exiles.

RENEGADE EXILES

Robust though it was, the Quakers' support network was not as effective as it could have been; as Friends lobbied and petitioned, the actions of two of the exiles—William Drewet Smith and Owen Jones Jr.—threatened the Quakers' already precarious position. Drewet Smith, the apothecary and disowned Quaker (he had married a non-Quaker), had been an unlikely exile. Though he professed solidarity with the other exiles, their cause was not his. "Despite all exiles agreeing to act in unity," Drewet Smith and Thomas Pike had tried to negotiate their own release separately from the others, making a separate application to Congress with aid from influential Patriot merchants in Philadelphia.[29] Other exiles took a dim view of this unexpected maneuver, which showed scant regard for their own feelings and prospects. It was not entirely a surprise, then, when Drewet Smith left Winchester in December without a word to the others and proceeded to Philadelphia.[30] He had escaped on horseback, in violation of the terms of the exiles' parole agreement with their guards in Winchester.[31] On his return to Philadelphia, he told General Howe of his medical work among the British soldiers and promptly joined the British Army.[32] Drewet Smith's escape occasioned a new fear among the exiles: that Patriots would perceive an escape attempt by any exile as an admission of guilt by all that they were inimical to the American cause. "I don't intend to sneak Home in a private manner," Henry Drinker wrote to Elizabeth, "but when I think the time is come, it shall be as openly & publicly as may be." The exiles' relatives feared that events such as Drewet Smith's escape would result in harsher punishment to those exiles who were left behind.[33]

Another shocking incident occurred later that week. On December 15, after more than two weeks' work, the Quakers agreed on another protest essay—titled "Observations on the Charges," a lengthy, dispassionate critique of Patriots' actions against them, signed by fifteen exiles—and a cover letter to the Meeting for Sufferings in Philadelphia suggesting that its members might print and publish it.[34] One of the fifteen proposed that they send it to Congress first. However, as soon as the exiles had arranged for and agreed on materials to send to Congress, the local county lieutenant, Joseph Holmes, interrupted them. He had learned from the Continental Congress's board of war that, since the exiles' arrival, the Quakers residing permanently around Winchester had "refused taking Continental Money."[35] The board of war had received and transmitted to the SEC a deposition from a York resident who had visited Winchester, where exile Owen Jones Jr. had given him fourteen half Johannes (quite a significant sum for any man to be carrying in specie). Multiple wealthier exiles may have entrusted these monies to Jones so that he could pass them to John Musser in Lancaster to exchange (at a presumably favorable rate) for Continental money, which the exiles could use to pay for goods and services.[36]

Charges of depreciating the currency were both common and serious. The discovery of Jones's actions caused the congressional board of war in York to order further punishment for the exiled men. They were to be sent to Staunton, Virginia, a hundred miles to the southwest, where they would be held in a common jail and prohibited the use of ink and paper.[37] The Quaker leaders quickly composed a protest to the board of war at York, and Holmes refrained from taking any actions to carry out Congress's threat until the protest was decided. Henry Drinker cryptically warned Elizabeth that he may be "debarred from communication" without elaborating why.[38] He did not mention Jones's currency violation or Congress's threat, though he expected the courier would update her in respect to those matters.[39] "The times are truly alarming," wrote Elizabeth when she learned the news.[40] On December 25, word came that Isaac Zane Jr. had persuaded the congressional board of war to give up their threat to send the exiled prisoners to Staunton.[41] Isaac Jr. had again saved the exiles from being confined deeper in the wilderness. The threat of congressional repercussions over this affair, however, would continue to hang like a sword of Damocles over the exiles and their families through December and most of January.

The exiled men engaged the best local lawyer they could hire: Alexander White, a London-trained attorney and confirmed Patriot whom the exiles described as "a gentleman of character in this neighborhood."[42] The exiles refined a protest essay for White to take with him to York, where he would ask Congress to release them. The Quaker leaders also gave White a letter of extensive background and instructions regarding their situation but allowed him discretion in pursuing relief. He left on December 21 for York, Pennsylvania, where a greatly reduced number of delegates to Congress continued to meet. Many had gone home for the duration of the Philadelphia Campaign, and John Adams had been sent to Paris as an ambassador.[43] "There were divers opinions about us [in Congress], but he [White] had some hopes of Success," Thomas Fisher reported.[44]

As the year came to a close, Henry Drinker reflected on his situation. "I am mercifully preserved in much calmness & ease of Mind," he wrote.[45] It presented a stark contrast to what Elizabeth and other exiles' families faced in Philadelphia. Winchester remained an island of relative tranquility on the outer edge of civilization, while a war in and around the city poured devastation on the homes and lives of their loved ones, coreligionists, and neighbors.

Chapter 7

QUAKER HOME FRONT

Through the invasion and occupation of Philadelphia, war had finally come to the very seat of the Friends in Pennsylvania, one of the largest and most important centers of Quakerism in all the British Empire at that time. A broadside posted on September 10, 1777, captured the Patriot view of what was at stake.

PROCLAMATION

The time is at length come in which the fate of ourselves, our Wives, Children, & Posterity must be speedily determined; General Howe, at the head of a British Army, the only hope, the last resources of our enemies' has invaded this State. . . . He appears to have risked all upon the event of a movement which must either deliver up to plunder & devastation, this Capital of Pennsylvania & of America, or forever blast the cruel designs of our implacable foes. Blessed be God, Providence seems to have left it to ourselves to determine whether we shall triumph in victory & rest in freedom and peace, or by tamely submitting, or weakly resisting, deliver ourselves up as prey to an enemy, than whom none more cruel & perfidious was ever suffered to vex & destroy any people.

Thomas Wharton, junior, President.

Attest,

Timothy Matlack, Secretary.

God Save the People.[1]

While residents fled and Henry Melchior Muhlenberg, the Lutheran prelate, compared the coming of the British Army to "a vial of wrath" being poured on the region, Quakers in the city hoped that the British would restore some order and save them from "the violent people," as Sarah Logan Fisher had repeatedly called Patriots but not the British.[2] The exiles' families heard the firing of ordnance from rifles and ships' cannons and saw the marching of troops to the north, south, east, and west. Provisions grew scarce, the required currency scarcer. Yet it was the human privation that mattered the most, as families coped with separation from loved ones.

One of the longest and largest military engagements of the entire war, the battle at Brandywine extended from early in the morning into the evening of September 11 and involved fifteen thousand troops on each side. It ended with a surprise as Howe surreptitiously and with the aid of local Loyalists tried to turn Washington's right flank. Only a hasty and effective retreat enabled Washington to emerge with a mere defeat. It was not a crushing blow, and American troops sustained good morale. General Howe remained at Quaker George Gilpin's house (a cousin of exile Thomas Gilpin and his brother, another George Gilpin who will be introduced later) in the Birmingham Meetinghouse area for five days after the battle, taking care of his wounded. In Philadelphia, Elizabeth Drinker noted "the great quiet we enjoy at our end of the town" (figure 9).[3] The Drinkers lived very close to the Delaware River and its wharves, usually a bustling beehive of activity loading and unloading ships, now grown quiet as shipping came to an abrupt halt pending the outcome of the British invasion of Pennsylvania. Happily for Drinker, other members of the Quaker community mitigated the silence. "Our sympathizing Friends are kind in frequently coming to visit us," she wrote. On average during the period of the exile, Drinker received about a dozen visitors at home in the course of a day, twenty or more at the busiest times.[4]

The quiet did not last for long, as no one in the city knew when Howe would arrive. Residents had reason to be anxious: six days after the British had arrived in New York one year previously, nearly one-third of the city's habitations went up in flames. Philadelphians were understandably nervous about what might happen in their city.[5] Sarah Logan Fisher, twenty-five and pregnant, described how skittish her neighbors had become: "Two nights ago, the city was alarmed about two o'clock with a great Knocking at People's doors and desiring them to get up that the English . . . would presently be in the City . . . Waggons rattling, horses galloping, women running, children crying, delegates flying & all together the greatest consternation fright and terror that can be imagined . . . all the Congress moved off before 5 o'clock."[6] Elizabeth Drinker also noted a general alarm in the middle of the

FIG. 9 | Elizabeth Sandwith Drinker (1735–1807) was a diarist, letter writer, women's mission member, and Henry's wife. Even when a British soldier was quartered in the house, it was the site of many informal meetings to exchange news of the exiles and the "tumult" surrounding them. She mostly did her writing late at night and was anxious for her husband's health. Silhouette, Historical Society of Pennsylvania portrait collection [V88]. Reproduced with permission from the Historical Society of Pennsylvania.

night of September 22, waking nearly everyone, when someone in her neighborhood had thought, mistakenly, that the British were arriving. They were not. Not yet. Elizabeth did not tell Henry of the disruption.[7]

Even on the eve of the city's capture, the American army was still making life difficult for Philadelphia's Quaker residents. On September 24, Sarah Logan Fisher reported that Lieutenant Colonel White and a "Captain Hamilton" came to the Fisher family's store "with armed men and forcibly broke open the store door & took away a large quantity of goods & said it was by General Washington's orders." Allowing for the mix-up in rank, this was likely Lieutenant Colonel Alexander Hamilton, an aide to Washington whom the commander in chief had sent to Philadelphia to supervise the collection of goods for the army.[8] Fisher found "this arbitrary conduct of theirs . . . unprecedented before in any age or country whatever."[9]

Diarist Robert Morton feared the city's remaining Patriots more than he did the approaching British Army. He spent the nights of September 24 and 25 sitting up as a guard in order to satisfy others who were "afraid of the City being set on fire." On the second day, two men "were taken up who acknowledged their intentions of setting the city afire."[10] Those Patriots who remained in Philadelphia "resolved on burning the Town and actually got together great quantities of Combustibles for the purpose, to prevent which the Loyalists . . . went thro' the different wards to seize all Arms & destroy such Combustibles."[11]

The next day, September 26, came the entrance into town of the British soldiers. Philadelphians Enoch Story and Phineas Bond led the light horse, followed by "soldiers [in] clean dress and their bright swords glittering in the sun. After that came the [regiments of] foot, headed by Lord Cornwallis. Before him went a band of music, which played a solemn tune, . . . 'God Save great George Our King.'"[12] A man with a face familiar to many Philadelphians, Joseph Galloway, rode alongside Cornwallis. Phineas Bond, Esq., who originally was on the hostiles list, had accepted parole, then renounced it. Given a second chance, the SEC offered him the opportunity to go to the West Indies. Instead, he guided the enemy's forces into his home city. According to Morton, the British arrived "to the great relief of the Inhabitants who have too long suffered the yoke of arbitrary Power; and who testified their approbation of the arrival of the troops by the loudest acclamations of joy."[13] "What a satisfaction it would be to our dear Absent Friends, could they but be informed of it," Elizabeth Drinker observed.[14] It is startling that a pacifist neutral, as the Quaker leaders publicly proclaimed themselves, would welcome the presence of either army.

British officers and their American Loyalist allies did attempt to quell fears among the city's sympathetic residents, which included some of the roughly one thousand Quakers who remained.[15] Galloway announced that no provisions would be taken from "well affected citizens" (Loyalists).[16] As early as August 29, Howe had issued strict orders to his men, including his Hessian troops, that any troops caught plundering property would be severely punished.[17] He executed two men on the spot, but word was already filtering into the city of the widespread plundering after Brandywine, and promises that those well affected to the British would not be harmed were just not kept. According to Morton, on September 25 General Howe sent a letter to Thomas Willing, a former Philadelphia judge, commanding him to advise city residents to remain at home if they wished to be left alone.[18]

By October 1, a soldier who had stolen some property from Mary and Israel Pemberton (Morton's aunt and uncle) was scheduled to be executed. Mary Pemberton "petitioned the General for a mitigation of the punishment."[19] Her Quaker beliefs trumped any attachment she may have felt to Howe.

Unsurprisingly, then, Philadelphia Quakers watched both armies warily. The banks of the Delaware River were rife with gunfire on September 27. No one on shore was hurt, but one man on the river "had his head shot off." Some mariners were taken prisoners. The next day, Elizabeth Drinker noted that "the Americans" were building a battery on the New Jersey side of the Delaware River opposite her part of Philadelphia.[20] On September 29, some British officers "[numbered] the Houses with chalk on the Doors." Some historians have noted that these chalk marks were to indicate whether the occupant was a rebel or Loyalist, but Drinker did not know or record that.[21] On October 1, the Americans lurked around Frankford, where the Drinkers had a country house. A large number of Friends in and near Burlington, New Jersey, were also taken into custody for questioning.[22] Though Elizabeth noted these developments in her diary, she said little in her letters to Henry, alluding to the occupation only as "the difficulty that now lies in the way of hearing from thee."[23] With censors of two armies standing between them, she was circumspect. But she also may have wished to spare Henry from further worry.

Among the events that Elizabeth did not share with Henry were several upsetting interactions with the British Army. In early October, British officers came to the Drinker household, telling her they were taking a census. The men told Elizabeth the count was necessary "in case provisions should be scarce each may draw their provisions with the army." Then she heard that James Bayard, the seventeen-year-old son of her friend John Bayard, a non-Quaker then speaker of the Assembly, had been arrested by the British as a spy and confined. In Henry's absence, she asked his business partner, Quaker Abel James, for help in extricating the son.[24]

There were, however, indications that Drinker and other Quakers were sympathetic to their occupiers. On October 3, Drinker noted that there were in town conflicting rumors about which side had won the Battle of Saratoga in upstate New York. Beginning in September, British General John Burgoyne faced off against Continental Army Generals Horatio Gates, commanding, and Benedict Arnold.[25] Drinker and some of her friends did not know what to believe at this point, but Sarah Logan Fisher was content to think on October 9 that the British had won at Saratoga. "A most agreeable piece of intelligence," she wrote, "to all the real well-wishers of America [the Loyalists] & as great a damp to its pretended friends, such as Washington, the Congress, Council, & all . . . perhaps infernals would not be too harsh a name, for surely their characters deserve to be stamped with the blackest dye—who wish to raise their own fortunes by sacrificing thousands of lives & the total ruin of their country."[26]

As civilians adjusted to their new reality, another battle loomed. By October 3, General Washington had suffered a solid defeat at the Battle of Brandywine, and days later a savage beating had been administered to General Wayne's troops at the Paoli Massacre. The capital city had been yielded without even firing a shot. Washington had already lost nearly five thousand men, either dead, wounded, or taken prisoner. Recruitment lagged, so the prospect of augmented forces could not be depended on. Many of Washington's own troops were shoeless and wore ragged clothing. Many farmers, some Quaker, would not sell the army meat for the troops or forage for the animals, as the Continental currency was devalued. Washington had garnered a surprise victory over the Hessian forces at Trenton the year before, taking over nine hundred prisoners, and defeated the British force at Princeton, but they had been battles against a detached regiment of Germans and a small rear guard of British. Now, he was up against the main body of the British Army, well equipped and handsomely outfitted, including a complement of Hessian mercenaries (25 percent of the overall force). Nevertheless, at six o'clock that evening, his troops moved out of their temporary camp and marched as far as twenty miles, mostly at night, to see if they could surprise the British at Germantown. It was a gamble.[27]

The first volley in the Battle of Germantown fired off at 5:30 a.m., and it was over by 10:00 a.m. A dense fog first favored the Americans insofar as it contributed to their surprising the British. Later, it hindered the Americans in their rout. The losses for the two armies, according to Thomas J. McGuire, favored the British, with the Americans losing about one thousand and the British only about six hundred.[28] It was a costly win for the British but a moral victory for the Americans. Howe did not finish them off, and he paid a steep price in casualties.

That day was a busy one for both Elizabeth Drinker and the city around her. It was the last official day of the PYM, which she and her family had attended every day that week, along with many out-of-town guests. The sounds of the beginning 5:30 a.m. salvos of the furious firefight in

Germantown were heard among the early rising Quakers. The cannon fire was particularly audible, and rumors flew among the nervous but stalwart Friends. One of the more gruesome reports described a dozen or more dead Americans lying on the front lawn of the house owned by former chief justice Benjamin Chew (a former Quaker, now a straddler confined in exile on an iron plantation in New Jersey).[29] Dr. James Hutchinson wrote to his uncle Israel Pemberton that "thy Place in Germantown has suffered considerably by the army, which has last occupied it, but all possible care has been taken to make the devastation as little as possible."[30] A doctor on the American staff, Hutchinson would discreetly not reveal in his letter which of the two armies that had occupied Pemberton's abode had left it devastated. Weeks later, Henry Drinker still imagined Elizabeth "surrounded & accompanied . . . by thousands of armed Men & frequently tried by the Din of War and the alarms which they occasion."[31]

October 5 was First Day, and Elizabeth Drinker attended meeting both in the morning and the evening, especially as many "Country Friends" were still visiting among them. Soon thereafter, shots rang out. In the evening, Drinker witnessed "the heaviest firing that I ever heard [for] upwards of two hours." People thought it was by the British troops engaged in a battle with three hundred American forces on the Mud Island Battery (now known as Fort Mifflin), fortifications of the Patriots in the middle of the Delaware River, south of the city. With troops wounded at Germantown still in the city and other skirmishes continuing to break out, Drinker ministered to soldiers on both sides. She recorded that she went to "the Play-House [a small theater in the neighborhood], the State-House [today's Independence Hall], and one of the Presbyterian's Meetinghouses to see the Wounded Soldiers."[32] On other days she sent her servants to do similar work. Not long after, her friend Sarah Logan Fisher sent a tub of broth "to the poor wounded Hessians."[33]

Both of the Presbyterian churches were used as hospitals for British soldiers, probably in deference to the city's two Anglican churches, while captured Americans were held at the State House. Henry Melchior Muhlenberg recorded that the British Army used the German St. Michael's church as a "garrison church" for the German soldiers, and the Zion church became a hospital.[34] Droves of British were brought into Quaker-run Pennsylvania Hospital, much to the chagrin of its managers.[35]

The British Army may have treated Quaker meetinghouses in the city more carefully than it did other houses of worship. No Quakers complained in writing about damages done to their three city meetinghouses at the hands of British soldiers (they had complained mightily about the Americans doing so). Muhlenberg also noted that the British Army "spared the Quaker meeting houses."[36] One nineteenth-century history of the city stated that "when the British occupied the city they [the Quakers] were treated with special consideration and respect on account of their well-known loyalist tendencies."[37] This possibility of preferential treatment provides circumstantial evidence for an insidious rumor: that the Quakers made a tribute payment to the British general. Quaker Major-General Nathanael Greene reported in a letter that General Howe required tribute money from the sect when he entered the city. Greene wrote that "the Quakers voluntarily lent Howe [£]5,000 sterling at his arrival . . . it is said that he laid them under the necessity of lending him [£]20,000 more."[38] Muhlenberg also reported it. In November 1777, two visitors informed him "that the British had demanded £20,000 in gold and silver as tribute from the Philadelphians. The Quakers had offered £4000 to £6000, but this was not deemed enough."[39] No Quaker sources confirm this exchange, and hard evidence is lacking. Regardless of the rumor's veracity, these two reports reveal that intelligent and influential observers believed the rumor true, which could have sorely affected the reputation of Quakers. Indeed, the very fact of Quakers staying in Philadelphia in the face of an invasion "fed the suspicion already circulating that Quakers had an understanding with the British and had insured their property with them."[40] Major-General Greene was so irritated by the Quakers' behavior that he was willing to take seriously a rumor that "several of the Friends say they wish G Washington's army was cut [in] pieces that there might be peace."[41]

At night, Drinker continued to hear firing on the battery on the Delaware River. That fight would go on until November 16, when the British were able to capture the battery from an undermanned force of determined Patriots on Mud Island.[42] Despite this victory, General Howe was getting edgy. His troops had been unable to get British ships up the Delaware to Philadelphia, and an alarming rumor held that General Washington would try to enter the city. If true, it would undoubtedly trigger a violent confrontation.[43] Unbeknownst to those in Philadelphia, the British forces fighting at Saratoga under the command of General John Burgoyne laid down their arms on October 17, agreeing by a "convention" (a contractual agreement) struck with American forces under generals Horatio Gates and Benedict Arnold not to fight again, thus surrendering to the American forces 5,791 officers and soldiers, along with many field artillery pieces.[44] The news would soon strike

Philadelphia, though for the time being Drinker confessed to her diary that "we hear a lot of news, but know not what to depend on."[45]

Closer to home, uncertainty and hardship continued to reign at the end of October. "Provisions are so scarce with us now," Drinker recorded. "The fleet not yet up, nor likely to be soon." The British would have liked to bring up fresh provisions on their flotilla of ships waiting farther downstream, but there was still much fighting on the Delaware River. The Pennsylvania government sought to prevent the entrance of the fleet by live fire as well as by Robert Smith's numerous chevaux-de-frise.[46] This was one of several strategies both armies developed to deprive the other side of food and supplies. The Americans made sure as little food and other provisions as possible were allowed to pass into the city, where the British would pay hard money for them; the British countered by sending troops into the countryside to round up provisions to bring into the city and prevent the Continental Army from availing itself of these goods. The decisions of all regional farmers, among them many Quaker farmers, whether to sell provisions to the armies became intensely political. At one point, a friend of the Drinkers was taken by "the Americans, bringing provision[s] to Town [for] our Yearly Meeting, and carried to Washington's camp, where 'tis said he is to be try'd for his life." (He was released on October 20).[47] Later that fall, Henry's brother Daniel Drinker lent his horse and cart to fellow Quaker Thomas West to bring goods back to town from the country, but the horse and cart were "taken by the Americans, so that Dan[ie]l has met with a loss," as had West.[48]

Necessities like food and firewood became scarce, as it was hard for suppliers from the countryside to obtain entrance into the city. "If some things don't change before long," Elizabeth Drinker opined, "we shall be in a poor plight."[49] Scarcity, skyrocketing prices, depreciated Continental currency, and lack of the old species of provincial currency combined to make life difficult. In the meantime, "the Hessians go on plundering at a great rate."[50]

On October 21, Drinker could see from the garret window atop her three-story house the action on the Delaware. Men crossed in flat-bottomed boats to resupply the Patriots while British ships fired on the fort. Two thousand Hessians crossed over to New Jersey to attack Fort Red Bank, also called Fort Mercer, opposite Mud Island, to help bring the Patriots on Mud Island to heel. The British resupply ships were not able to get upriver yet, and the occupiers had asked residents for blankets, now become scarce implements of war desired by both armies. Drinker continued to shepherd her four school-age children to their school, shop for food and other scarce provisions, manage a household of eleven persons, and check with the families of other exiles for news. All around her day after day was fraught with enormous consequences: arrest, imprisonment, loss, theft, wounding, destruction, and death.[51]

On October 21, twenty-five hundred Hessians crossed the Delaware River into New Jersey, and the next day they were driven back two or three times. In endeavoring to storm Fort Mercer at Red Bank, two hundred were slain and many more wounded. Now known as the Battle of Fort Mercer, the altercation, evidently within sight of the Drinker house, included the burning of two English ships, the sixteen-gun *Merlin* and the sixty-four-gun HMS *Augusta*, which exploded. A Continental Army officer stationed near the Merion meetinghouse compared the event to an earthquake.[52] Drinker, at Fifth Day (Thursday) meeting at noon when the explosion occurred, later echoed the earlier report that "it appeared to some like an Earth Quake."[53] Thomas Paine was on the road between Germantown and White Marsh and reported later to Benjamin Franklin that the sound was "as loud as the Peal of a hundred Cannon at once."[54] It was the largest of the four hundred ships there and the largest ship ever lost by the British navy in an American war.[55]

The American troops at Red Bank repulsed an attack by powerful Hessian forces, and a five-hour battle ensued between the British and American fleets on the river itself. Henry Drinker's partner, Abel James, tried to catch a glimpse of the action from the Drinkers' roof, but all he could see was smoke.[56] German troops killed, wounded, and captured amounted to 374, while only 37 American soldiers were killed or wounded.[57] Patriot soldiers again secured the fort at Red Bank. "Many of the Inhabitants of this City," Drinker wrote, "are very much Affected, by the present situation and appearance of things, while those on the other side the question are flushed, and in Spirits."[58] Presumably, she contrasted those in favor of the British with the Patriots, who were giddy at the destruction the Royal Navy had suffered.

It was getting cold in Philadelphia, and the occupiers could be cruel. Anyone found on the streets without a lantern between the beating of tattoo (calling soldiers to quarters at night) and reveille (the bugle call waking the military at sunrise) was subject to arrest and detention. Citizens were ordered to rake and sweep the streets in front of their houses every Saturday afternoon. A permit was required to sell a blanket. Only British soldiers could cut wood, and they everywhere tore down fences and sheds of all kind for their own use.[59] In late October, Quaker Tom Prior was arrested by the

British "on suspicion, as 'tis said, of sending intelligence to Washington's Army."[60] On November 1, a "poor [British] Soldier hanged this afternoon on the Common, for striking his Officer."[61] Quaker shipping merchant and minister William Brown also had an unfortunate encounter with a British officer. In typical Quaker custom, Brown declined to doff his hat. The officer struck him on the head with the flat side of his sword, giving him a wound from which he never entirely recovered.[62]

Joseph Galloway had often promised General Howe that Pennsylvania Loyalists would flock to the British side, but recruitment lagged. The presence of the British Army did attract Loyalists who wanted its protection, some of whom also enlisted. Most accounts estimate that three thousand Loyalists joined the British during the occupation, only fifteen hundred of whom fought for them.[63] Some—not all—were Quakers, though this was the group on which commentators tended to focus. From his perch outside the city, Henry Melchior Muhlenberg charged in his journal that "the Quakers are said to be very busy and to have enlisted five hundred recruits to reinforce the British troops. They act like the monkey who wanted to draw roasted chestnuts out of a fire and used a cat's paw to do it."[64] Unwilling to face danger on their own, Muhlenberg suggested, Quakers let others fight their battles. Contemporary observers may have fumed when the PYM decided to send six Quaker leaders as a peace mission to visit in person generals Howe and Washington, fresh from the blood and gore spilled at the Battle of Germantown. The five ministers and one elder with their broad-brimmed hats embarked on horseback with no weapons and no pass but with a great sense of moral purpose, good intelligence, and good sources. They knew where to find General Howe—safely ensconced in a stately Quaker mansion, called Stenton, which some of them had likely visited before and in which General Washington had also recently stayed, using it as his headquarters one night. Some of the Quaker exiles in Winchester knew the mansion especially well. Some local neighbors in Philadelphia likely thought Quakers had welcomed the invaders.

Chapter 8

QUAKER PEACE MISSION

Despite the widespread British invasion of the area, the PYM of the Religious Society of Friends refused to change the place or date of its regular, annual spiritual and business meeting "as a public testimony . . . of an unshaken Zeal for the Cause of righteousness."[1] Before the meeting broke up on October 4, its members decided to send a delegation of six weighty Quakers—five ministers (all merchants) and one elder (a farmer)—to visit each army's commander in chief on behalf of their fellow Quakers. These men held strict religious credentials equal to those of the exiles, even if some had a lower public profile. The 'elder,' though the youngest, was farmer Warner Mifflin; the merchant-ministers were William Brown, Samuel Emlen, James Thornton, Joshua Morris, and Nicholas Waln (figure 10).[2] The PYM directed the mission to "lay before the generals" its members' peace testimony, rebutting the charges recently made public by Congress in the publication of the Spanktown Papers and elsewhere that the Quakers had taken on a partisan, warlike loyalism. The six Quaker leaders were to reassure the military to the contrary while delivering to the generals the biblical admonition that they should "beat their swords into plowshares, and their spears into pruninghooks: nation shall not lift up sword against nation, neither shall they learn war any more."[3] They were further instructed by the PYM to protest the innocence "of the banished Friends . . . [and] to speak on behalf of truth and our religious society, as best wisdom may dictate and make way for them."[4] George Churchman, a Quaker activist in southern Chester County, reported to the exiles that these two visits by Friends to the generals were made "in order to remove prejudices against our Society."[5]

FIG. 10 | Nicholas Waln (1742–1813), a London-trained lawyer as a colonist, quit law practice to serve as a Quaker minister when, in 1772, he experienced a religious epiphany. He was a member of the peace mission to the generals, an adviser to the women's mission, and a clerk who signed the PYM 1789 letter to President Washington. Silhouette by Joseph Sansom, Friends Historical Library of Swarthmore College [Thomas Gilpin [Jr.] Profile Album, PA 033].

The members of the peace mission brought with them a printed broadside of a PYM testimony dated October 4, 1777, and reiterated their coreligionists' innocence. This committee's audacious mission was to defend the faith, defend the exiled men, and seek peace.

The members of the peace mission left the city on Second Day, Monday, October 6, and first went to see the real stranger to the area, General Howe, at his headquarters in Germantown. Ironically, Sir William Howe and his brother, the admiral, had been simultaneously commissioned by King George III not only as warriors but also as "peace commissioners," with authority (limited, it turned out) to make peace with the colonists. Howe had taken up residence at Stenton, the former home of the late James Logan, a Quaker intellectual and colonial administrator who was the grandfather of Sarah Logan Fisher, the wife of exile Thomas Fisher.[6] This was a difficult and dangerous journey as the delegation sallied forth through enemy lines in the midst of a shooting war without permission and without an armed guard or "passport" from either army. To these Quakers, accepting a pass from soldiers would have been equivalent to condoning war.

Contemporaneous descriptions suggest a stark contrast between the two groups. The men of war, clothed in vibrant red coats with gold or silver and white braid and shiny accoutrements, swords dangling at their sides next to polished high leather boots, were a powerful sight to behold. On the other side of the meeting space stood the five ministers and one elder, wearing coats with long skirts of dark gray or green, in black beaver hats, with their talk of "thee" and "thou." Their sect's strict practice as a matter of firm principle was never to take off their hats in the presence of such men as judges, kings, or generals or otherwise show any signs of deference to personages of exalted station.[7] It was their way of saying that before God all men were equal.

At least one of the Quakers stood out. He was not the eldest or the most experienced man among them, nor one of the weighty ministers. To the contrary, he was, at age thirty-two, the youngest by more than a decade and a rising voice in their councils. He was quite new to the inner circle of the PYM and not even a resident of Pennsylvania but of the flat land of central Delaware. Like the others, he was wealthy, via both inheritance and marriage, although unlike them he came from a rural farm. Though charming and humble, he was above all "utterly impossible to intimidate."[8] Contemporaries noted his well-known "ability to talk his way out of tight situations."[9] He appears to have been someone even the British would have had to look up to: one contemporary pointed out that he was "a great fellow near seven feet tall."[10] His name was Warner Mifflin, and not only did he have these fine qualities and a reputation as a good negotiator, but he was also the second cousin of a general in Washington's camp, Quartermaster General Thomas Mifflin. He was also related by marriage to a man traveling in the entourage of advisers in General Howe's camp, Joseph Galloway, an uncle to Warner Mifflin's wife.[11] Although these latter facts may have influenced his selection as spokesman, there is no evidence that either familial connection or even his great height helped him in this delicate endeavor.

Among the committee's members, Mifflin seems to have reflected on the experience in writing more than the others. "With no passport or shield to protect us from any merciless attack but our own innocence, sheltered by the wing of divine preservation," Mifflin later wrote, the men rode horseback together toward the British camp.[12] As he told it, Mifflin's sense of religious duty prevented him from feeling any terror riding in between the contending armies. On entering the camp, he "had to . . . observe the brutal revenge that appeared in the countenances of the soldiery against each other."[13] The members of the peace mission found the strength to persevere in a higher power "to whom the winds and sea are subservient."[14] A later descendant of Mifflin maintained that "all authorities agree that he [Mifflin] was seized by the British soldiers in his journey through the lines and spent some time in a guard house, from which he was released and treated with the utmost respect by General Howe."[15]

The actual meeting with Howe remains shrouded in mystery, a fact that detractors may have taken as evidence of Quaker perfidy. A friendly visit to representatives of the government that many Quakers felt had been unfairly usurped certainly invited suspicion. In their later report to the PYM, the six emissaries said only that they had conferred with Howe, delivered one of their testimonies, and departed.[16] There is no further description of their meeting with General Howe and no direct evidence of how they couched the discussion of the exiled Quaker leaders, whether they had discussed Quaker miller Roberts's aborted rescue attempt, how the six had been received by the British commander and his staff, or what, if anything, they had requested of the general. Members of the committee of six were "sensitive to Patriot charges that Quakers to the last man were proto-Loyalists." They later reported that they stuck to their script and gave out no intelligence.[17]

Making their way from Howe's field headquarters to the American camp without a passport, Mifflin wrote, "was like taking my life in my hands." Arrayed in their recognizable, drab Quaker garb, the committee members risked arrest by both sides as spies. Mifflin later wrote to the Quaker Major-General Nathanael Greene that some of the men in Washington's camp may have wanted to see the members of the peace mission dead. Again, however, because he was serving his faith, Mifflin "felt terror removed from me . . . I was not ashamed nor afraid at any time to Face the Head General of Either Army." According to Mifflin, the justness of their cause was so apparent that "we were at last treated as Ambassadors from some Prince."[18]

Quakers were on General Washington's mind as he and his troops camped at Pennypacker's Mill on Perkiomen Creek, American field headquarters from October 4 to October 8.[19] In a highly unusual move, General Howe had sent a letter to General Washington on October 3 complaining about the destruction by American troops of mills in the vicinity owned by "peaceable inhabitants," a common term for Quakers. Howe pleaded an "abhorrence of such Proceeding . . . [due to] a Regard to their Sufferings" (using the Quaker term for damages), chiding Washington to put a stop to it.[20] On October 6, Washington fired back a letter telling Howe that he was "at a loss to understand the design of your letter . . . remonstrating against a . . . common practice of Armies. . . . I am happy to find you express so much sensibility to the sufferings of the Inhabitants, as it gives room to hope, that those wanton & unnecessary depredations which have heretofore in too many instances marked the conduct of your Army, will be discontinued for the future." He reminded Howe of the burning by British troops of a mill near Head of Elk and another near the Schuylkill River, as well as the particularly brutal destruction of Charlestown, Massachusetts, in 1775, which included a savage cannonading from British man-of-war ships. This was remarkable correspondence, as most of the communication between the commanding generals was confined to routine prisoner exchange requests.[21]

Washington had a variety of interactions with Quakers on October 6, two days after the battle and a day before he was to receive the Quaker contingent. Washington had signed a warrant authorizing a man to collect blankets, shoes, and stockings "from the Quakers & other disaffected Inhabitants," suggesting Quaker intransigence.[22] By contrast, Washington's spymaster, Major John Clark Jr., had obtained valuable intelligence on the situation in Philadelphia, both from Cadwalader Jones, a Quaker "on whom I can rely" and several other Friends (unnamed), some returning home from the yearly meeting.[23] Finally, Washington had also instructed the local county lieutenant that if any man (in an area where Quakers were prevalent) was caught going into the city to join the enemy, their horses and cattle should be seized for his army's use.[24]

Despite his irritation with Quakers, Washington not only met with the six men but also invited them to partake of a midday meal with the general staff. The Quakers later reported quite expansively of the meeting that they "had a very full opportunity of clearing the Society from some aspersions . . . invidiously raised against them . . . we were kindly entertained by General Washington and his officers . . . all the officers then present, and there were a pretty many, being fully satisfied as to Friends clearness."[25] No one objected when the Friends distributed their testimonies, though General Washington "chastised Friends for depreciating the Continental currency by refusing to accept it in business transactions."[26] Some historians have concluded from this report that the committee of six convinced the officers of the spuriousness of the Spanktown Papers.[27] But it was perhaps an optimistic view; if the meeting did anything at all, it clarified Quaker intentions only among a few of the skeptical general staff present.

Additional sources provide another window into the meeting of the Quakers with General Washington. General John Armstrong, a sixty-year-old Cumberland County, Pennsylvania, Presbyterian, was with Washington that day. In a letter of October 8 to Pennsylvania's SEC President Wharton, Armstrong commented on the Quakers' interview with Washington: "We lost great part of yesterday with a deputation of Quakers from their yearly meeting, . . . declaring their own and the innocence of their Body, desiring prejudices against them might be removed as a Society, seeking in the world only peace, truth, and righteousness, with equal love to all men, etc. . . . The General was for sending them to you [the Council] and to Congress who had banished their friends."[28] If Armstrong was for that, Washington had thought better of it, treating them likely better than Armstrong thought befitting. Only a few miles down the road in the Patriot-held countryside, Lutheran prelate Henry Melchior Muhlenberg wrote in his diary on October 9 that according to an informant who lived nearby, "five prominent Quakers fled from Philadelphia to the American camp and pleaded with his Excellency General Washington for protection; he allowed them to appear before him and sent them to the guards."[29] Muhlenberg was quite dismissive of the Quakers as Christians, and his thirdhand report was likely inaccurate. But Muhlenberg, like other Patriots, may well have related it that way because that was how he felt it should have happened.

Washington took the precaution of having the Quaker deputation leave his headquarters and go first to nearby Potts Grove for a couple of days before reentering occupied Philadelphia, "within which time . . . such alterations might have taken place as to render [their] return less exceptional" to the Continental Army. By then, the American troops would have moved, and the committee could not reveal any useful intelligence to the British guards at the city gate. The circumspect Quakers carefully complied. In Potts Grove, they were "hospitably entertained" by a Potts family member, Thomas Rutter, the contractor for American cannon balls and other ordnance who had earlier hosted the exiles themselves.[30]

As the men tried to pass into Philadelphia, a Hessian guard questioned two of them who were traveling together. Becoming harsh and angry, the guard conducted the two to General Wilhelm von Knyphausen, a sixty-year-old military veteran and commander in chief of the Hessians, who appeared to the Quakers friendlier than the guard but who spoke no English.[31] He saw to it that the Quakers were conducted to Howe's tent. Noting that it was the Quakers returning from their mission, a secretary to Howe ordered that they be allowed into the city.[32]

In her diary for October 11, 1777, Elizabeth Drinker reported simply that the commission to visit General Washington had returned to the city. The next day, she went to Quaker meeting, where Samuel Emlen, one of the peace mission members, was also present. She noted later that "SE [Samuel Emlen] related some particulars of their reception at Washington's camp, as I had little expectations from their application, am not so much disappointed—as little has come of it."[33] Her diary scrupulously does not mention whether he told her how the visit to the British camp went.

Three months later, in mid-January 1778, two members of this committee, William Brown and Nicholas Waln, were sent with seven other Quakers to visit General Howe, this time to complain about the "Violence, Plunderings, and Devastations committed on the city" by the British Army.[34] The Quakers complained to the general again later that spring, this time about theatrical performances they deemed immoral. Quakers were every bit as nettlesome to British authorities as Adams had once found them toward the Patriot cause.

While the available evidence sheds little light on General Howe's reception of the Quakers or their presentation to him, it reveals General Washington's willingness to treat them with politeness. Quakers had treated Washington and members of Congress with the same respect in 1774, when Miers Fisher and Samuel Pleasants hosted lavish dinners for delegates to the First Continental Congress in Philadelphia. Now, Washington was welcoming them to midday supper and at least giving them an ear. He was open to hearing even from dissenters—at least those of a certain elite rank in society—despite his occasional complaints about Quakers. Though it did not yield immediate, concrete results or a cessation of hostilities, the peace mission does not lack lasting significance. It is testimony to the persistence, seriousness of purpose, and courage of both individual Quakers and the sect as a whole. Despite their ambivalence to earthly politics, they saw themselves as a significant enough third party to the conflict to stand up to the military of both sides and advance the cause of peace at the possible cost of their lives. Patriot observers, by contrast, might have seen gall and foolhardiness in the peace mission's actions. They may even have feared that the visit to Howe proved the Quakers' collusion. If non-Quaker critics ever thought that national security was at stake, this foray was the time when it potentially hung most starkly in the balance—even when weighed against the pursuit of religious liberty.[35]

Chapter 9

QUAKER ORDEALS

ELIZABETH DRINKER IN OCCUPIED PHILADELPHIA

By November 1777, Elizabeth Drinker had become a keen wartime observer. She was experienced at listening carefully and distilling the day's reports, and her diary became an accurate seismograph of the region's tremors, from the attacks on Fort Mercer across the Delaware River to the British and Hessian soldiers policing her very doorstep. In her diary, but not in a letter to her husband, she recorded that a British soldier came "to demand Blankets, which I did not in any wise agree to; notwithstanding my refusal, he went upstairs and took one, and with seeming good Nature begged I would excuse his borrowing it, as it was G. Howe's orders."[1] Drinker refused blankets to the British Army as she had to the Continental Army and militia. Blankets, though a simple component of bed clothing, had remained an implement of war. The fact that the British needed them, too, is evidence that the American blockade on the Delaware was working, and Drinker's refusal of these instruments of war to both sides suggests a firm and strict adherence to the peace testimony.

On November 21, Drinker had to deal with "an inferior Hessian Officer, an elderly man" who was quartered next door. He wanted to put his horse in the Drinkers' stable, and Drinker refused him this accommodation. Despite help from Harry, a formerly enslaved servant whom the Drinkers had manumitted, the German insisted on putting his horse in their stable. When Abel James, her husband's partner, stopped by, he offered to seek collaborator Joseph Galloway's intercession, as he had once before. James returned with the message that the top civilian authority in town would not allow other people's horses in the Drinkers' stable. Drinker closed the day, understandably, with a headache.[2]

Also in November, the Drinker household experienced the chaotic intrusion of a cantankerous and uninvited drunken British officer seeking the company of servant Ann Kelly. At first, he swore he had mistaken the house, then he shook his sword to threaten Drinker and her sister when they asked him his name and to leave the premises. Backing toward the kitchen, he continued in a quarrelsome way. Abel James's son Chalkley wrestled the sword away from the officer, and Drinker's sister locked it up. Then the intruder insisted he would not leave without his sword. Various neighboring men helped the women get rid of the intruder, who continued to swear and shout rude remarks. Drinker had to lock Chalkley in the parlor for fear he or the intruder would get seriously hurt. Finally, Harry locked the intruder out of the house, but the intruder remained outside the front door and demanded entry to drink a glass of wine with them. Abel James and another man talked with the intruder while Drinker locked and bolted all the doors in the house. Chalkley and a relative slept in the Drinker house just in case the intruder returned. By one o'clock in the morning, Drinker was still in a fright; indeed, she remained "in a flutter [over] Ann, and her Gallant" the whole next day.[3] All she conveyed to her husband was that Kelly "went off last week" with one of the British officers.[4]

British soldiers burned and plundered houses indiscriminately in November 1777. In a skirmish with British picket guards (troops stationed on the city's outskirts to watch for the approach of the enemy), the Americans hid in Fairhill, John Dickinson's house. As Drinker reported, "The English immediately set fire to such houses and burned them to the ground." Dickinson, despite having refused to sign the Declaration of Independence, for which he thought Americans not yet prepared, was by this time serving as a Patriot general in the Delaware militia. Descended from a long line of Quakers and married to a woman from a prominent Quaker family, many considered him a Quaker fellow traveler, but he believed in defensive war. The British viewed him from afar as "the ruler of America" and thus they had no incentive to save his houses either in Delaware, where the Loyalists had also captured and destroyed his home, or in Pennsylvania.[5]

In determining which houses to burn, the British seem to have considered military strategy more than politics. Drinker wrote that "the burning of the Houses 'tis said is a premeditated thing, as they serve for skulking places; and much annoy the Guards. They talk of burning all the Houses

&c within four miles of the City, [outside] the lines." From the top of the Drinker house, one "could see the Houses burning, and the Ships coming up."[6] Drinker did not record how she felt at this moment.

Robert Morton reported in his diary that twelve of the houses burned that day were Quaker mansions: "What is most astonishing is their burning the furniture in some of those houses that belonged to friends of government, when it was in their power to burn them at their leisure. Here is an instance that General Washington's Army cannot be accused of. There is not one instance to be produced where they have wantonly destroyed and burned their friends' property. They [the Americans] could have destroyed Benjamin Chew's house [Cliveden], and then would have injured a man who is banished in consequence of his kingly attachment."[7] The Hessians, too, committed cruel acts of destruction.[8] The young Quaker's sympathies, initially fiercely Loyalist, were evolving.

Unbeknownst to those in the city, including the British, on the night of November 24, with the knowledge that General Lord Cornwallis was in south Jersey with several thousand troops, Continental Army General John Cadwalader presented to the commander in chief and a council of general officers his detailed "Plan for Attacking Philadelphia." Congress had sent delegates to Washington with the idea of such an aggressive plan.[9] It called for a frontal attack on the westernmost part of the city while a couple thousand American troops sneaked into Frankford (to the northeast) and embarked by boat to land on the eastern flank of the city, within blocks of the Drinker house. The attack would have been on Thursday, November 27. After hearing from his generals in writing over the next two days, however, Washington decided against the plan.[10] Had the conditions for such an attack by American forces been favorable, the Drinker household would have been engulfed by soldiers from both sides fighting hand to hand in the streets of their neighborhood. Elizabeth Drinker had missed a close call and likely never knew it, but the mere possibility of the plan illustrates the state of uncertainty and alarm that hung over everyone in the city.

QUAKERS MOBILIZE

As the war persisted around them, Philadelphia Quakers continued to support their exiled brethren. The steps that Elizabeth Drinker took to secure acceptable currency for her husband in late November illustrate the complicated logistics of even seemingly quotidian tasks. The previous week, Henry had asked Elizabeth in a letter to send him "15 or 20 half Joannes," Portuguese gold pieces. On November 23, First Day, William Jackson, a Quaker minister, announced he was leaving town for Winchester the next day. In the market that day, Elizabeth exchanged "3 half Joes today for £60 Conti" and gave Jackson to deliver to Henry the £60 in Continental currency, roughly the equivalent in paper money, plus two pairs of worsted stockings for her husband. The next day, however, Jackson called on Elizabeth to tell her that, on reflection, "he was not free to take the continental money with him." Evidently, Jackson's Quaker scruples against war prevented him from having anything to do with Continental money, which most Quakers felt was tainted by war.[11] Elizabeth determined that she must seek another messenger to send the money to Henry.

Looking for news of a suitable messenger, she went to see, successively, Mary Pemberton, her uncle John Jervis (there she read a letter to him from his son, exile Charles Jervis), and Becky Jones (sister of exile Owen Jr.). Two weeks later, at Hannah Pemberton's, Elizabeth at last gave Thomas Lightfoot, the trusted messenger finally chosen, a letter and the paper money wrapped up "in HD's shirts" to carry to Henry.[12] Lightfoot was no ordinary messenger but an especially daring and defiant antirevolutionary dissident of strict Quaker principle, and, as an experienced surveyor, he knew the territory. He courageously risked his life and freedom acting as a courier for this significant sum of money, Continental currency or not, through the lines and two hundred miles away to Henry.[13] Individual Quakers retained the right to determine their own feelings about the Continental currency. Apparently, Elizabeth did not absolutely eschew the currency, nor did Lightfoot, at least in this dire situation.

With the two armies taking increasingly strict measures to cut off one another's food and other provisions, civilians suffered too. On November 12, Elizabeth Drinker recorded that with the present scarcity of provisions, "it is reported in the Country that 5/ [shillings] is given here for a Rat." She gave some "Beef and Biscuit &c." to elderly relative Edward Drinker's widow, as she "had heard she was in want."[14] In the first week of December, William Loague, a Quaker farmer, came into town from Chester County carrying flour and butter, but the next week he would no longer accept paper currency in payment, and Drinker decided not to buy his produce that week.[15] Intent on letting the British and others in the city starve, General Washington grew concerned about farmers taking provisions into the occupied city.[16] By late

November, however, the British Army had the supplies that English merchant ships brought into the harbor, so at least for the British soldiers there was a great abundance in the city. Few people had any silver or gold, even among the wealthy, to pay for special foods. As Robert Morton wrote on December 1, "Provisions scarce, people daily going out for it. Hard to pass the money."[17]

The Philadelphia Quakers were in such dire straits they even reached out to their brethren in the faith in London and Dublin. On December 16, the PYM tasked a group of eleven Philadelphia Quakers, including wealthy merchants Samuel Emlen, Abel James, Owen Jones Sr., Hugh Roberts (each a hostiles lister not exiled), and Richard Waln, along with John Drinker, hatmaker, to send a letter to Friends in London. The letter writers enumerated several sources of hardship: Congress and the Continental troops prevented provisions from the surrounding countryside coming into the city, and the British placed restrictions on currency and prioritized their army's and navy's requirements for provisions over that of the local populace. In addition, "The destruction and havoc made by the two armies for many miles around the city, is generally very great and afflicting; many of our peaceable brethren [have been] stripped of nearly their all, as to provision, livestock, bedding, and apparel." Soon, the Philadelphia men wrote, great privation would be rampant. They solicited their brethren in London and in Ireland to procure provisions, engage a proper ship, and send those provisions quickly.[18]

The London and Irish Friends must have made the arrangements at great risk to themselves. By so doing, they risked not only their financial investment but also the accusation of aiding nominal enemies of the Crown, despite the Philadelphians' claims to the contrary. Conversely, the Americans, had they intercepted the cargo, could have charged the Philadelphians with treason. Not only that, but if the shipment were seized by the British, Patriots could charge that the Quakers had contributed to feeding the enemy. The letter, however, was so carefully written by its draftsmen that neither the British nor the Americans could have used it as evidence that the Philadelphia Friends were Tories or Patriots, though likely the leading prejudice against Quakers would have prevailed.

OCCUPIERS AND RESIDENTS ENTANGLED

The British, by contrast, were newly flush with provisions. In the second week of December, a flotilla of British ships arrived with fresh goods and food, but the British still wanted to deny vital supplies to the American army, which they had recently failed once again to finish off in the Battle of White Marsh. In seeking to accomplish this goal, at Lord Cornwallis's insistence, they called on Quaker John Roberts, miller, who had earlier plotted to rescue the exiles. Roberts had left his wife and nine children in the suburb of Merion and decamped into the occupied city when a Patriot neighbor had threatened Roberts's life in response to his failure to pay taxes. Against Roberts's protestations, British officers forced him to lead a contingent of soldiers into the countryside near Roberts's own farm to search for and seize provisions and forage. The officers wanted Roberts along to identify which farms would reap the choicest harvests for their stealthy thievery. Roberts tried to pull his hat down, avert his eyes, and keep a low profile. He later maintained that he tried to protect certain neighbors whom he knew could not afford the ruinous loss that would result from having their livestock impressed and taken, but it seemed to Roberts that he could do no more. At the end of the raid, Roberts lamented to the couple hosting him in the city, Susanna (Suky) and Owen Jones Sr., the parents of exile Owen Jr., that the "distresses and cruelties [he witnessed] . . . were more than his nature could bear" (figure 11).[19]

New arrivals further complicated the relationship between residents and occupiers. General Howe's elder brother, Admiral Lord Richard Howe, commander in chief of the Royal Navy in North America, arrived in Philadelphia in late November with his secretary for Loyalist affairs, Ambrose Serle. Serle's mission in America was to seek out Loyalist sentiment and intelligence and report it back to headquarters.[20] To do so, Serle quickly inserted himself into Philadelphia's Loyalist society, which likely meant attending Quaker meetings. His diary for November 24 records: "Breakfasted with my Friend Mr. Galloway at Mrs. Wharton's, whose Husband, a Quaker [exile Thomas Wharton Sr.] with Mr. Pemberton & several others of the same religious Society, have been torn from their Families by the Rebels & sent into Virginia, where they have been imprisoned & treated very roughly on account of their supposed attachment to [the British] Government."[21] In the coming months, Serle became close with Galloway.

On December 18, British Major John Crammond, another of Galloway's associates, came to the Drinkers' door looking for living quarters for "some Officer of distinction." Drinker had already refused two similar requests on the basis that her husband was away. Drinker had a full load of responsibility at home, with ten people under her protection, all dependent

FIG. 11 | Owen Jones Sr. (1711–1793), a merchant and the last provincial treasurer of Pennsylvania, was targeted by Patriots for exile. Timothy Matlack intervened to add "Jr." to his name on a government list to protect this elderly Friend and substitute the namesake son, aged thirty-three. Owen Sr. and his wife, Susanna "Suky" Evans, hosted the refugee miller John Roberts and had to testify at his trial. Silhouette [FC 12.9], Historical Society of Pennsylvania. Reproduced with permission from the Historical Society of Pennsylvania.

on her to keep the household running. She again "pleaded off," though "he would have persuaded me that it was a necessary protection at these times to have one [i.e., a British officer] in the House." Crammond pledged to call back in a day or two. Drinker "fear[ed] we must have some [army personnel] with us, as many Friends have them, and it seems likely to be a general thing." The Pleasants family had also been approached to quarter an officer, though they hoped Galloway and his assistant commissioner, Enoch Story, could intervene.[22]

In the meantime, Major Crammond returned to the house and informed Drinker that he wished to take up quarters in her home himself. He prepared her to expect that "a number of Foreign Troops were to be quartered in the Neighborhood, he believed they might be troublesome." Crammond had liaison responsibility with the Anspachers among the Hessians. The two had a good conversation about the "malbehavior of the British officers, which he by no means justified." She told him frankly that she sought someone in the habit of early hours and little company. Before he left that day, Crammond informed Drinker that he and Galloway were well acquainted. Drinker was "straitened how to act, and yet determined; I may be troubled with others much worse, for this Man appears much of the Gentleman, but while I can keep clear of them, I intend to do so."[23] In comparison to other officers whom Drinker could have housed, Crammond was at least polite.[24]

Enoch Story dropped by that evening to tell Drinker that he might be able to exempt the exiles' wives from quartering "the military Gentlemen," despite the hardship it would pose for the army.[25] The prospect of quartering a British officer, even for a Loyalist and especially for a Quaker, was a daunting one. The family of exile Owen Jones had "been very ill used by an officer who wanted to quarter himself, with many others on them, he drew his Sword, used very abusive language, and had the Front Door split in pieces &c." Mary Eddy, mother of exiled Quaker ironmonger Charles Eddy, quartered some army personnel "who they say will not suffer her to make use of her own Front Door, but oblige her and her family to go up and down the Alley."[26] Eddy planned to complain to Galloway about the officer's insolence.[27] Ultimately, Story failed to exempt Drinker and the others from the onerous duty. Even Israel Pemberton's wife, Mary, now in her mid-seventies, could not escape this obligation.[28] Drinker must have worried that she too would be treated like Eddy and the Joneses.

Soldiers and others also imposed themselves unannounced and uninvited. A group of British soldiers and the wife of one took possession of the Drinkers' Water Street house. When Elizabeth Drinker learned that a group of men was tearing down the shed there, she sent her sister Mary to check on it. Mary told the trespassers, who were destroying the shed for its firewood, to desist. The men claimed that the house belonged to Patriots, but Mary "assured 'em it was not," seemingly proud that the Drinkers were neutral or Loyalist.[29] Scavenging for firewood occurred all over the city, no matter whether the home's owners were Tories or Patriots.

As the year drew to a close, Crammond came a fourth time and stayed for tea. Drinker later wrote, "We have agreed on his coming to take up his [abode] with us, I hope it will be no great inconvenience, tho I have many fears." One of Crammond's servants was to stay with him at the Drinkers', with two others boarding nearby. On December 31, Drinker announced that "J. Crammond . . . is now become one of our Family; appears [a] thoughtful sober young man, his servant also sober and orderly, which is a great favor to us."[30]

Late in December, both commanders in chief took stock of how the campaign was progressing. At Continental Army headquarters in the countryside at Valley Forge, barely twenty miles away from Philadelphia and barely two weeks into winter quarters, George Washington sat in his lodgings on the twenty-third and penned a heartfelt letter to the president of the Continental Congress. His view of the situation was not sanguine. "I am now convinced, beyond a doubt that unless some great and capital change suddenly takes place in that line, this army must inevitably be reduced to one or other of these three things: Starve, dissolve, or disperse. In order to obtain subsistence in the best manner they can; rest assured Sir this is not an exaggerated picture." Meager supplies, underclothed troops, and inclement weather all posed significant threats.[31]

General Howe, while waiting for his (secret) resignation of late October to be accepted in London, at this same time could report nearly sixteen thousand troops at his command and nearly three thousand Loyalists, perhaps a half of the latter now serving in his ranks, and more personnel on the hundreds of British ships docked in Philadelphia.[32] His army was situated comfortably in houses and churches in secure areas of the city.[33] Fresh uniforms had arrived, along with replacement swords, bayonets, rifles, ammunition, an abundance of rum from the West Indies, letters from home, and news of London. Meanwhile, Galloway reported to Howe that "thirty to forty colonists were dying daily of starvation or illness" in Philadelphia. He also claimed that "two thirds" of the Americans were Loyalists (an exaggeration) and that privation had reduced the Continental Army to a "miscreant troop."[34] Howe's officers were looking forward to the new year, when they would establish a theater and begin to put on plays mocking the enemy. Howe had reason to impart his words with a rosy glow.

Most Philadelphia Quakers did not truly belong to either camp, yet they could not help but be affected by the presence of both armies. Reduced to suspicion, persecution, and exile, members of this group could only look back on their once hegemonic political status. A laundry list of their woes was a depressing image. No longer were they a force to be reckoned with in Pennsylvania. Now they had no place in government, their 1701 Charter of Privileges had been revoked, they were fined for their military exemption, and they had no right to vote without taking the oath of allegiance. Their leadership had been arrested and banished *unheard*, soldiers were quartered in their homes, and their faith community would disown them if they accepted compensation for crops or livestock seized by either army. Plus, if they sold to Washington's army, they might be paid in Continental currency, already on its way to worthlessness. A wise and well-respected Quaker thinker residing in southern Chester County, George Churchman, reflected on the year's events and recorded in his diary, with the characteristic restraint of a Quaker: "This endeth the year 1777, a year which exhibited a series of trials such as were hitherto never experienced by the People called Quakers in Pennsylvania or other parts of the American continent."[35]

Chapter 10

WINTER STRESS

_____

In Winchester, the fallout from Owen Jones Jr.'s attempted currency manipulation continued as 1778 began. With the assistance of their attorney, Alexander White, the exiles had protested the board of war's decision to send them farther southwest to Staunton.[1] In December, White met on behalf of the exiles with delegates to Congress in York, Pennsylvania, where Congress had fled from Philadelphia. He sent three letters back to Winchester while there, but only the first was optimistic. In the latter two he was "more doubtful." White also carried his message on the exiles' behalf to the SEC in Lancaster, but the Council "considered us as prisoners of Congress." At least according to Henry Drinker, however, SEC members thought "it was doubtful whether our arrest had answered any good end & that the continuing our Imprisonment was not likely to serve the public cause."[2] If so, this was either an attempt to pass the buck or a major admission by the Pennsylvania government that the exile had failed its purpose. As of January 24, the exiles' protest had still not yet been considered. Meanwhile, the governor of Virginia had directed that the exiles be removed to Staunton pursuant to the board of war's instructions and the accusations of currency violations against Owen Jr., but the local authorities would not execute that order pending board of war consideration of the exiles' appeal. Given their circumstances, this was an uptick in their fortunes.

This exchange reflected the incessant interplay between the two levels of governmental authority, and it is quite possible that Congress and the SEC intentionally created confusion to avoid responsibility for their actions. They _knew_ these measures were extraordinary. They _knew_ what laws and legal procedures normally applied. This incident appears to have been a deliberate obfuscation, even though no direct admission has surfaced.

According to James Pemberton, White related that views among congressional delegates diverged widely: "Some are for our discharge, condemning the whole proceeding as arbitrary and unjust. Others for discharging us because if we were dangerous men at the time of our being taken up, we could now do less harm in Philadelphia than where we are. Others were for discharging us, because if we pursue our own inclination, to go where we choose, and go to Philadelphia now in possession of the British, and within their lines, our estates would be confiscated as persons joining the enemy. Some were candid enough to say that they knew nothing could be proved against us."[3] Henry Drinker grasped divergent possibilities: "If Justice, & humanity are not wholly banished from the Councils of our Oppressors, or even a desire in them to save appearances, we may expect to be moving homewards ere long—but on the contrary if they harden their Hearts & are determined to continue their Tyranny, then we may experience a further trial of our Faith & patience."[4]

In Winchester, Thomas Fisher recorded in his diary that a visitor named John McGill told the exiles that he thought it would hasten their release if they would all promise not to protest or publicize their treatment on their return to Philadelphia—at least while the war lasted.[5] The exiles may have received this advice with a good degree of skepticism; there is no sign of discussion of it in any of their correspondence or diaries, and the record they left suggests it would not have been well received.

On January 23, Congress received a petition from six Quakers, including Isaac Zane Sr. and John Parrish, both of whom had recently visited the exiles. The petition handed to the congressional representatives asserted, among other claims, that the exiles' wives were in dire straits, suffering greatly.[6] Increased communications led to greater awareness of the situation facing those who remained in Philadelphia. Drinker, for example, knew of his wife's many "difficulties, tryals & close provings." He felt that he was failing to perform "the Offices due from me in the tender Relation I stand, as Husband, Father & Friend to my beloved wife & precious Offspring."[7] Congress appointed three delegates—all lawyers from states other than Pennsylvania—to hear the petitioners.[8]

The board of war agreed to suspend the previous order to send the exiles forward to Staunton, at least until Congress had a chance to consider the Quakers' latest protest, which the six Quakers discussed with the committee of three congressmen. Apparently, several members of Congress thought that orders for the removal of the exiles from Winchester to Staunton were, Henry Drinker wrote, "grounded on weak frivolous pretexts, & were upon the whole hasty & cruel . . . having declared fully & freely to several of our Friends, that the depriving us of our liberty in the first Instance was altogether wrong, & that the continuing our confinement is an increase of that wrong." Outside of the political establishment, "all Ranks of people agree . . . that our Imprisonment & Banishment is universally condemned almost without exception." Some members of Congress may have been embarrassed to admit error, while other Patriot authorities continued to see the exiles as "dangerous Men & unfit to be entrusted with Liberty to return to the City & our Families."[9]

In England, Jabez Maud Fisher—young Tory, Quaker naturalist writer, and younger brother of the three exiled Fishers—was seeing the sights while visiting manufacturing facilities of interest to the family firm, Joshua Fisher & Sons. A series of Loyalist-tinged public statements in 1776 had gotten him in trouble in front of Philadelphia's revolutionary committee before his father, Joshua, had precipitously bundled him onto a ship bound for England, out of harm's way. There, he later received a package from a Philadelphia friend, Dr. Thomas Parke. It contained "the Pamphlet published by our banished Friends," which had already been reprinted in England and circulated widely. These were copies of the eloquent protest Israel Pemberton had written while confined at the Freemason's Lodge in Philadelphia. This protest, which criticized Congress and the new Pennsylvania government, was evidently used as fodder by the British ministry in London to call into disrepute the rebel Patriot cause in America.[10] Jabez called the exile a "barbarous Deed," which people of all classes held "in merited Detestation and even with horror, a Proceeding so contrary to that Spirit of Freedom . . . and so derogatory to every Principle of Right."[11]

In London, meanwhile, news of the crushing defeat of General Burgoyne and the British troops at Saratoga had arrived. Parliament began to doubt the ability of Lord North, the prime minister, to lead the war and convened a top-level review. By January, its conclusions were in: General Howe had failed to coordinate with General Burgoyne, with disastrous results; Howe should have opened up the 1777 campaign much earlier, possibly April, rather than July 23, when he and his troops sailed from New York Harbor.[12] According to John E. Ferling, the British had concluded that "America could not be conquered militarily, but American independence

might be prevented."[13] Major Carl Baurmeister may have been less optimistic. At British headquarters in Philadelphia, he reported that the American soldiers had "been told . . . that their steadfastness and patience through
one more campaign will secure their independence once and for all. . . . The
Americans are bold, unyielding, and fearless. They have an abundance of
that something which urges them on and cannot be stopped," a prescient
observation.[14]

The British, however, were not going anywhere, at least for the time
being. In the first week of January 1778, British Major John Crammond and
his considerable entourage—three servants to handle his personal needs,
three Hessians to serve as messengers and orderlies, three horses, three cows,
two sheep, and two turkeys for his and his guests' culinary pleasure—settled
into the Drinker home. In his first week there, he invited five Anspachers,
Hessians from a certain principality, to dine with him.[15] Elizabeth Drinker
remained largely unperturbed; she found that "our new guest behaves unex-
ceptionably, and much like a Gentleman."[16] Henry, by contrast, resented the
intrusion and feared Crammond's influence on the children.[17] Elizabeth's
acceptance of the situation likely stemmed from her knowledge that it could
have been much worse: she could have been stuck with someone like the officer who had wooed Ann Kelly, the Drinkers' indentured servant, away from
the home some days before, neglected to pay Elizabeth the £20 that the servant's remaining time was worth, and spoke rudely to her on the street.[18]

This unpleasantness aside, Philadelphia was more peaceful than earlier
in the occupation. Since December 9, the British Army's winter quarters
had fully set in, and much less cannon fire and combat were heard around
the city. Rumors also indicated that good news lay on the horizon. Elizabeth Drinker had learned "some information which leads us to hope better
things than your Letters intimate, but some of us are fearful of disappointment." With Congress considering the exiles' protest, it "was thought by
most, that they [the exiles] would be acquitted." Though Congress had not
yet responded to the exiles' protest, this news spiked the rumor that the
exiles were either about to be discharged or already had been.[19]

Except for foraging and occasional raids, the soldiers experienced light
duties during the winter. The British officers in Philadelphia attended dinner
parties, theatrical performances, musical concerts, gambling casinos, and
dancing assemblies late into the night. General Howe and his mistress, Betsy
Loring, were often seen chauffeured around town in exile Israel Pemberton's
fine coach.[20] With abundant English goods now available for purchase with

the right kind of money, Elizabeth Allen, the wife of Loyalist James Allen, reported that "everything is gay, and happy, and it is like to prove a frolicking winter."[21] Teenage Loyalist and poet Rebecca Franks, after moving back to the city from a country estate, bragged to a friend, "I've been but three nights alone since we moved to town, [and] I begin to be almost tired."[22] Quaker women, however, maintained their prewar habits as best they could, and Drinker and her cohort preferred quiet visits with friends to raucous parties with strangers. Some Quakers saw the behavior of the British shameful displays of "vanity and dissipation." Indeed, there were many "very bad accounts of the licentiousness of the English officers deluding young girls."[23]

By the end of January, the bad news seemed to overwhelm the good. While a rumor of John Pemberton's death turned out to be untrue, Drinker and her friends learned that John Parrish and John James had been held in Lancaster jail since the previous month.[24] Another rumor claimed that the men in Winchester were deprived of writing paper and implements, an example of their persecutors' "cruelty and hardness of Heart." For the exiles' families in Philadelphia, hearing from the exiled men by letter was "our greatest Consolation," and reliable communication was difficult enough as it was.[25] From John James, who returned to town on January 27, Drinker learned, incorrectly as it turned out, that the exiles would indeed be sent southwest to Staunton—"cruel orders," she thought. Lawyer Alexander White sent Hannah Pemberton a letter to share with the families of the other exiles describing the futility of dealing with Congress. As Elizabeth Drinker wrote to Henry, friends and family members in Philadelphia came to believe that "there is not much to be expected from those in . . . [whose] power" the exiles were held.[26] After all, "even our persecutors well know the innocency and goodness of Heart of many whom they endeavor to Afflict—poor Men." If legislators knew from the beginning that the exiles were innocent, what could persuade them to release the men? Drinker slept little during this month and complained that her mind was disturbed. She suffered more headaches.[27]

Indeed, Congress had again refused to release the exiles, despite some members' desire to do so.[28] Congress deliberated for more than a month before offering in late January 1778 yet another oath, upon the signing of which legislators promised to release the detainees. The oath was this seemingly harmless one: "I, A. B., do swear (or affirm) that I acknowledge myself a subject of the State of Pennsylvania, as a free and independent state, and that I will in all things demean myself as a good and faithful subject ought to do." The exiles had refused to subscribe oaths in the summer and fall of

1777, and they continued to do so in the new year. This new oath seemed to them like a method for Congress to excuse its own behavior. Henry Drinker sarcastically excoriated Congress as "the Great body, these Guardians of Liberty. . . . How insulting. Did they not make the same offer in Philadelphia when we protested against that ensnaring proposition [release in exchange for signing a parole] & their Tyranny[?]" Realizing that his letter might be read by Patriot censors and wishing to avoid charges of "interfering in State Affairs," Drinker dropped the subject.[29]

In the meantime, military matters continued to percolate in Philadelphia and elsewhere. Joseph Galloway's spies provided a tremendous amount of intelligence to British officials in early 1778, so they knew exactly how destitute and naked Washington's soldiers were during their time at Valley Forge.[30] Washington expected Howe to attack and was perplexed when he did nothing. Howe's inaction frustrated Galloway and other Loyalists, including Sarah Logan Fisher.

In Paris, Benjamin Franklin, sometimes even clothed in the garb of a Quaker, which he knew the French fancied, sought the French king's help for the American effort.[31] Franklin, John Adams, and another former delegate to the Continental Congress, Silas Deane, represented American interests. While many felt that Franklin's warm diplomacy was the deciding factor, Adams insisted that Burgoyne's defeat and Washington's daring attacks at Trenton, Princeton, and Germantown had achieved "more in Europe, than all our Ambassadors."[32] French military leader Charles Henri Hector, comte d'Estaing, noted the esteem in which French citizens held Washington.[33] On behalf of the new republic, the ministers signed a Treaty of Alliance and a companion Treaty of Amity and Commerce with King Louis XVI on February 6, 1778. France promised substantial loans, supplies, ground troops, and its navy. The treaties also opened the way for a similar alliance with Spain.[34] This news would not reach America's military and congressional leaders until May; when it did, it would have a profound effect on the playing field in the fight for control of Philadelphia and of the thirteen colonies.

Chapter 11

SHADOW OF DEATH

February and March 1778 were months of illness among the exiled men in Winchester and anxiety among their relatives in Philadelphia. Meanwhile, Congress and the Pennsylvania authorities continued to toss responsibility for the exiles back and forth. Partial rumors of these developments filtered to Winchester and Philadelphia and sometimes seemed to bode well for the exiles. As early as February 1, for example, Elizabeth Drinker learned some good news from Friend Elizabeth Morris: a vote in the Pennsylvania Assembly, led by a non-Quaker supporter, went positively for the exiles' chances for release, though its specific provisions were unclear. Another rumor suggested that exile Samuel Pleasants (whose wife, Mary "Molly" Pemberton Pleasants, had recently given birth) may return home on parole. But Henry Drinker, and likely the other Quaker leaders, had previously rejected such a conditional form of release that did not apply to them all, and the rumor soon turned out to be false. With changes at Philip Bush's inn, several exiles moved to the homes of individual Quakers; that trend continued in February, so they were greatly dispersed throughout the area (map 2). The exiles' lives remained in serious danger, and that motivated their female relatives to begin plans to send a delegation intended first for medical aid and then, in unprecedented fashion, also for political redress.[1]

Rumors of shifting political tides thus did not equal release, and growing sympathy in the Assembly for the exiles was hardly universal. In January, the Assembly had extended the sunset provision for the Banishing Law until late April. In late March, Henry Drinker heard that "Congress have ordered the Board of War to deliver up the Gentlemen of Philadelphia now

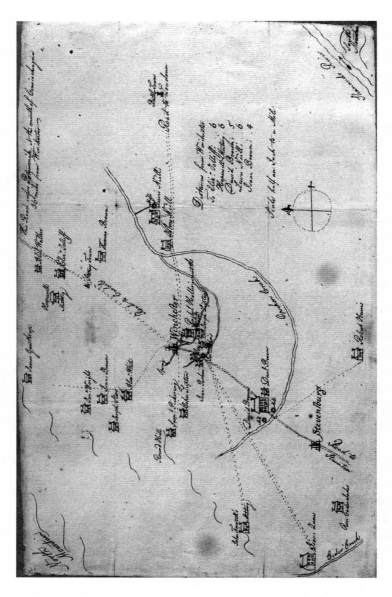

MAP 2 | Map of Winchester area, March 1778, drawn by exile Thomas Fisher, showing the location of homes where exiles lodged after they left Philip Bush's inn/residence. Winchester lies in the center; below left is Isaac Zane Jr.'s house; at the center top is Hopewell Friends Meetinghouse, where Thomas Gilpin and John Hunt are buried. Logan-Fisher-Fox family papers [1960], Historical Society of Pennsylvania. Reproduced with permission from the Historical Society of Pennsylvania.

prisoners in Winchester, to the order of this State who mean shortly to send for them & bring them to tryal on the charge formerly exhibited."[2] Since no formal charge had ever been leveled at them, this news caused some consternation. The exiled men knew nothing further, including "what proceedings have been had on these new Orders. . . . [But] this may be one of the last Letters I may write from [here]."[3]

Continuing enmity extended to the exiles' friends. When the SEC in Lancaster learned that Dr. Thomas Parke, James Pemberton's son-in-law and a Continental Army surgeon, and James Morton, Pemberton's stepson, were setting out to visit the exiles without permission, the Council directed that the men be arrested and held.[4] Even a committee of soldiers at Valley Forge suggested in a letter to president of Congress Henry Laurens that Parke and Morton should not be allowed to reenter Philadelphia.[5] Rarely, it seems, was the Quaker exile far from the minds of observant participants in the war at all levels.

Accordingly, as individuals and in groups, Quakers again petitioned both levels of government on the exiles' behalf while the PYM continued to send delegations to lobby politicians as well. Alexander White, the exiles' lawyer, petitioned Congress with reasons why the exiles should be "set at Liberty, on the [grounds] of Humanity, justice and good Policy."[6] Unfortunately, "those are things [the Congress] seem unacquainted with," Elizabeth Drinker noted tartly.[7] Quakers Thomas Lightfoot, Robert Valentine, and their wives (Lightfoot's wife was a public Friend, or traveling minister; Valentine's an elder) also visited the Pennsylvania Assembly to lobby for the exiles, the second such time and the first time a mission had included women. "We have heard that T. and S. L. [Thomas and Susannah Lightfoot] etc. have been to the Assembly," Elizabeth Drinker wrote to Henry.[8] She reported "that they had a hearing and were favorably received—that two [delegates] were appointed from the Assembly and one from the Governor . . . to go to Congress and straighten out whose prisoners these men were," so that the correct arm of government could release them.[9] There was said to be growing public sentiment for it. The next day, however, Elizabeth heard that the Lightfoots and Valentines were in Lancaster jail. This could have been a false rumor, or the men could have been caught without oath certificates (women needed none). Their status, and the status of their request, was still unclear days later.

In mid-February, the PYM appointed a special committee to visit the SEC, which "when convenient admitted some responsibility for the exiles."[10]

Isaac Zane Sr., who shared this news with Elizabeth Drinker, was prepared to return promptly to Lancaster to push for release of the exiles. On February 24, the SEC reported that six Quaker men, led by Warner Mifflin, petitioned in person for release of the exiles and of four other Quakers held in the Lancaster jail. The Assembly admitted the men but asked them before they spoke whether they acknowledged the Assembly's legitimacy and authority to pass and enforce laws. The Quakers replied that they had not come with answers to such questions and withdrew from the room. They returned the next day, but the Assembly pronounced their oral responses evasive and unsatisfactory, and they were instructed to petition in writing.[11] The SEC held an hours-long conference with the men, which ended without satisfaction. If the Quakers found the law in this instance "grievous or oppressive," the Council, the executive arm of government, concluded, they should petition the Assembly instead.[12] Congress had tossed the ball to the SEC, and now the SEC tossed it to the legislature. The SEC also found it convenient to tell the petitioners that the exiles in Winchester were still under the jurisdiction of Congress, while the prisoners at Lancaster were under the jurisdiction of the court. No relief—or at least no immediate relief—was granted.[13]

Unfortunately, for some of the exiles, release could not come soon enough, as illness spread among the men. Henry Drinker was one of the exiles experiencing many different debilitating symptoms. In early February, he wrote that he "felt stitches about my Breast, a pain in my Head, a fullness & other indications that Bleeding was needful." The previous day, Dr. Thomas Parke, after an eventful trip to Winchester, "opened a Vein it left me weak & fainty for a while and totally indisposed to write." Fevers, kidney problems, and disrupted sleep also plagued him, as did a "swelling on the left side . . . more painful than I had ever known it."[14] Drinker's health eventually improved, but others' did not.

Death and its shadow spread over the exiled men, many of whom were relatively elderly or susceptible to illness. Fifty-year-old exile Thomas Gilpin, according to Israel Pemberton, had been exposed to the weather one day and caught a "violent cold." He weakened over a period of weeks, ran a high fever, and on March 2 passed away despite efforts to nurse him back to health and the love and support of his three Fisher brothers-in-law and friends.[15] Gilpin had been the owner of many mills, a transatlantic merchant, and an eager and capable scientist, inventor, and member of the American Philosophical Society. In short, he was an especially useful member of society. He was also a husband and father of as many as nine children.

Thomas Fisher reported that in exile Gilpin was "a reading Genius seldom idle."[16] Over the course of the exile, Drinker wrote, Gilpin had been "easy & engaging, & his last Moments appeared much resigned & given up to the awful solemn call."[17] In his last days, Gilpin asked brother-in-law and fellow exile Miers Fisher to draft a will for him. Reciting Gilpin's current residence as Winchester, Virginia, the will explained that "he with a number of others, had been unjustly banished." According to Israel Pemberton, on reading the draft, Gilpin, a moderate man, asked Fisher to alter the phrase. Gilpin felt that it reflected badly on those who had imprisoned him, and he did not wish to cast aspersions on others. As Pemberton recalled, Gilpin then reaffirmed his faith: "There is but one true religion arising from faith in God, and in his son Jesus Christ, and hope in his mercy. A monitor placed in every mind, which if we attend to, we cannot err." In Gilpin's final hours, according to Pemberton, "he several times desired those about him to be very still, as he hoped he should also be; after which he said very little, his breath grew shorter, and without sigh or groan, or any sensible emotion, he quietly departed at half an hour after midnight." Pemberton may have overemphasized Gilpin's piety in the face of death, but the circumstances certainly warranted a dramatic rendering.[18]

The next trial was the "case of our beloved Friend John Hunt," whose leg had developed a "mortification"—gangrene. "Unless his disorder takes a turn soon, he cannot long survive," Henry Drinker wrote to his wife.[19] Other exiles were also ill: the young Owen Jones "has been poorly," the still younger Charles Eddy "has had a swelled Face," and the middle-aged Edward Penington suffered from rheumatism, while the more elderly Thomas Wharton Sr. also "had his complaints," and the only slightly younger Israel Pemberton was ill for several days. Middle-aged Samuel Pleasants "has been confined to the house, [with] a slow fever." The exiles believed that suffering had its uses, but this much illness caused great anxiety back home. Drinker was uncertain, moreover, when or how the men would request and obtain medical and other supplies for what they expected to be a longer stay in confinement. To his mind, "many difficulties seem in the way."[20]

The two doctors who attended the even more seriously ailing John Hunt on the twenty-first decided that his life could only be saved by amputation of the leg. Adam Stephen, a doctor trained in Edinburgh, Scotland, who lived twenty miles from Winchester, performed the surgery with the help of a second doctor. He sawed off the leg without anesthetic. While dressing the amputation, Dr. Stephen told his patient, "Sir, you have behaved

FIG. 12 | James Pemberton (1723–1809), a Quaker activist, former legislator, and clerk of PYM committees, wrote a journal of the exiles. In 1790, he succeeded Benjamin Franklin as president of the Pennsylvania Society for the Abolition of Slavery. Carte de visite copy of engraving, David McNeely Stauffer Collection on Westcott's History of Philadelphia [#1095], Historical Society of Pennsylvania. Reproduced with permission from the Historical Society of Pennsylvania.

like a hero!" to which Hunt replied, "I have endeavored to bear it like a Christian."[21] Hunt regained a lively appearance some days later, but then he weakened, and a "paralytic affliction" came over him. Hunt maintained a serene exterior, and he bore "the amputation of his Leg above his Knee . . . with admirable serenity & fortitude."[22] Despite occasional improvement, by the end of March, Hunt was "verging fast towards a City, none of whose inhabitants shall say they are Sick," a subtle reference to heaven. It would be "a heavy loss to the Church & his friends."[23] On the ninth day after surgery, Hunt "departed this life very easily" at the age of sixty-seven.[24] He had labored for forty years in the gospel ministry while also carrying on a mercantile practice, and his ministry had been "often favored with great power . . . singularly manifested in our meetings for worship," James Pemberton wrote (figure 12).[25] Under the circumstances, Henry Drinker urged

Elizabeth to prepare for his own death. All they could do was to be "entirely subjected to the Divine Will."[26]

On April 3, the *Pennsylvania Evening Press*, a newspaper with a Loyalist cast, ran a rare double obituary (despite the deaths of hundreds, even thousands, of soldiers and civilians in the interim), only the second obituary they had printed since the previous September: "Mr. Thomas Gilpin, formerly a reputable merchant in this city, and Mr. John Hunt, an emigrant minister among Friends, lately died in the back woods of Virginia, whither they had been banished with several other wealthy and loyal inhabitants by the rebel government of this province, at the instigation of congress."[27] This was a jibe meant to embarrass the Patriots. For all the obstacles to travel and communication, the news of the two deaths had traveled fast.

Chapter 12

"ENTIRELY AN ACT OF OUR OWN"

_____

Amid the tragedies that befell the exiles in the early months of 1778, a germ of an idea was developing among the women in the exiles' families. On February 3, Susanna 'Suky' Jones, wife of Owen Sr. and mother of exile Owen Jr., told Elizabeth Drinker that she wanted to go see "G. Washington on account of her Son; she hinted as if she would like me to go with her. . . . Tho' my Heart is full of some such thing . . . I don't see the way clear yet."[1] This exchange was the first suggestion that the women would eventually make a dangerous trip to visit their "dear Friends" in exile, though Drinker needed more convincing.

Taking political *action* was new for Drinker, but she and several of the other women involved in the mission were nonetheless skilled politicos. As literary scholar Kacy Dowd Tillman argues, diaries, though today often imagined as private, functioned "not only as historical artifacts" but also as "literary texts that [women] writers used to construct the war's narrative." In this view, Loyalist women's diaries were "as vital as the books and pamphlets that have been credited with the formation of America's national narrative." Railing against the perfidy of the Spanktown Papers, for example, Sarah Logan Fisher engaged in a form of "discursive resistance" and participated in "Friends' communal rebuttal of Sullivan's accusations against them" (figure 13). The communal nature of Quaker diaries was not just symbolic. Quakers often meant for their diaries to be read by others. Fisher sent her diary to her husband, Thomas, to read to his fellow exiles. Exile James Pemberton once noted that he "wrote to my family, and sent my diary from

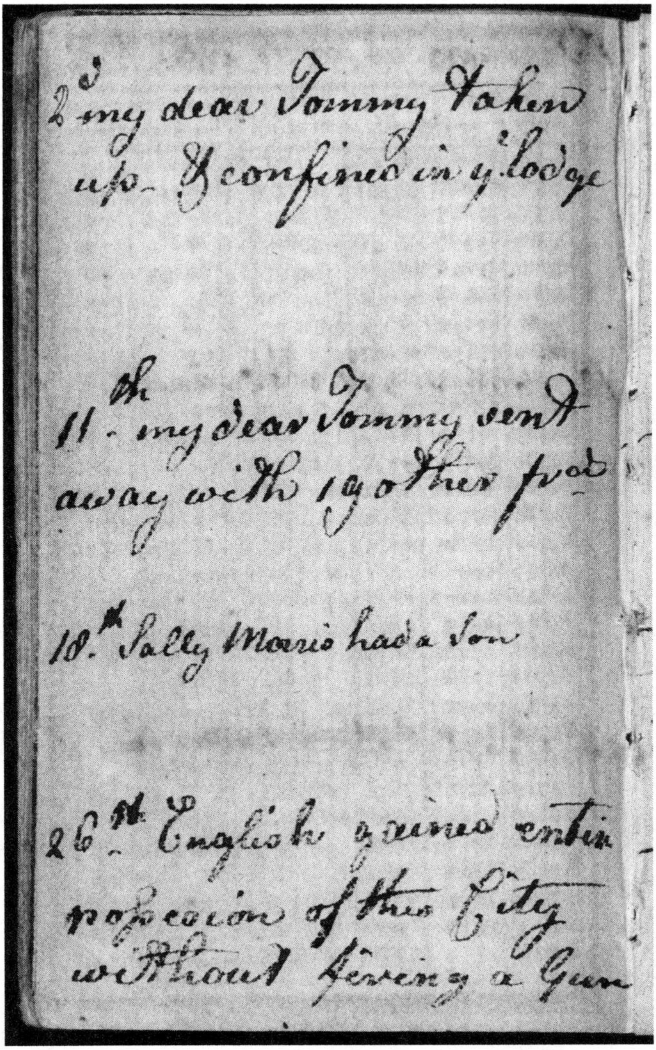
2d my dear Tommy taken
up- & confined in ye lodge

11th- my dear Tommy sent
away with 19 other frds

18th Sally Morris had a Son

26th- English gained entire
possession of this City
without firing a Gun

FIG. 13 | In her diary for September 1777, Sarah Logan (Mrs. Thomas) Fisher (1751–1796) wrote of her husband, Thomas, a wealthy transatlantic merchant and strict Quaker: On the 2nd, "My Tommy taken up & confined in ye lodge." On the 11th, though he had been accused of no crimes, "My Tommy sent away with 19 other Fr[ien]ds." On the 26th, "English gaines entire possession of this City without firing a gun." Pocket diaries such as *Poor Will's Almanack* became literary texts passed among Friends disseminating Quaker narratives of the war. Courtesy of The National Society of The Colonial Dames of America in the Commonwealth of Pennsylvania (on deposit at the Library Company of Philadelphia).

the time of my leaving Reading." This circulation of texts inevitably contributed to the development of a dissident political identity and narrative.[2]

News on February 5 that Quaker John Hough and Colonel George Gilpin, Thomas Gilpin's brother, had petitioned Congress in support of the exiles emboldened Drinker. According to John Parrish, some of the exiles' most ardent opponents had softened their stance. The time may have been ripe for action. Drinker wrote, "I have been much distressed at times when I have thought of my being still here, when perhaps it might be in my power to do something for my dear Husband . . . I hope it will please the Lord to direct us to do that which is right. It would be a tryal on us to leave our Young Familys at this time, . . . I believe, if we could conclude on the matter we should leave, and trust in kind providence."[3] It was a courageous belief at such a time. Both armies impeded easy movement, and the SEC might think that family members of suspected Loyalists planned to aid the enemy. Still, she wanted to do "that which is right," which meant taking action for her husband.[4]

As late as the fourteenth, Elizabeth Drinker still vacillated. Suky Jones, "full of the notion of [the women] going to Congress, gave me several broad hints, which I could not give into."[5] Part of her concern derived from a lack of news. The SEC censored mail from the exiles, searching all people who entered or exited the city. Elizabeth feared that a letter intended for her from Henry was missing.[6] Another time Elizabeth sensed that letters may have been censored as they passed "through Washington's camp," which increased her unease. The other women's "letters were all opened, Israel Pemberton's excepted; and S. Pleasants' envelope was sealed again."[7] Elias Boudinot, the American commissary of prisoners, forwarded the letters. This news triggered in Elizabeth the fear that there were probably other letters sent her that were detained somewhere, and perhaps they contained bad news.

The indispositions, illnesses, and deaths among the exiles, along with the diminished flow of news from Winchester caused by the lengthening of time between letters received and the failure by Congress and the SEC to release the men, were all conspiring to exercise a pull on the heartstrings of their families in Philadelphia. "It is whispered here that one of your Company is no more, and that several others are unwell," Elizabeth Drinker wrote to Henry amid rumors of illness and death. "Oh! How much I fear on account of my dearest Henry; this matter is not confirmed and many won't believe it."[8] Elizabeth "could willingly ask our cruel persecutors, what happiness or advantage has, or is likely, to accrue to them, from our distresses, I am persuaded they will find it far otherwise."[9] Slowly, she was being drawn into Suky Jones and Molly Pleasants's plan, which included an attempt to bring the Quaker leaders home.

The women's plans, whispered about for months, now gained momentum. Phoebe Pemberton (James's wife) and "M. P." (more likely Drinker's close friend Molly Pleasants than Pleasants's stepmother, Mary Pemberton) "came to consult me about drawing up something to present to those who shall acknowledge our dear Friends as their prisoners." Congress and the Council still cunningly tossed jurisdiction over the prisoners back and forth as convenience dictated. The women's "intention . . . tho we do not yet say so is to take it ourselves, 2 or 4 of us."[10] This was the moment when the women entered the formal political realm. It was a bold, risky proposition.

Elizabeth Drinker first solicited her brother-in-law John Drinker's help, but he said only that he would think about it. While visiting Mary Pemberton (Israel's wife), Drinker learned that the rumors about Thomas Gilpin's death were true. Several others, including John Hunt and her husband, were still ill. The exiles had "no medicines, Wine, Sugar, Vinegar, nor many other necessary articles" at Winchester, and she feared what may have happened to her husband in the three weeks since her last letter from him.[11] At Molly Pleasants's home, she and Drinker discussed sending medical necessities—their first priority—to Winchester. They went together to see Rachel Hunt, who was at that moment writing a letter to her husband, whose death was then imminent. She was not planning to go to Winchester for fear that she would learn during the trip that her husband had died, "which would be more than she could [bear]." Drinker returned home "much distressed."[12]

The women were increasingly driven to take action on their own. John Drinker had consulted Owen Jones Sr., who had counseled that the women should wait longer before sending provisions to Winchester. Elizabeth Drinker disagreed. Along with a letter, she sent her husband a quire of paper, some spices, rhubarb, and herbs via courier George Logan, Sarah Logan Fisher's brother.[13] Molly Pleasants, with help from her stepmother, Mary Pemberton, wrote a paper to send or take to Congress. The Quaker minister and former lawyer Nicholas Waln had also drafted a letter, but the women did not approve of his version or of him writing what they were to deliver. They convened on the afternoon of March 31 at Mary Pemberton's large home. In addition to the exiles' female relatives, at least five weighty Quaker men attended: paroled hostiles listers Joshua Fisher and Abel James, Owen Jones Sr., frequent Patriot target John Drinker, and Waln. Waln read aloud the petition that the women alone drafted, which the authors and others then signed. Four of them—Suky Jones, Phoebe Pemberton, Molly Pemberton Pleasants, and Elizabeth Drinker—were chosen to carry the petition to Washington at Valley Forge, the Council and Assembly in Lancaster, and Congress in York.[14]

Together, Drinker and Pleasants went to Owen Jones's home "to settle matters for our journey." There was much to arrange, including child care. Despite her concerns, Drinker had "concluded in my mind, that to the care of kind providence, and my dear Sister I must leave my dear little ones, and the Family generally." Drinker's sister Mary Sandwith at first had balked at assuming the responsibility, but Drinker hoped Sandwith would come around.[15] Mary Pemberton wrote to General Washington to announce the women's imminent departure for Valley Forge.[16] In contrast to the PYM's men's peace mission before them, members of the party also requested from the British Army a pass to leave the city, though Drinker did not note that delicate fact in her diary.[17]

Soon thereafter, Nicholas Waln called on Drinker with the petition, amended to reflect the death of John Hunt.[18] The text of the petition is an instructive departure from the language and tone most often used by the leading Quaker men. On behalf of "the wives, parents, and near connections of the Friends in banishment," the women's petition addressed both state and national persecutors. The authors still did not know who, Congress or Council, was most directly responsible for the exiles' plight. Their salutation, which clearly and respectfully addressed revolutionary officials and bodies, acknowledged the new state government and the elected delegates to Congress that had arisen out of the conflict with Britain.[19]

The women also appealed to the common ties they had with Patriot men—"Christian charity and compassion"—and reminded them of the golden rule.[20] They addressed the illnesses of several exiles and the deaths of two, alluding to the "unspeakable grief & irreparable Loss" some of the women had already suffered. They reminded the Patriots that many of them, too, had "wives and tender children and must know . . . in the time of trial and distress none are so proper to alleviate & bear a part of the Burthen as their affectionate Husbands." They never mentioned the war or Pennsylvania's deep, internecine, partisan divide between Patriots and passive and active Loyalists. Their tone avoided sanctimony (or subtle disdain), and they did not seek to glorify their own ancestors' founding of the colony as the men had.[21]

The women advocated straightforwardly the reasons that the exiled men ought to be released: they were guilty of no crime and faced persecution

FIG. 14 | Sarah Redwood (Mrs. Miers) Fisher (1755–1847) was a signer of the women's petition. During the First Continental Congress, on September 7, 1774, she cohosted with her husband, Miers, a reception and sumptuous dinner for delegates. John Adams, future chief justice Thomas McKean, and future prosecutor and governor Joseph Reed attended. Pastel portrait by James Sharples, Friends Historical Library of Swarthmore College.

solely for their religious beliefs. Throughout their lives, the exiles had "evidenced their strong attachment to their native country, and a benevolent disposition to mankind in general." The authors also insisted that their petition was "Entirely An Act of our Own, we have not Consulted our absent friends . . . [we] Request you take no offense at the freedom of Women so deeply interested as we are in this matter—And that divine Benevolence may so influence your Hearts as to Grant our Earnest Request in which we doubt not you will find true peace in the Hour of Retribution, & it will be an Inexpressible satisfaction to you." These "Suffering & Sorrowful Friends" produced a powerful plea that drew its great strength from its gendered and straightforward approach.[22]

Nineteen of the women signed, one female relative for each of the remaining eighteen men, with Charles Eddy's mother and sister signing (figure 14). Though Rachel Hunt signed at least an early draft, she likely in her state of grief was never asked to sign the final version mentioning not one but two deaths. It was an exceptional document by all counts, finalized against an appropriately dramatic backdrop of a "storm of thunder and Lightning, wind and rain."[23] This petition may be the first recorded instance in the history of Pennsylvania as a state, and possibly in the new republic, where women alone took collective political action to right in a public way a perceived governmental wrong.[24]

The next day, Owen Jones Sr. sent word to the women that Quaker minister Israel Morris had offered to accompany them. Though Owen Sr. seemed to support the offer, Drinker was skeptical. Ultimately, the women agreed to accept Morris's offer only under certain conditions. He could come along, they told him, only if he would escort them "and advise when we asked for it, . . . but [he] hinted that he thought it necessary that he should appear with us before Congress, which we by no means consented to— and he acquiesced." The women wanted to proceed their own way, as they believed their strategy had the best chance of success.[25]

As she prepared for her trip, Drinker continued to worry about her husband's health. Recommending two home remedies for serious illness, she also sent him a small package of provisions: "vinegar, a large Phial of thieves vinegar, to prevent infection, two single nightcaps, two pocket Handkerchiefs and Nancy's small almanac," plus an old jacket. Even the night before her departure, she said nothing in her letter about her mission, which the women had promised not to mention.[26] On April 2, Drinker went to see Rachel Hunt, who was again writing to her husband. Rumors of John Hunt's passing had circulated for days, though Rachel still hoped he would recover. When Drinker left the Hunts', however, she learned definitively "that John Hunt was no more—that the Account of his death was just come to Town." Anthony Benezet's wife, Joyce, and Mary Pemberton assumed responsibility for informing Rachel, while others sought suitable horses, drivers, and a carriage.[27] Later that day, Rachel seemed "to be composed tho in great affliction." With all that was going on around her, Drinker felt her "Heart is afflicted and fluttered very much." Still, that night Drinker kept to her regimen and wrote in her diary, giving the full names of the more than thirty persons who flooded her house that day. "May the Almighty favor our undertaking," she closed.[28] The next day, she and the other women would set off on a perilous journey, one of consequence unlike any other, to rescue the remaining prisoners of Congress so dear to them.

Chapter 13

"ABLE POLITICIANS"

On April 5, 1778, at about two o'clock in the afternoon near the wharves in Philadelphia, a large number of Friends met to say goodbye to the small caravan.[1] Susanna 'Suky' Jones (mother of Owen Jr.), Phoebe Pemberton (wife of James), Molly Pemberton Pleasants (daughter of Israel and wife of Samuel), and Elizabeth Drinker departed in a carriage with "4 Horses, and two Negroes who rode Postilion," with minister Israel Morris riding alongside. The women and their entourage crossed over the Schuylkill ferry easily and went ten miles seeing only two or three persons on the road as they made their way to the home of John Roberts, miller, where they stopped for the night. There they were "kindly entertained by the Woman of the house and her daughters, the Owner being at this time a Refugee in Town" in the home of Suky Jones, who could relay news of him.[2]

Suddenly, a scouting party of nearly one hundred American troops arrived at Roberts's house. Two officers entered the house claiming to have heard "there was Ladies from Philadelphia. . . . They [the officers] were about the House and in the Barn when we went to Bed—which leaves us under some apprehension concerning the Carriage and Horses."[3] The general staff at Valley Forge had heard of the Quaker women's mission—word of any unusual movements traveled fast, and Washington had already received a letter from Mary Pemberton giving him notice of their goals. Members of the Continental Army were especially on alert to suspect Quakers, as Washington had warned his troops that Friends were currently holding a quarterly meeting and that "the plans settled at these meetings are of the pernicious tendency."[4] The soldiers likely looked in the barn to make sure that this modest party of suspected Tories had nothing with them that looked like a British contingent, even in plainclothes.[5] The Test Act required only white men to take the oath and carry an oath certificate, so this party of women and two Black servants could in certain ways move about more freely than white men.

On leaving the home of John Roberts the next day, the women's mission proceeded to the American picket guard at Valley Forge, which sent two or three men to escort the women to an officer, who then gave them a pass for army headquarters, where they arrived in the early afternoon.[6] They were there to apply for a pass to send a wagon west with medical supplies and, if allowed, to accompany it themselves. Mary Pemberton, who at age seventy-four did not make the journey, had written a very polite introductory letter to General Washington in advance of the mission.[7] Washington, along with other delegates to the First Continental Congress, had dined with the Pembertons in Philadelphia in 1774. Pemberton wrote the letter before the women's departure, addressing the general in inimitable Quaker style as "Esteemed Friend" and asking him to provide protection for the two wagons to pass through the lines and deliver medical supplies to the exiles in Winchester. One of the exiles, she added, had already met his death in Winchester (Thomas Gilpin), indicating she wrote it before news of John Hunt's death arrived. She did not reveal the political part of the mission.[8]

General Washington sent a letter that day to SEC President Thomas Wharton Jr. in Lancaster, enclosing Mary Pemberton's request. He brought attention to her request to accompany a wagon of supplies to the exiles. Washington carefully told Wharton that as the persons concerned were prisoners of the state of Pennsylvania, "I did not think it proper to comply with her request." He was not going to interfere with state business, but he "did not doubt that her application would meet with your ready concurrence . . . I dare say you will extend the indulgence as far as may be requisite and consistent with propriety." The "indulgence" requested was passports for two wagons, one for the medicines and one for the women to accompany it.[9]

Elizabeth Drinker recorded that the women's mission arrived at Washington's headquarters at 1:30 in the afternoon. The Quaker women requested an audience with the general. Martha Washington came and sat with them while they waited. She was, Drinker confided, a "sociable pretty kind of woman." General Washington then appeared to meet the women and "discoursed with us freely, . . . but not so long as we could have wished. . . . He told us he could do nothing in our business further than granting a pass to travel on to Lancaster."[10]

Despite being short on positive encounters with Quakers and long on negative ones, the commander in chief invited the women to join him and his staff for the midday supper, usually served at 3:00 p.m. (He had similarly invited the six-man Quaker peace mission to a midday meal with his general staff the previous October.) Among their fellow diners that day were between fifteen and twenty-two officers, including the Quaker Major-General Nathanael Greene. The guests, Elizabeth Drinker recorded, "had an elegant dinner, which was soon over; when we went out with the General's Wife up to her Chamber, and saw no more of him [General Washington]."[11]

The Washingtons' hospitality likely derived from several sources. The general knew these were women of a certain rank in society, they provided welcome company for his wife while she visited the encampment, and he was a man open, capacious, and unfailingly polite. Both George and Martha, moreover, had powerful personal reasons to sympathize with the members of the women's mission. On October 19, 1777, the exiles in Winchester had received a surprising visitor: Colonel John Augustine Washington, a younger brother of the general. This visit may have particularly surprised Israel Pemberton, who wrote to family in Philadelphia that he had contacted George Washington about the plight of the exiles and that "Washington refused to do anything for them."[12] The commander in chief appeared to enjoy corresponding with his younger brother, sending him fairly frequent letters.[13] While in Winchester, the exiles recorded that Colonel Washington read to them an account of British general John Burgoyne's ignominious defeat at Saratoga, New York, that month and General Howe's vulnerabilities in his Philadelphia Campaign.[14]

No source indicates the reason for the younger Washington's visit. It seems unlikely that a confirmed Patriot and a family member of the commander in chief would have any affinity for these pariahs and suspected Tories. He lived in Westmoreland County, probably two days' ride from Winchester. George Washington acknowledged receipt of a letter from his younger brother dated October 26, 1777, seven days after the latter's visit to Winchester, but unfortunately this letter does not survive.[15]

Another visitor to the exiles with a personal connection to the commander in chief was Colonel George Gilpin, who arrived in Winchester on December 28, 1777. George Gilpin had been raised in Quaker ways by his elder brother Thomas, the exiled milling entrepreneur, though as an adult George attended the Anglican church near his home in Alexandria, Virginia. Exile Thomas Gilpin had written to his brother on October 3, when Colonel Gilpin was in the Philadelphia area with General Washington.[16] His stay, which also included trips to York and Lancaster lobbying on behalf of the exiles, was one of the longest visits with the exiles of any individual; it lasted until February 26, 1778, nearly a full two months.[17] Leaving that day to visit his own family, George Gilpin missed witnessing his brother's death by mere days.

Colonel Gilpin's visit coincided with a leave of absence from his military attachment, with which he had fought since 1775 at the side of his Virginia neighbor, General George Washington (Gilpin had corresponded with Martha Washington just before he left home to join her husband). Gilpin had served at Dorchester Heights, Boston, in 1775 and remained with the general all through the New York and New Jersey campaigns. In later years, Thomas Gilpin Jr., the exile's namesake son, would claim that Washington *sent* George Gilpin to Winchester to check on his brother. After the war, Washington and George Gilpin dined and stayed overnight at each other's homes. Gilpin represented Washington's interests in a project seeking to improve navigation on the Potomac River and ultimately was so close that he served as one of the six pallbearers at Washington's 1799 funeral. Unbeknownst to previous historians of the Quaker exile, George Gilpin was not only a longtime friend and colleague, he was also a part of Washington's personal family. The Gilpins and Washingtons considered themselves descended from ancestral families in England related by marriage (and Gilpin's brother Thomas had actually traveled there). Colonel Gilpin also married in succession two sisters, Catharine and Jane Peters, cousins to Martha Washington.[18]

When the members of the women's mission arrived at Valley Forge in early April, it had been one month since the death of Thomas Gilpin. The women likely mentioned it to Martha Washington, or she may have known already. There is some evidence that Martha conveyed to her husband a favorable impression of the Quaker women and their plight. British spies at Valley Forge even concluded that "through this lady's [Martha Washington's] kindly intercession, all Quakers were released."[19] The general, however, may not have needed this encouragement: he was capable of the most humanitarian and humane of acts, especially when his personal and military family were concerned, and he surely knew of the Quaker women's connection to Thomas Gilpin and his younger brother George.

General Washington dictated a second letter to President Wharton early the next morning. Asking Wharton only for a pass for the women, he reminded Wharton that women connected to the exiles had requested permission to go to York. Their intention, Washington noted, was to visit Congress to "endeavor to obtain the release of their Friends." This was Wharton's first inkling of their political mission. He left the decision up to Wharton but "imagine[d] their request may be safely granted." Washington again made the generosity of his desires clear.[20]

Washington concluded his letter with these seemingly unnecessary and poignant two lines: "They [the women] seem much distressed. Humanity pleads strongly in their behalf."[21] Washington hardly needed to invoke humanity's plea in order to obtain from the SEC president a mere permission for the women to pass through the lines. His letter to Wharton recalled a similar incident earlier in the war. Benjamin Franklin's son William, the Loyalist colonial governor of New Jersey, had been arrested and was confined in his own exile in Middletown, Connecticut, at the behest of Congress and the Patriot faction of the New Jersey legislature. The younger Franklin's wife was dying in New York, and he wrote to General Washington to plead for help in securing a pass to visit her. In his response, Washington claimed that he could not intercede, but he forwarded William Franklin's plea to Congress, recommending a favorable response. The commander in chief's letter read, "Humanity & Generosity plead powerfully in favor of his Application."[22]

Both Thomas Gilpin's namesake son and other historians have argued that Washington wanted Wharton not only to grant the passes but also to release the exiled men, though the text is ambiguous. Only the backstory of the relationship with Colonel Gilpin strongly suggests that Washington meant to influence the release of the exiled men.[23] Through the sympathetic window of their multifaceted relationship with Gilpin, George and Martha Washington likely knew more about and took a greater interest in the fate of the Quaker exiles than previous historians, even Thomas Gilpin Jr., have realized. These overlapping connections also provide one possible explanation for why John Augustine Washington, the commander in chief's younger brother, had earlier visited the exiles in Winchester in the winter of 1777.[24]

The morning of April 6, 1778, Washington gave the Quaker women the pass he received from President Wharton, which would allow them to proceed only as far as Lancaster.[25] For reasons explored here, Washington's exile-related Quaker interaction, including with members of the men's peace mission in the fall and the women's mission in the spring, were consistently on a higher level of sensitivity and humanity than any of his other interactions with local Quakers. While sometimes he was highly provoked by Quaker behavior, at other times broader humanitarian considerations tempered his response, and he trusted and respected his half dozen Quaker officers.[26] Washington's treatment of Quakers was nuanced and multilayered. It varied, understandably, depending on his own priorities and objectives at the time as well as on social class and personal connections.

After dining among the generals at Valley Forge, Drinker and the three other Quaker women by chance encountered at headquarters Isaac Penington (exile Edward Penington's son) and Charles Logan (exile Thomas Fisher's brother-in-law). The men had been taken into custody the previous day while carrying a packet of letters and supplies for the Winchester exiles from their Philadelphia families. They gave the letters and the rest of their baggage to the women before being released.[27]

On April 9, as the delegation approached Lancaster, its members met several Friends coming from a nearby Quaker meeting, among them James Webb. A former legislator, Webb owned an inn on the Conestoga River where the women were to lodge for some days. Webb had been one of several Lancaster Quakers who signed a report in September 1777, the very month the Quaker leaders departed into exile, describing the local militia's wanton destruction of the Quaker meetinghouse there.[28] At Webb's, the women received a surprising piece of news, long rumored but never before confirmed: plans for the men's release were underway. As early as February 28, as Elizabeth Drinker contemplated taking action on behalf of her husband and the other exiles, she and two other women, also relatives of exiles, had ducked into the meetinghouse to read a letter from exile Thomas Wharton Sr. Wharton "expressed . . . an expectation of a release e're long; in what manner I don't rightly understand, . . . it is talked of a forfeiture of their Estates, or by acknowledging themselves to be Subjects of the King of Great Britain."[29] This possibility presented a mixed bag to the exiles and their families. The possible loss of estates suggested the legislative convictions of treason by bill of attainder, a medieval practice for convicting people of crimes and seizing property by legislative fiat.[30] The Pennsylvania Assembly announced the first bill of attainder treason convictions in newspaper proclamations just days later than Wharton's letter, in early March. Among the convicted were three men whom General Howe had appointed to serve as the superintendent and two magistrates of the city, Joseph Galloway, Anglican judge John Potts Jr.,

FIG. 15 | Samuel Shoemaker (1725–1800), a merchant and former mayor of Philadelphia, was targeted for exile. He took parole, promising not to harm the local government; later, however, he accepted an appointment by General Howe to serve as a magistrate during the British occupation. He self-exiled to England, where he once chatted amiably with King George III, and returned to Philadelphia in the 1790s by permission of the Pennsylvania government. Silhouette, Friends Historical Library of Swarthmore College.

and Quaker merchant Samuel Shoemaker (figure 15). The exiles and their loved ones longed for release, but these circumstances were unacceptable. Thomas Wharton Sr.'s letter provided the first indication that the members of the women's mission would have to put their negotiating skills to use in securing more favorable release conditions for the exiles.[31]

Inside the Council, rumors slowly turned into reality. On March 7, Thomas Wharton Jr. asked Congress to place the exiles again under the control of the state of Pennsylvania. The SEC now feared that "the dangerous example which the longer continuance of the prisoners in banishment may afford on future occasions has already given uneasiness to some good friends of the independence of these States."[32] In the face of opposition even among Patriots, Wharton and the Council found that banishment on suspicion only set a dangerous legal precedent. Unless Congress could provide a reason to prolong the exile, Pennsylvania authorities desired that the jurisdiction of the exiled men be returned to them—and the men themselves returned to Pennsylvania.

The congressional board of war voted March 16 to give over control of the prisoners to the SEC, which failed for a couple weeks to inform Congress of its plan for the exiles' release. With this information finally in hand, the board of war, by its chairman, Major-General Horatio Gates, instructed the Virginia authorities to release the men to Pennsylvania authorities on April 8. At Lancaster that same day, now knowing that the women would arrive soon, the Council made arrangements for the men's release and return to Pennsylvania; two days later, Thomas Wharton Jr. formally dispatched two men, Francis Y. Baily and Captain James Lang, to collect the exiles in Winchester, take them to distant Shippensburg, Pennsylvania, and there set them free. Baily and Lang were instructed by the SEC to treat the men "with that polite attention and care which is due from men who act on the purest motives, to gentlemen whose stations in life entitle them to respect, however they may differ in political sentiments from those in whose power they are." Wharton's words would likely have rung hollow to the exiles themselves.[33]

The women had forded three rivers that day before arriving at Webb's, surely exhausted, around 5:00 p.m., but they had no time to waste. Traveling to Shippensburg, inconveniently located eighty miles west of Lancaster, would have significantly burdened a group that had already traveled far from home at great personal cost—especially since the SEC, contrary to its earlier promises to cover the expense of the exiles' journey and appeal to Congress to bear the additional costs of confinement, had that same day ordered that "the whole expense of arresting and confining the Prisoners sent to Virginia, the expense of their journey, and all other incidental charges [are to] be paid by the said Prisoners"![34] This would be a rude shock if communicated to the former exiles. The women dried off, had the muddy carriage cleaned, and departed an hour later for nearby Lancaster. They drove directly to President Wharton's door, where the exiles' chief nemesis suddenly gave their female relatives an audience. The SEC president was hardly unknown to them, though no prior face-to-face interactions had occurred. All Drinker recorded of the conference was that it had been "not very satisfactory." Afterward, they were offered tea with the Council president's wife, which they apparently accepted before returning to Webb's "by Moonlight."

That night, SEC secretary Timothy Matlack, a disowned Quaker who had long ago been a schoolmate of Elizabeth Drinker, visited them at Webb's and promised to consider sharing the women's petition with the Council.[35]

The next day, the women returned to Lancaster, where half a dozen local Friends met them. The women also met again with Matlack, Drinker wrote in her diary, "who undertook to advise us and perhaps with sincerity." They lobbied three of the twelve individual Council members and tried to visit another, who was not at home.[36] They even went to Matlack's home, where his wife, Nelly, "seemed much pleased to see us." They were also stopped "in the street, and at every place we came" by politicians, curious people, and seeming well-wishers from Philadelphia in their own self-exile from the captured city.[37] Matlack asked the women to wait until the time was right for them to appear before the Council; meanwhile, he agreed to deliver their petition. After an hour of waiting, Matlack informed the women that their presence "was not necessary." The Council would not see them as a group. This had to be a disappointment.[38]

Yet the women's presence in Lancaster was fortuitous and significant. In a surprising turn of events, the SEC quickly changed its tune and offered the women the option of release of the men at Lancaster. The next day, Pennsylvania officials changed their instructions and now called for escorting the exiled men safely back to the temporary state capital instead of to remote Shippensburg. Timothy Matlack explained the decision in a letter to James Pemberton: "It was intended to have set you at liberty at Shippensburg, but at the request of your wife, (Phebe Pemberton,) Susanna Jones, Mary Pleasants, and Eliza Drinker, the first resolution was altered. . . . The time of their arrival was very lucky, as a few hours of delay would have lost the opportunity of obtaining this alteration, which appears to me much in your favor."[39]

As a gauge of the strength of the women's advocacy and assertiveness, Matlack wrote to a Quaker friend after the incident: "The zeal and tenderness of these good women are so great that it is with some difficulty and strong persuasion [his own] they are restrained from making further solicitation [of Council members] before the arrival of their husbands which would in my opinion be unfavorable for them rather than advantageous."[40] Matlack himself had to persuade the women not to insist on seeing the implacable Scotsman, SEC Vice President George Bryan. With "a little practice," Matlack told James Pemberton, the women could become "able Politicians."[41]

Matlack could not see the members of the women's mission as the skilled politicians that they already were, though he heartily approved of their actions. Like other Quakers, Matlack was raised in a culture that believed in women's spiritual equality and valued their worldly authority, albeit unevenly. They could, for example, preach and hold their own business meetings, a rarity among Christian denominations for the era. On learning of Elizabeth Drinker's participation in the mission, Henry was "[pleased] to learn that thou had surmounted all difficulties and given up to be a party in the Embassy [the women's mission]. . . . A Query has arisen amongst us, who was the Spokesman of your Committee & whether you did as the Apostles formerly, depart from the presence of the Council rejoicing[?]" Even he and the other exiles struggled to fit these bold and unprecedented actions into narratives with which they were already familiar. Unlike the apostles in biblical times, the women's "Embassy" did not leave the Council chambers rejoicing, but they had won a significant victory. Just as importantly, as Henry learned later, there was not a spokes*man*; it was, the women had declared proudly, "Entirely an Act of our Own."[42]

Chapter 14

RELEASE AND RETURN

With the emerging spring, hope, too, returned, though tinged with skepticism. Back in Winchester, exile Thomas Fisher for the first time "saw Peach Trees in Blossom [and] Apple Trees in warm situations not in small leaves."[1] The escorts sent from Lancaster had only arrived in Winchester on April 17, and most of the remaining exiled men left Virginia ahead of them two days later.[2] Henry Drinker revealed how he felt at the prospect of release: it "seems like clearing their hands of us." He blamed "our continuing here in Bonds" on the SEC, which the exiles knew was purposely delaying the release.[3] "Will it be," Henry asked, "an unfair conclusion, if we are yet held in captivity, after all these steps, that they were merely to save appearances & a Juggle among them [Council and Congress] to abuse us and deceive the people, who are become very uneasy at our hard usage—many now speaking their Minds on this matter plainly & loudly."[4] Still, he eagerly awaited "meeting my beloved Wife in a short time & embracing her in the unbounded Affection which has invariably accompanied me during our long separation."[5]

Even as the release materialized, the members of the women's mission continued to seek information about and amelioration for their relatives. On the thirteenth, Drinker learned from Israel Morris of the "dangerous illness" of exile Edward Penington. To Drinker, this message portended ill of her husband's health. The next day, Drinker sought out lawyer Joseph Reed, the source of the Penington information. Reed, a former aide to Washington and a zealous Patriot, and his wife, Drinker wrote, "appeared kind, but I fear tis from the teeth outwards." She also sought out George Bryan, despite Matlack's attempts to dissuade her. She met again Major-General Nathanael

Greene and Colonel Clement Biddle, both disowned Quakers of the Continental Army. These men "all make a show of favor," Drinker recorded in her diary, but she either did not learn or chose not to reveal any new information.

On the twenty-first, the women had another conference with their nemesis, President Wharton, which Elizabeth Drinker again found "not altogether agreeable." They then called on SEC Vice President George Bryan, who, surprisingly, seemed sympathetic. Matlack delivered to the women what Drinker called the "sham release," a paper by which the SEC discharged the exiles without absolving them of any of the unofficial but implicit charges of treason or misprision of treason made against them in Congress and by Congress's publication in newspapers of the infamous Spanktown Papers.[6] Hearing the news in the letter from Elizabeth, Henry, moving more slowly, finally left Winchester on April 21 with his good friend and Quaker minister John Pemberton and the militia escort.

As Israel and James Pemberton made their own journey to Lancaster through York, where Congress met, they stayed overnight at James Updegraff's home. Next door they encountered Major-General Horatio Gates, then head of the board of war. According to James Pemberton, Gates told them that "if I had been in Philadelphia at the time of your being arrested and sent into exile, I would have prevented it." Gates had been in upstate New York commanding the American forces that earned British General John Burgoyne's surrender at Saratoga, after which Gates served for some months as head of Congress's board of war—in effect, General Washington's superior. His statement must have come as a surprise. Gates gave the former exiles a letter to ensure a speedy crossing of the Susquehanna River by the ferry operator. Once they reached the crossing, another disowned Quaker, General Thomas Mifflin, offered the former exiles the same kindly assistance.[7]

The prospects of returning home were now real. On the twenty-fourth of April, Elizabeth Drinker and Phoebe Pemberton called on Matlack and Bryan again, asking if the SEC would reconsider how the exiles were to be discharged. The two men took this request, presumably for a full discharge, more like an exoneration, a new political negotiation, to the Council. Matlack eventually reported back to the women that "nothing further could be done, towards granting their request."[8] The infinitesimally slow process of release and the refusal to hear the women's ongoing pleas in person were more evidence of the SEC's intransigence toward the exiles.

The women then went out to a tavern for dinner in town. Exile James Pemberton's servant Richard entered the tavern, followed by Pemberton

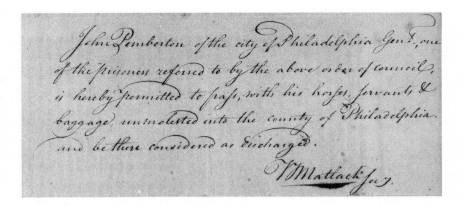

FIG. 16 | Colonel Timothy Matlack (1736–1829), who served as the scrivener on parchment of the Declaration of Independence and later as the secretary of the SEC, wrote out a "pass" for each prisoner that would serve as a "discharge." The Quaker leaders wanted an exoneration, and John Pemberton argued for one, but Matlack and the SEC would not budge. Pasted into a copy of Thomas Gilpin [Jr.], *Exiles in Virginia* (extra-illustrated first edition), William L. Clements Library, The University of Michigan.

and exile Samuel Pleasants. Elizabeth Drinker learned that while Henry was well, he could not travel as fast as the others and likely would be arriving later. At one o'clock the next afternoon, April 25, "My Henry arrived at J. Webb's, just time enough to dine with us; all the rest of our Friends came this day to Lancaster." She found him "much heartier than I expected, he looked fat and well."[9] In sixteen years of marriage, the two had been apart for longer than any other time—seven months and fourteen days.[10]

The twenty-sixth was First Day, and Henry and Elizabeth Drinker went to meeting in town. Minister John Pemberton prayed aloud at the meeting. The formerly exiled Friends met and agreed on a written plea to the SEC the next day asking to be "reinstated in the full enjoyment of the liberty of which we have been so long deprived."[11] In the evening, Quaker lawyer "Billy [William] Lewis came . . . according to the request of us Women."[12] The women may have consulted him on whether anything could be done to move the Council to soften its stance. The following day, the Quaker men applied to the Council, offering up their written plea for a "proper discharge," which they did not get. Nor did the Council agree to a face-to-face meeting. The Council granted only a pass to Potts Grove, where the group could apply to General Washington, again accommodating, for permission to return to occupied Philadelphia (figure 16). John Pemberton protested the SEC's cruel rebuff, but it was in vain.[13]

It is not hard to imagine the tension that a face-to-face meeting would have engendered. The exiles wanted a full exoneration; facing the SEC, Pemberton would have noted acidly that the exiles had been dragooned on faked evidence, with no criminal charges ever having been made. Had they only had a hearing, they could have refuted the veracity of the Spanktown Papers and the widespread allegations of disloyalty. Council members likely would have reasserted their belief that the rampant insinuations in newspaper coverage provided enough evidence that the exiles had betrayed the country of their birth. Members of the SEC may have been envious of the exiles' quiet sojourn in rural Virginia while their neighbors back home were plundered, firebombed, or worse in the British-occupied city. At the very least, they likely would have seen the exiles' pleas as caviling arguments from wealthy, entitled men who had suffered hardly at all (though they would have had to overlook that two good men had died in exile). They likely hated the thought of letting these men reenter the city while the British were still there (what might they reveal?). In the end, the result likely would have been the same: neither side would have given an inch. The exiles received the least generous release the Council could give them and still be done with these men. The Patriots likely had only one regret: that someone in the Assembly had been squeamish about the continued exile and caused its early termination.

On the return trip, the Quaker caravan of former exiles, members of the women's mission, and servants made only two stops. The first was in Downingtown, Chester County, at the home of Robert Valentine and his wife, Rachel Edge Valentine, he a weighty public Friend and she an elder in Uwchlan Friends Meeting. In March, the Valentines and neighbors Thomas Lightfoot and his wife, Susannah, also a public Friend, had lobbied the Pennsylvania Assembly together. Though the Valentines and Lightfoots "had a hearing and were favorably received," they landed in jail as a result of their activism.[14] The women's mission had also stayed with the Valentines on the way to Lancaster. Now, a much larger party—perhaps twenty persons or more—arrived, some only dining and passing through. The Fisher brothers' party stopped for a midday meal at "our kind Fr[ien]d Robt Valentine's," according to Thomas Fisher's diary, while the Pembertons and Drinkers reached there in the evening and stayed the night.[15] The Valentines may have had to utilize not only their home but also Valentine's Mill, the farm and six stone buildings they owned in the village three miles west of town (known since the 1850s as Edge's Mill).

Frisson filled the Downingtown air when women's mission member Suky Jones voiced a serious concern, and she and several others "had a meeting." She and her husband, Owen Jones Sr., had hosted John Roberts, miller, in the city. Should the Patriots retake Philadelphia, or Roberts be captured by Patriots, he would surely feel the Patriots' wrath. His participation in the Cornwallis raid had not gone unnoticed by Patriots. Quaker historian Francis G. Brown has noted that the Quaker caravan could likely have made the city in one day from Downingtown, but after a meeting with the Valentines, Lightfoots, and other weighty Friends on the morning of their departure, instead they split their trip in two and planned to stop again at the Roberts' home in Merion.[16] There they had a chance to counsel the Roberts family. After an early breakfast at the Roberts' home on the thirtieth, they held a "setting," a time of silent worship seeking inward light. Then minister John Pemberton stood and spoke to the family, likely in poignant testimony.[17]

Later that morning, Henry and Elizabeth Drinker and the others departed for home. Israel Morris had gone ahead to Valley Forge, where he obtained passes that, after stating the names of the exiled men, read, "Having been discharged by the Executive Council of this State have permission to return to Philadelphia unmolested."[18] On the thirtieth of April, the Drinkers and the others "were welcomed by many before, and on our entrance in to the City—where we arrived about 11 o'clock, and found our dear families all well for which favor and Blessing and the restoration of my dear Husband, may I ever be thankful." That day, for one time in her many years of diary keeping, Elizabeth Drinker had "such a number of Friends to see us . . . that it is not in my power to enumerate them."[19]

This joyful homecoming could not erase the past eight months. Two of the exiles, one disowned and one non-Quaker, had fled Winchester early and joined the British Army, and two of the Quaker leaders had escaped their mortal bounds confident of their everlasting life. But the other sixteen had endured the entire two hundred and thirty-eight–day exile: up to nine days in the Freemason's Lodge, eighteen more days on the journey west, and two hundred and eleven days in Winchester or en route back to Lancaster and Philadelphia. Their treatment—epithets, public shamings, forced neglect of the successful businesses of which they were justifiably proud—seemed calculated to abase precisely this group of men, whose religion demanded they not defer to anyone. Patriots may not have consciously realized the particular cruelty they enacted on the exiles, but they were surely motivated by a desire not only to punish dissidents or protect their own interests but also to thoroughly humiliate members of a group that had long asserted its superiority. Thus, the physical hardships and material privations of the exile ultimately paled for the Quaker leaders in comparison to the spiritual and political indignities: the affront to the peace testimony and, perhaps most galling of all, the fact that they were forced to remain *unheard* in their own defense. Unheard by Congress, by the Council, and by the courts. These were the most galling of all. But spiritual suffering is difficult to quantify, and the exiles could not have expected a sympathetic reception from their fellow citizens on the home front, many of whom had suffered even more privation, horror, and material devastation as collateral damage of the two armies' extended presence.

Back in Philadelphia, the exiles found British officers still quartered in their homes. More than an annoyance, these unwelcome guests could have reminded both the exiles and their Patriot neighbors of the reason for the exiles' plight: supposed collaboration with the enemy. It was not a good look, and Patriots likely gave them steely stares for it. By the second week of May, the exiles and their family members found the city's British occupiers preparing for a celebration. May 18, Elizabeth Drinker recorded, was again "a day [that] may be remembered by many."[20] This was the day of the *Meschianza* (medley in Italian), a lavishly expensive combination regatta, gala, costumed ball, and entertainment with elaborate scenery, intended as a loving tribute by the British officers and men to their beloved general, Sir William Howe, on his departure. Writing about the Meschianza in his diary, General Howe's Hessian aide-de-camp, Captain Friedrich von Muenchhausen, remarked, "Everything was as splendid and magnificent as possible and all, even those who have been in Paris and London, agree that they have never seen such a luxurious fete."[21]

Most Quakers strongly disapproved of this revelry. "How insensible do these people appear," Elizabeth Drinker commented, "while our Land is so greatly desolated and Death and sore destruction has overtaken and impends over so many."[22] Yet some also feared what would happen should the Patriots retake the city. Hessian Major Carl Baurmeister, sitting in British headquarters, wrote home to his superior in mid-June: "The Society of Friends have endless worries. They are expecting an unbearable fate should the [British] army completely withdraw from the city."[23] Baurmeister boarded in the home of a prominent Quaker, so he likely had good sources. His hosts and others may have come to rely on the protection the British Army could provide from Patriots' harassment and constant requisitions. Late in the occupation, the British were well-supplied and had stopped making requisitions of the populace.

In London, General Sir William Howe's resignation, which had been written and sent in the strictest of confidence in late October, had been accepted privately in February, and suddenly on May 8 General Sir Henry Clinton from New York arrived in Philadelphia to take Howe's place as commander in chief of British forces on the continent.[24] "War is declared with France," Elizabeth Drinker, speaking like a British subject, declared on the eighth, though England would not officially declare war on France until June 17.[25] By contrast, the American soldiers at Valley Forge celebrated the news that France had joined with them against the British, largely as the result of both smart generalship by the Americans in the Philadelphia Campaign and smart work by the American minister plenipotentiary, His Excellency Benjamin Franklin, who had labored in Paris with fellow commissioners John Adams and Silas Deane.[26]

As British attaché Ambrose Serle prepared to depart Philadelphia on June 3, he had a "long Conversation upon the affairs & Politics of this Country" with former exile Israel Pemberton, whom he referred to as "first man among the Quakers here" and "My Quaker." Serle related that Pemberton, while of the view that Parliament had no right to tax America, "was equally averse to the violent Proceedings of the People here and particularly to the atrocious Act of Independency." The two disagreed on the rights of Parliament, but "it was an agreeable amicable Conference, in which we mutually expressed our Wishes for Accommodation & a speedy Termination to the Horrors of War. He mentioned that [generals] Gates, Washington, & some other principal officers of the Rebel-army freely gave out their Desire for a Treaty, when he passed through their Camp on his Return home: But the Congress cannot part with their Power & sink into former Obscurity."[27] Serle was the very man who had been tasked by the Howe brothers with collecting from Loyalists their military intelligence and their views of the war. If Israel Pemberton indeed revealed Gates's statements to Serle, it would have been more than enough for Patriots to convict him of high treason. The exiles' journal confirms the fact that Gates had confided his desire for peace at the Quakers' chance meeting with him in York on April 24, and the fact that Howe had used Pemberton's fine carriage to display around town his

American mistress would not have helped Pemberton's case.[28] Patriots likely did not spot the visit between Pemberton and Serle, and thus it remained unknown for at least another century.

The American authorities may also have turned a suspicious eye to a ship that arrived in port shortly thereafter. The ship of sorely needed provisions from England and Ireland, which the Quakers had ordered in their letter of December 16, 1777, had arrived in the harbor around June 6, twelve days before the British evacuation.[29] According to John Pemberton's diary, it was "with provisions for poor Friends," but no source reveals what happened to it.[30] The French ambassador to the new republic sent back to France a note that said the Quakers in the city had bought British goods at a favorable price and were selling those same goods for much more, thereby implying that they capitalized on the ill fortune of their neighbors, but he might have meant this shipment and mischaracterized how they distributed its contents.[31]

On June 8, Major Crammond went to bed at the Drinkers' home but was awakened at one o'clock the next morning in order to accompany his two regiments of Anspachers, who embarked on a vessel in the harbor. Elizabeth Drinker and her sister watched the regiments pass by their house.[32] By the thirteenth, a report circulated that all the British would leave Philadelphia within two days. Three regiments of Hessians boarded vessels that day. Enoch Story, an administrator of the occupied city, stopped by and told the Drinkers that he was departing with the fleet.[33] Whether the Drinkers had been invited to join the exodus, as many Loyalists had been, is unknown. It was highly unlikely that they would have gone. The Quaker leaders were firmly rooted in Philadelphia and bore no shame for what had happened to them. And even some of the most notable Loyalists who did leave for England at this time returned to Pennsylvania later or applied to do so.[34] But the Quakers certainly anticipated the evacuation sadly. Sarah Logan Fisher, who earlier had welcomed the British, recorded that "the English who we had hoped & expected would have stayed & kept possession of the city, are near leaving us & it is said are going to New York, and we may expect some great suffering when the Americans again get possession."[35]

By the early morning of June 18, Elizabeth Drinker observed, "there was not one Red-Coat to be seen in Town." The look of the city on the evacuation of the British was a greatly depressing sight. One visitor to financier Robert Morris found "nothing but wanton desolation." The very air was "fouled by stench, filth, and clouds of flies . . . the Town [is] exceedingly Dirty

& disagreeable, stinks Intolerably," another Morris acquaintance wrote to a friend. The floor of the State House had been opened for use as a latrine. Close by, British soldiers had dug a great open pit where they dumped the bodies of dead prisoners and starved horses. Like other returning residents, Morris was shocked by the devastation the city and its residents had experienced, including the "lank bodies . . . thin visages and meager carcasses" of those who endured the occupation.[36]

The British had "not been gone a quarter of an hour before the American Light-Horse entered the City," brandishing swords, galloping about the streets, and warning people not to be caught outside on the streets at night.[37] Meanwhile, angry Patriots formed citizens groups to gather evidence against any collaborators and bring them to justice.[38] As the SEC saw it, however, Philadelphia residents were not doing enough to help the Patriot government discover conspirators; it remarked on "a great unwillingness in the People of the City to give the necessary information against the disaffected."[39]

Some persons now brought forth charges they had suppressed during the occupation. On August 5, the PYM's Meeting for Sufferings delivered a petition to the Pennsylvania legislature admonishing the Assembly for its "punitive measures against Quakers who were but following the dictates of their religious beliefs."[40] News of the petition spread quickly. In this highly charged environment, the sheriff took Quaker John Roberts, charged with high treason for his role in Lord Cornwallis's December foraging mission, into custody on August 10. Roberts had dutifully approached his local magistrate and affirmed his allegiance to the state of Pennsylvania on June 19, but doubts about his loyalty and past actions swirled among Patriots.

Two delegates to Congress, representative of many others, expressed great frustration with the Quakers the same month. Josiah Bartlett of New Hampshire wrote that the "majority of the Quakers remain the same dark, hidden hypocrites as formerly."[41] Samuel Adams of Massachusetts, a cousin of John Adams, remarked to a friend: "Nothing can equal the barefaced falsehood of the Quakers and Tories of this City, unless perhaps their Folly."[42]

On August 13, the Quaker petition was reprinted in the newspaper and "ignited a firestorm of indignation" from Patriots.[43] An anonymous letter printed in a newspaper and signed only "Philadelphiensis" asked whether "piloting the enemy for the specific purpose of showing them where the Americans were, that they might kill them, consistent with your peaceable principles?" The letter writer was likely referring specifically to John Roberts's ride at the head of a British provisioning and foraging party in December 1777.

At Roberts's arraignment on August 20, Chief Justice Thomas McKean, who had earlier expressed a policy of leniency for Pennsylvanians attainted of treason but had also gone behind the Quaker exiles' backs to undermine his own habeas ruling, denied bail to prisoner Roberts.[44]

Steps away from the PYM's annual gathering, the two-day trial of John Roberts began on September 30, 1778, before Chief Justice McKean (acting then in capacity of a trial judge).[45] Roberts had a distinguished three-man legal team, two of whom were delegates to the Continental Congress and signers of the Declaration of Independence: James Wilson, a future US Supreme Court justice, and George Ross, who had been a county prosecutor for the Crown for twelve years.[46] William Lewis, the same capable, Quaker-raised young attorney who had consulted with the former exiles and their families, assisted.[47] The prosecutor was Joseph Reed, a London-trained lawyer who had served as an aide to Washington and would soon become the second president of the SEC. Despite such capable defense counsel, Roberts was convicted of high treason by a jury of his peers—one that, because Quakers were constrained by their faith not to serve on juries that might condemn to death another Quaker, included no members of his faith.[48]

Roberts's supporters had hoped for clemency, and several thousands signed petitions to the SEC, but all the clamor was futile.[49] The SEC would not be moved. Nor was McKean in his sentencing statement accommodating. He was eloquent if not merciful: "Treason is a crime of the most dangerous & fatal Consequences to Society; it is of a most malignant nature; it is of a crimson color, and of a scarlet dye. . . . What punishment . . . must he Deserve who joins the enemies of his Country, and endeavors the total destruction of the lives, liberties, and property of all his fellow Citizens?" McKean also focused on the absurdity of Roberts's effort to rescue his exiled coreligionists: "Your offering to put yourself at the head of a troop of horse of the enemy, and to effect this rescue at the risk of your life, was a strange piece of conduct in one who pretended that he was conscientiously scrupulous of bearing arms in any case."[50]

Speaking directly to Roberts, McKean then gave the definitive contemporary, radical Patriot view of the Quaker exile. "It is in vain to plead that you intended to relieve some Friends who were ordered under guard to Virginia, for Government was then doing a necessary and usual Act in like cases for its preservation, the retaining men whose going at large was thought dangerous to the Community, and putting them for a time under gentle confinement. . . . Alas! Happy had it been for you had you fallen under the indulgent restraint and been sent also to Virginia."[51] When the SEC heard of the statement, it asked McKean to prepare his remarks for publication in the newspaper.[52] In suggesting that Roberts would have been better off had he been exiled to Virginia, McKean thus spoke for the elected Pennsylvania government, expressing its view that Roberts exemplified why the Pennsylvania government had exiled those seventeen peaceable Quakers in the first place. In McKean's view, if the government had not exiled the Quaker leaders, there may have been more stories like Roberts's: of willful men following their religious tenets but committing foolish acts that aided the enemy, wittingly or unwittingly risking the lives of their fellow citizens and encouraging the British Army in their efforts.[53] As punishment for his actions, Roberts was sentenced to be "hanged by the neck until dead" on November 4. McKean added: "May God be merciful to your Soul." Quaker Abraham Carlisle, a neighbor of the Drinkers and a master builder, convicted of treason for serving the British as a gatekeeper at the northeastern entryway into the city, was also sentenced to be hanged at the same time.[54]

With the day set for Roberts's and Carlisle's executions approaching, Henry Drinker had much work to do. He and John Pemberton, members of the PYM committee of inquiry into both cases, approached George Bryan, the acting president of the executive council (President Thomas Wharton Jr. having died in office the previous May), and the next day the two of them, joined by minister John Parrish, went to visit another member of the Council, Joseph Hart. Arguing only for compassion and clemency for Roberts, they pleaded for a stay of the execution of a man whom they knew had strayed from the Quaker code. They likely rendered the members of the Council impatient and, knowing that Bryan had evidenced no sympathy whatsoever for the Quaker exiles, Pemberton recorded afterward that there was almost no reason to expect mercy. To forgive these two men after so many less wealthy men had their entire properties confiscated or ruined by the armies would in the Patriots' view undermine the newly established legal system.[55]

Elizabeth Drinker recorded on October 28 the sorrowful scene that ensued that day: Former hostess to the women's mission and the returning exiles, "Jane Roberts, wife of John Roberts, Owen Jones and Wife [he who had nearly been an exile, she a women's mission member], and James Thornton [peace mission minister] were there this morning. HD and self went with them to visit our neighbor Ann Carlisle, when James [Thornton] had something to say to the afflicted women, by way of Testimony, which I thought encouraging." The wives of the convicted traitors had also pleaded for their husbands' lives with the Patriot authorities. Drinker wrote, "Tis hoped and believed that their lives will be spared, it would be terrible indeed should it happen otherwise."[56]

The two convicted men were taken to Center Square, the corner of Broad and High Streets, then west of most of the inhabited city. Walking behind the plain pine boxes in which their bodies would be buried, and without much fanfare, they climbed the steps. Roberts bore the execution well, garrulous as he was inclined to be, standing before the gibbet and speaking out loud "for some time" before the deed was done. They cut him down within the hour after the hanging. Elizabeth Drinker recorded—stunned—that "they have actually put to death; hanged on the Common, John Roberts and Abraham Carlisle this morning about noon—an awful solemn day."[57] Henry Drinker attended Roberts's funeral, at which Nicholas Waln preached at length before Roberts was lowered into the earth next to his namesake father and grandfather in the graveyard of the Merion Friends Meeting.[58]

Of the 491 men in Pennsylvania who had been attainted for treason during the revolution, only 131 were tried (many having fled the jurisdiction), and only three were convicted. Two of them Quakers, these men suffered the ultimate penalty permissible by law. There are several reasons why they were shown no quarter: First, Pennsylvania's leaders believed that political goals had to be met in order to demonstrate authority and show the citizens of Philadelphia the consequences of opposing the Patriot cause.[59] Secondly, it was a signal that the Quakers had been sidelined while other—previously less prominent—groups had attained positions of power.[60] Thirdly, it was tolerable because Quakers were viewed as noncitizens of Pennsylvania because they had claimed rights to the protection of government, primarily legal due process, without being bound to share in the burdens of that government (taxes, loyalty), a charge that had been made before the exiles were sent away.[61] Also, as long as they failed to sign the oath, they had no vote. In the Patriot view, protecting the fragile new nation required constant, unflinching vigilance.

Perhaps led by the example of Congress and Pennsylvania state authorities, zealous Pennsylvania Patriots outside of Philadelphia believed they could, with impunity, round up other groups of dissidents and abuse them for their various refusals. While officials did not explicitly link these actions to the Quaker exile, these persecutions followed in its wake and shared many similarities. Most importantly, Patriots targeted the German Protestant sects—Moravians, Mennonites, Schwenkfelders, and German Baptist Brethren—who held similar nonviolent, pacifist beliefs and had allied themselves with the Quakers early in the war. In Lancaster County in October 1777, armed militia members rounded up thirteen Moravian men in Lititz and forcibly marched them as a group to a jail in Lancaster city. In Bethlehem in April 1778, Northampton County lieutenant John Wetzel detained nineteen men, including twelve Moravian Brethren, and had them roped together at their necks and dragged through the streets. Wetzel also targeted Mennonites who had refused to swear allegiance to the state. In Germantown on May 21, 1778, Pennsylvania militia officers arrested printer and German Baptist Brethren bishop Christopher Saur II, who had risen to political prominence decades earlier by marshaling the German votes that kept the Quakers in power in Pennsylvania until the revolution. Rousting him from bed in the middle of the night, the officers stripped Saur naked, cut his hair and beard, painted him red and black (the colors of an early Saur publication), and marched him barefooted through the fields and valleys to the jail at Valley Forge. Unheard of before the Quaker exile, each incident echoed the public, arbitrary, malevolent humiliation of the merchant princes of the Quaker exile. Political chicanery in service of the persecution of minorities once commenced is not easily contained, then or now.[62]

In 1779, the Philadelphia Meeting for Sufferings appointed a committee of men to inquire into the Carlisle and Roberts cases for whatever lessons might be learned and conveyed to others of their faith.[63] David W. Maxey finds that "of all the contemporary judgments reached concerning the fairness of Roberts' trial and its outcome, none was the subject of more careful deliberation" than that of this committee.[64] The committee completed its report in August 1779, but its members kept it hidden away in their possession, fearing that publication might lead to reprisals. In the history of the sect, the committee noted, members had often been persecuted and martyred for their faith. It was uncommon, however, for Friends to be put to death who, by contrast, did not hold fast to their religious testimonies. The PYM had warned Roberts often enough that his actions violated the peace testimony, and the PYM had published "exhortations . . . admonitions & cautions to all among us to avoid . . . [becoming] entangled in the confusions prevailing."[65] Despite repeated warnings from their coreligionists,

Roberts and Carlisle were, in the emollient wording of the committee, so "overtaken . . . that they have involved themselves in difficulties, and distress, . . . and their families subjected to great affliction, & adversity."[66]

The committee, however, maintained an odd stiffness and resolve regarding the present government of Pennsylvania, to which its members still refused to grant any validity or legitimacy. They referred in their report to "the British army" three times but called the state government and the American forces the British Army's "opponents" and "persons in power who held the authority over" the men found guilty.[67] They had learned nothing from the women's petition.[68] Ironically, they were caught up in what Henry Drinker, in one of his earlier letters, had charged Congress with: the refusal to admit and correct a mistake.[69] They had also refused to acknowledge anything akin to what Henry Melchior Muhlenberg had privately acknowledged as early as 1776—namely, that the British government no longer had the power to protect people in Pennsylvania, and that it must be a sign that God had raised up a new government to which one should now owe allegiance.[70] The report was kept quiet until 1785 and only then entered into the minutes of the Quaker meeting.[71]

Quakers were still under great threat of mob violence. When in late 1781 Washington's victory at Yorktown was celebrated in Philadelphia, all citizens were once more asked to illuminate their windows. Friends did not, and Patriots again attacked their houses. "Scarcely one Friends House escaped," Elizabeth Drinker recorded. The mob shattered seventy panes of glass at the Drinker home, splintered window sashes and front parlor panels, burst open the front door, and stoned the interior of the house and furniture. Men stormed in and tried to frighten the women and children. Some "fared better, some worse . . . 'tis a mercy no lives were lost." This went on for three hours.[72] John Drinker, a hatter, "lost half the goods in his shop and was beaten. The mob threw flaming materials into one house, shot off guns in another."[73] Yet Quakers had begun to accept their unhappy lot. Loyalist Quaker Anna Rawle recorded in her diary this plaintive lament: "It seems universally agreed that Philadelphia will no longer be that happy asylum for the Quakers that it once was. Those joyful days when all was prosperity and peace are gone, never to return, and perhaps it is as necessary for our society."[74]

In the meantime, in 1784 the Quakers did receive a small token of good news—a state government agency found that the Pennsylvania government had been wrong to suspend habeas corpus in its treatment of the exiles.

As it happened, Pennsylvania included an ultra-democratic governmental agency in the liberal state constitution of 1776. That new constitution had called for an elected "Council of Censors" (twenty-one men) to oversee the work of the executive, the SEC, every seven years.[75] Thus, with the war settled, the Council of Censors was elected, met over a period of months, and produced a published report.[76] The report declared two parts of the Banishing Law of 1777 unconstitutional: the part of the law that indemnified SEC members for their actions against the Quakers and the part of the law "which restrained for a time, the full operation of the writ of HABEAS CORPUS."[77] This was an altogether surprising outcome by an unexpected actor in the drama, and it was not even a result of Quaker protests or lobbying. Ironically, the Quakers had adamantly opposed the constitution of 1776 because it had abrogated the Charter of Privileges of 1701, yet in the end the new constitution had vindicated them. Retroactively negating the suspension of habeas was, though too little too late, an elegant validation of the Quaker leaders' many forceful protests and a nod toward reconciliation to begin the postwar era.

It was not until 1789 that the real reconciliation between temporal government and the Religious Society of Friends in America occurred. With the US Constitution already ratified by most of the states, a national president elected and sworn in, and the Pennsylvania state constitution of 1776 about to be replaced by the more moderate constitution of 1790, the PYM, seeing now an orderly government organized to rule over the country, reverted to its custom of sending a delegation to meet with the new leader of the country. This was a practice their distant ancestors had once followed with kings of England in the late seventeenth century and their more recent ancestors with the proprietary Penn family governors in Pennsylvania. These meetings were intended to welcome the new leader and to make sure he was well acquainted with the presence, accomplishments, and most pertinent beliefs of the Religious Society of Friends. These included the peace testimony and the testimony against oaths as well as the Quakers' prominence and good intentions in the community. In September 1789, the PYM appointed a committee to write a suitable letter to George Washington, who had been inaugurated in New York in April of that year.[78]

Former lawyer and peace mission member Nicholas Waln signed the letter in his current role as minister and clerk. The authors began by acknowledging that the "Almighty . . . [had] permitted a great Revolution to take place in the Government of this Country." They believed, in accordance with the Bible, that only God could take down or raise up a government. In 1776, 1777, and 1778, they had not yet been ready to acknowledge that God had done that. With this letter, they reversed their position. Now that a formal national constitution had been adopted and ratified and a chief executive elected by the people, the Quakers finally admitted who the prevailing power was and acknowledged that it constituted a legitimate government.[79] They now acknowledged "those in Authority over us," a somewhat different formulation than Henry Drinker's previous reference to "those in power over us." Though they referred to them as "Rulers of the People" and not elected administrators of a nation of laws, the Quakers had made great strides forward.

The society was quick to warn the new president that "we can take no part in carrying on War on any Occasion, or under any Power, but are bound in Conscience to lead quiet and peaceable Lives in Godliness and Honesty amongst Men, contributing freely our Proportion to the Indigences of the poor and to the necessary Support of civil Government."[80] Yet their esteem for Washington was clear in the blessings they heaped on him:

> We feel our Hearts affectionately drawn towards thee, . . . with Prayers that thy Presidency may, under the Blessing of Heaven, be happy to thyself and to the People; that . . . Divine Providence may condescend to look down upon our Land with a propitious Eye. . . . And it is our earnest Concern, that he may be pleased to grant thee every necessary Qualification to fill thy weighty and important Station to his Glory; and that finally, when all terrestial Honours shall fail and pass away, thou and thy respectable Consort may be found worthy to receive a Crown of unfading Righteousness in the Mansions of Peace and Joy for ever.[81]

This was praise as fulsome as the society had ever given any government, wary as its members had been of government since the sect's founding. Ten days after they presented this letter to the new president, Washington appeared before them in Philadelphia to read his own prepared reply. The Religious Society of Friends in America took this gesture as a particular sign of mutual respect, as well they might.

In his remarks, Washington thanked them for their affectionate regards to him and to his administration and expressed his hope that the government would serve people of all religions. One of the purposes of government, he wrote, was "to protect the Persons and Consciences of men from oppression. . . . The liberty enjoyed by the People of these States, of worshipping Almighty God agreeable to their Consciences, is not only among the choicest of their *Blessings*, but also of their *Rights*." His audience particularly treasured the word "conscience."[82] The new president went on to assure the Quakers most importantly that

> your principles & conduct are well known to me—and it is doing the People called Quakers no more than Justice to say, that (except their declining to share with others the burthen of the common defence) there is no Denomination among us who are more exemplary and useful Citizens. . . . I assure you very explicitly that in my opinion the Consciencious [*sic*] scruples of all men should be treated with great delicacy & tenderness, and it is my wish and desire that the Laws may always be as extensively accommodated to them, as a due regard to the Protection and essential Interests of the Nation may Justify, and permit.[83]

Again, he likely pleased the Quakers with his reference to conscientious scruples, a phrase pacifists used to describe their core tenet against war. Even with the last caveat regarding accommodation to defense needs, which listeners may well have expected the commander in chief to add, the reconciliation had been effected.

After the war and through the first three decades of the new republic, Patriot men and women who had survived the revolution, especially those who served in the military, and their descendants were justly proud of the nation they had founded. At the same time, Quakers began to develop their own mythology of the exile and the surrounding revolution. Since Quakers had been or claimed to have been disaffected to both sides during the war, their heroes of the period were different from those of their Patriot neighbors. In order to maintain a record of their kinship ties and connections to the recent history of the tumultuous 1770s and 1780s, Quakers seized on the art form of the silhouette and the album of silhouettes. At Charles Willson Peale's enterprising Philadelphia Museum, located first in his home at Third and Locust Streets, later on the second floor of Independence Hall itself—near the geographical heart of the PYM—Black silhouette artist Moses Williams and other artisans of the craft cut the silhouettes of affluent people. The albums assembled by elite Quakers included silhouettes of their family members alongside those of former exiles, including James Pemberton and Henry Drinker, as well as Owen Jones Sr. and minister and former lawyer

Nicholas Waln, who supported the exiles. According to material culture scholar Anne Verplanck, "The albums constitute a private counternarrative of the Revolutionary era . . . [through which] Quakers preserved and interpreted their past and their roles in the nation's history."[84] In the following years, Quaker schools would encourage students to "question authority and to practice non-compliance," obeying their leaders only "if their worldly laws concurred with God's divine law."[85]

The Quaker exile was one strategy employed by the Patriot leaders of the Continental Congress and Pennsylvania to enable those governments to survive the British invasion. In taking political prisoners into preventive detention by means of denying them habeas corpus (despite its illegality), exiling them to the frontier, and later attainting others, Patriots drew on that darker strain of English law. Surprisingly, Patriots had borrowed a strategy formerly used by kings and Parliament to stifle dissenting voices. But the exile also signified another kind of event—it signaled the demise of William Penn's holy experiment, a government begun in 1681 and led for nearly a century largely by men dedicated to Quaker values.

CODA

Reintegration, or Not

Despite what they had endured, all the most prominent Quakers among the exiles continued to reside in the Philadelphia region. One Quaker exile, not among the leaders, removed to England for two decades and then returned. Some of the exiles were able to reintegrate into a changed society, and some never did, remaining in opposition. Twenty men had been exiled on September 11, 1777. Two exiles (a disowned Quaker and a non-Quaker) escaped, one in December and one in February, and two (among the Quaker leaders) died in exile, both in March, leaving sixteen men who suffered the entire exile and survived it.

Of those who survived the exile, at least five did not reintegrate into society. The man once jeeringly called "King of the Quakers" and "King Wampum," Israel Pemberton (1715–1779), formerly one of the leading taxpayers of the city, returned to the city and his wife, Mary. She died in the fall of 1778, and his death followed in April 1779. Family members attributed both deaths to the rigors of the exile and the absence of the caring attentions of each to the other. General Howe had used Pemberton's carriage to cart his mistress around town, soiling Pemberton's reputation among non-Quakers even further. Likely unbeknownst to the other exiles, Pemberton had on June 3, 1778, probably divulged vague military intelligence to Howe's Tory outreach secretary, Ambrose Serle, a fact disclosed only in the 1890s when Serle's journal was first published in London.[1] Pemberton had not been popular among non-Quakers before the exile—congressional delegates from South Carolina to Massachusetts had referred to him derisively—and it is likely his status remained unchanged, though because his conversation with

Serle was never revealed contemporaneously, he was never officially accused of treason and never suffered the property loss that would have entailed.[2]

Thomas Wharton Sr. (1731–1784) was described as "speechless" when he returned home to his wife, Rachel, nine children, and a much diminished business. He had written a bitter letter in January 1778 to his namesake younger cousin, the president of the SEC, blaming him for "all Hardship and Distresses" of the exiles, which, he said, "lays at your door." He and his brother Isaac were successfully prosecuted for misprision of treason, and the Patriot government confiscated most of their assets. Wharton undoubtedly struggled to distance himself from the fact that the British used his grandfather Wharton's mansion as the showpiece of their much-despised revelry, the Meschianza. Once home, Thomas Sr. found great satisfaction in the letters he received from his thoroughly disgraced Loyalist friend Joseph Galloway in England, which galled Galloway's left-behind wife, Grace Growden Galloway, whose inherited assets her husband had placed in his own name, exposing them to forfeit. Thomas Sr. lived to see fellow exile Owen Jones Jr. marry his daughter before he suffered two strokes and died in 1784.[3]

Charles Eddy (1754–1804), ironmonger son of Mary Darragh (a relative of Patriot diarist Christopher Marshall), was attainted by the Assembly and self-exiled to England in 1779. He signed a Loyalist petition there and frequented the so-called Pennsylvania and New York coffeehouses in London, where notice of ships carrying mail from their American namesakes would first be received; here, in the mid-1780s, he sat in the company of Samuel Shoemaker and other American Loyalists, including city administrator Enoch Story, Brethren printer Christopher Saur III, Anglican clergyman Thomas Coombe, and fellow exile William Drewet Smith, waiting anxiously for news from Philadelphia. Eddy likely heard Joseph Galloway share stories of his testimony in Parliament critical of Howe's conduct of the war, and Shoemaker may have bragged that an old friend, painter Benjamin West, introduced him to King George III, to whom Shoemaker in his diary naïvely attributed an absence of warlike impulses or intentions. Eddy returned to Philadelphia and his Quaker meeting in 1796 with his wife and at least five children.[4]

Among the former exiles who failed to reintegrate were the two escapees. William Drewet Smith (before 1756–after 1785), the disowned former Quaker and pharmacist, escaped exile in December 1777 and returned to his wife, Margaret Stedman, in Philadelphia, where he conferred with General Howe and joined the British Army. He served fellow Loyalists in New York before self-exiling to Canada, from where he filed a claim for his losses with the British American Loyalist Claims Commission.[5]

The one non-Quaker, British-born Anglican Thomas Pike (1735–after 1786), dancing master and instructor in the use of the small sword (and trained equestrian and musician), escaped exile on horseback from Winchester in February 1778. He rejoined his wife and children and, after conferring with General Howe, self-exiled to England, where he filed voluminous petitions with the British American Loyalist Claims Commission. With incidental help from an unlikely source, Henry Laurens, once president of the Second Continental Congress (whom he knew when he taught dancing in Charleston, South Carolina), Pike eventually garnered from Parliament a Loyalist award of £70 per annum.[6]

Two of the exiles did not have the opportunity to reintegrate into postwar society. John Hunt (1712–1778), British-born Quaker minister and merchant (of tobacco and general merchandise), died in exile of natural causes, on March 31, 1778, his leg amputated by a Scottish-born surgeon who had been serving as a major-general in the Continental Army. The newly remarried (1777) Hunt left behind a grief-stricken second wife, Rachel, a previously widowed fellow minister, and as many as nine children.[7]

Thomas Gilpin (1728–1778), milling entrepreneur, merchant, and scientist, died of natural causes on March 2, 1778, while in exile, leaving his wife, Lydia, and their two young sons and a daughter to survive him (other children having died young). Like Hunt, Gilpin was laid to rest in an unmarked grave in the burying ground next to Hopewell Friends meetinghouse north of Winchester, Virginia. One of his two sons was instrumental in seeing the Chesapeake and Delaware Canal, which the father had first surveyed in the 1760s, completed in 1830. The other son, his namesake, published privately in 1848 *Exiles in Virginia*, a compilation of the official governmental papers (many of them carefully preserved by the exiles themselves) related to the exile of these twenty men, alongside the exiles' numerous protests and their own journals of their ordeal (see figure 17). This remarkable book preserved the story of the exiles for future generations, ultimately helping to make the present book as complete as possible.[8]

Most of the thirteen other former exiles reintegrated themselves into society once the war was over, though not always immediately, smoothly, or completely. Samuel Rowland Fisher (1745–1834) was one such case, convicted of a lesser charge of misprision of treason and jailed before he found his path later in life. His trial and conviction were instigated by a vengeful Timothy

Matlack. In March 1779, a year after the exile had ended, Samuel's brother Thomas Fisher, formerly exiled, and John James, who had avoided arrest, had a run-in with the famously short-tempered Matlack. As Samuel had recounted it, Thomas and James had followed a routine practice of Friends' meetings: to visit a young Quaker former soldier, in this case Timothy Matlack's son Billy, hoping he might repent and reembrace the peace testimony.[9] The two men had a civil conversation with Billy before Timothy encountered them at the front door. On being told the nature of the visit, Matlack started to hurl invective and beat the two men with his walking stick, chasing them into the street until the instrument broke.[10] When a notice of the incident appeared in the newspaper, Matlack felt compelled to explain his behavior.[11] He also sought vengeance. Matlack had been aware of an allegedly traitorous letter from Samuel Rowland Fisher to his younger brother Jabez that had been intercepted and seized.[12] No action had been taken to bring Samuel to trial for this offense. As a result of and in direct retaliation for the incident with Thomas Fisher, Matlack urged the sheriff to take Samuel before the judge to put him in jail. Tried for misprision of treason amid vague accusations of intelligence sharing and currency depreciation, Samuel would neither acknowledge the legitimacy of the state government nor defend himself. The jury failed twice to convict Fisher, but McKean pressured the jury into coming back a third time with a conviction, which they did. Fisher spent two years in jail before he was pardoned and released.[13] In 1782, Samuel petitioned the government to be allowed to travel to England to settle the estate of his younger brother, Jabez Maud Fisher, who died there in 1779 at age twenty-nine, never having seen his family again after his precipitous departure in 1775 (see figure 18). The Fishers' father had sent Jabez there to shield him from Patriot reprisal for his publicly expressed Tory sentiments.[14] The SEC slammed the door on the nettlesome Samuel, denying his petition.

Samuel Fisher married a Quaker from a prominent Rhode Island family and served the community as a manager of the Pennsylvania Hospital and of the Philadelphia and Lancaster Turnpike. He survived the exile by fifty-four years.[15] Samuel passed his diaries to Thomas Gilpin Jr., the author, editor, and compiler of *Exiles in Virginia*; the journals then passed to Samuel's daughter Deborah Fisher Wharton, who passed them to her son Joseph Wharton (1826–1909). Wharton was one of the preeminent American industrialists of his age. He cofounded Bethlehem Steel Company and donated the funds to create the Wharton School of the University of Pennsylvania.[16] In the Fishers' case, a broad-brimmed, principled, arguably law-abiding but cantankerous dissident paved the way for a fully reintegrated leading industrialist of the Gilded Age in three quick generations.

Samuel Pleasants (ca. 1736–1809) returned home to his wife, Mary "Molly" Pemberton Pleasants (ca. 1736–1807), an author of the women's petition. After his return, agents of the Pennsylvania government visited their home to seize furniture in payment of an unpaid tax. As time wore on, however, the Pleasants family prospered in the new republic. Five of Samuel and Molly's ten children lived to at least the age of thirty and either became prominent businessmen or married men who were.[17]

Edward Penington (1726–1796) left Winchester "exceedingly broken and look[ing] like an old man." He returned to his wife, women's petition signer Sarah Shoemaker (Samuel's sister), and his sugar firm, but he continued to face persecution for his Quaker beliefs. In 1782, celebrating Patriots intentionally damaged his house. He was, however, elected to the common council of the city, and he sold salt to the Washingtons during the president's residence in Philadelphia. Some time after 1793, Edward and Sarah Penington sat for portraitist James Sharples. [18]

James Pemberton (1723–1807), merchant and lifelong Quaker activist, remained active in Quaker and community life, succeeding Benjamin Franklin as president of the Pennsylvania Abolition Society. His service on the Quaker Meeting for Sufferings since the 1750s continued unabated until months before his and his wife's deaths in 1807. He served as a member of the American Philosophical Society and on the board of the Pennsylvania Hospital. He had also served as an overseer of the Philadelphia public schools continuously since the 1750s. He had suffered a stroke in 1754, which he bore, in the language of the day, "with Christian resignation," and it seemed not to impede his activism.[19]

John Pemberton (1727–1795), Quaker minister, had felt the sting of Thomas Paine's public accusations. Before he took a post–Revolutionary War trip to Europe to carry on the Quaker outreach, he carefully notified the SEC that he was going abroad, and with no intentions of partisan activity. He cofounded the first Quaker meeting in Germany at Bad Pyrmont, where he died and was buried in 1795. He left twenty bequests to charities and over a hundred to individuals in the Philadelphia area, with fellow exile Henry Drinker among his executors.[20]

Thomas Fisher (1741–1810), merchant, returned to his wife, passionate diarist Sarah Logan Fisher (1751–1796), their son, and a newborn baby girl, Hannah. Sarah Logan Fisher was disappointed to be ruled again by Patriots, men she called "violent," but she was also disappointed by General Sir William Howe's inability to crush the rebels. Her husband, who kept his own diary, proved more discreet. He led the merchant firm as his father's successor and owned extensive western lands and interests in paper mills. He also served as a member of the American Philosophical Society, on the board of Pennsylvania Hospital, and as first treasurer and cofounder of the Westtown School, to ensure a guarded education to young Quaker children. He continued, too, to serve his Friends meeting, as evidenced by the unfortunate story of the run-in with Timothy Matlack mentioned earlier.[21]

Miers Fisher (1748–1819) carried on a legal practice, which had some business in aiding Quakers to claim compensation from Britain's American Loyalist Claims Commission. He also was busy in the family's mills and its many businesses and even exchanged favors with Benjamin Franklin. He was elected to the common council of the city in 1790, to the state House of Representatives, and to the board of the Bank of North America. He was also active in the Pennsylvania Abolition Society as a pro bono lawyer.[22] In 1790, he served on a committee of Philadelphians who preselected for the new president, George Washington, a house of appropriate grandeur in which to reside. Fisher served as one of the principal intermediaries on the delicate matter of an appropriate sum for rent between Washington's personal secretary, Tobias Lear, and the committee managing the house.[23]

Henry Drinker (1734–1809) and his wife, Elizabeth Sandwith Drinker (ca. 1735–1807), saw men come to their house after the exile and seize furniture to account for their failure to pay taxes and fines during the war. The Drinkers also saw five of their nine children survive to adulthood. Henry dissolved his former partnership with Abel James and, relieved of merchant activities, remained as active as ever in Quaker affairs. After his return from exile, he and James Pemberton traveled to New York in 1786 to implore Congress to prohibit the importation of enslaved persons. In 1790, Henry Drinker and John Pemberton were part of a PYM delegation that brought a petition against the slave trade to the First Federal Congress in New York City. Drinker was also elected to the common council of Philadelphia in 1790. He corresponded with President Washington concerning his idea to produce sugar without the need for enslaved labor (via the sap of maple trees) and in connection with Quaker efforts to continue to support Native Americans in treaty talks with the government. He even lobbied Governor Thomas McKean, the former chief justice, on the move of the state capital from Philadelphia to Lancaster. He was elected to membership in the prestigious

American Philosophical Society in 1786. After the exile, Elizabeth Drinker continued writing; her personal journals, which span nearly fifty years, are celebrated as among the best sources of knowledge of daily life in eighteenth-century America. Elizabeth included in her diary that on June 9, 1778, "a little past one this morning," "sister and self stayed at ye door" and "J. C. [Crammond] bid us adieu as they went by [to sail for New York], and we saw no more of him." Three years later, on October 28, 1781, she recorded that "Js. Crammond a young Officer who had liv'd 6 months with us, while the British Troops were in this City, and Behav'd so in our Family as to gain our esteem" had died after being ill for eight days. Elizabeth died in 1807, not long after the death of a daughter. Henry died in 1809, leaving four children and numerous grandchildren and further descendants. Their direct descendant Catherine Drinker Bowen (1897–1973) was a bestselling biographer who won the National Book Award for nonfiction in 1958 and was elected to the American Philosophical Society on the basis of her multiple books of history and biography, including a biographical work on John Adams. The book never mentioned how central Adams had been in the exile of her own ancestor.[24]

Owen Jones Jr. (1755–1825), young merchant, rejoined his father's firm and in 1780 married the daughter of fellow exile Thomas Wharton Sr. He thrived at the business and served as an executor to his father-in-law and to another fellow exile, Thomas Affleck.[25]

Thomas Affleck (1745–1795), Scottish-born cabinetmaker, returned to his wife and family and again took up his craft. He continued to be among the first rank of furniture makers in Philadelphia for nearly two decades, making fine furniture for Congress Hall and many prominent families. He died in 1795, and a son, Lewis, struggled to carry on the business after him. Highly prized examples of Thomas's fine furniture are found today in the diplomatic reception rooms of the US Department of State, in the Philadelphia Museum of Art, and in the Metropolitan Museum of Art in New York, among other prestigious collections.[26]

William Smith (before 1742–after 1805), broker, returned home and was prosecuted a second time for alleged inimical behavior under scrutiny, but again Patriot officials could prove nothing damning against him, and he was discharged. He owned property directly adjacent to property of the Jervis family, and he and his wife were among the people frequently in attendance at the Drinker household in the years after the exile.[27]

Charles Jervis (1731–1806), hatter and first cousin of Elizabeth Drinker, had been disciplined for marrying out of meeting—he married Elizabeth

Boore at Christ Church (Anglican) in 1766—but he made amends and rejoined his Quaker meeting. The following year, Jervis was appointed an Overseer of the Poor. At the time of his arrest, he and Elizabeth had five children. Jervis likely made the hostiles list for refusal of the Continental currency, but aside from his connection with the Drinkers no other reason has been found. Though a hatmaker by trade, Jervis became a successful real estate broker, and the Jervis family was not poor. Elizabeth Drinker had often approached her uncle John Jervis, Charles's father, when she had financial matters on her mind, and census records identify Charles as a gentleman. In his postexile life, Jervis served on a relatively large scale as a realtor and attorney for both his own account and for others leasing or selling real estate; his clients included Judge William Moore, a leading Chester County Tory; Henry Drinker; and Israel Pemberton's son Joseph. Since the Test Act forbade non–oath takers from conducting certain types of business, Jervis may have had to associate himself with a non-Quaker, oath-taking colleague for these tasks. He was also among the approximately one hundred founding members of the Pennsylvania Abolition Society. In 1800, Jervis "engage[d] the attention of [Friends] Overseers for neglecting to attend our Religious Meetings, and also for not paying a considerable sum of Money awarded to his sister," though this disciplinary inquiry was discontinued in 1801. Jervis spent the rest of his life in Philadelphia's Chestnut Ward, dying there in 1806. He was buried in the Arch Street Meeting House cemetery.[28]

Elijah Brown (1740–1810), a disowned former Quaker and heavily indebted merchant, returned to his wife, Mary Armitt Brown, and their eight children. In October 1777, his wife's brother-in-law, merchant Richard Waln, who provided financial support for Elijah's family during the exile, was arrested as a Tory and given a choice: go to jail, declare his allegiance to the revolution, or take the loyalist pathway to British-held New York. He took the last option.[29] Elijah's family was thereby thrown on the mercy of the Quaker meeting. Elizabeth Drinker and Sarah Logan Fisher aided the family in this crisis, and Waln returned home in December. In February 1779, Brown attempted to rejoin the meeting by condemning his former conduct and repenting. The meeting asked James Pemberton to investigate Elijah's complicated affairs and mind. While Elijah never was allowed to rejoin, he wrote a piece of fatherly advice for his children on the value of a steadfast adherence to Quaker values. In 1784, he was imprisoned in jail for nonpayment of his debts.[30] After release, he called himself a conveyancer and helped manage family real estate. The "quirky" and "eccentric" Brown had not been considered a "man of reputation" before the exile, and his status thereafter remained unchanged.[31] His son Charles Brockden Brown (1771–1810), six years old when his father was forcibly arrested on the morning of September 3, 1777, failed to complete his law studies and instead became America's first professional writer and gothic novelist, with tales inspired by the many times as a child in 1776 and thereafter that his family felt persecuted by clamorous and frighteningly aggressive Patriots for not illuminating their windows during Patriot fasts and celebrations. Well known as a man of letters, Brockden Brown sometimes wrote on issues of national importance. In 1809, he published a plea to Congress to lift a controversial embargo. In it, he both drew on and distanced himself from his Quaker background, from which he, too, had been disowned: "Some, observing the city where I thus make my appearance, may think my pacific doctrine, my system of rational forebearance and forgiveness carried to a pitch of *Quaker* extravagance. The truth is, I am no better than an outcast of that unwarlike sect [disowned], but cannot rid myself of reverence for most of its practical and political maxims. I feel a strong inclination to admit to an equality of rights and merits, men of all nations and religions." Brockden Brown died that same year.[32]

Sometimes full reintegration took multiple generations. Elijah's great-grandson, Henry Armitt Brown (1825–1878), became a lawyer, a Yale-educated historian, and an "eloquent and impassioned speaker" often called on to orate publicly on special occasions.[33] He was chosen to deliver the oration in Carpenters' Hall in September 1874 for the ceremonies marking the centennial of the opening day of the First Continental Congress. Four years later, in 1878, Armitt Brown was called into service again to deliver an oration at Valley Forge on the centennial of the last day of the Continental Army's fateful revolutionary encampment. In both cases, he spoke with elegiac eloquence and patriotic fervor, each oration more than equal to the task. In neither instance did he mention how his great-grandfather Brown had fared during the revolution. Mimicking in part the words and tempo of the Gettysburg Address, Armitt Brown's sixty-page 1878 speech celebrated Americans' perseverance and eventual triumph in the Philadelphia Campaign: "We come to contemplate the sources of our country's greatness; to commune with the honored past; to remind ourselves, and show our children that joy can come out of sorrow, happiness out of suffering; light out of darkness, life out of death." He referred only once to Quakers in his oration at Valley Forge, noting ironically in passing that "Quakers from the Valley turned soldiers for their country's sake."[34] True, some did.

Inscribed in bronze lettering inside the National Memorial Arch erected in 1917 at Valley Forge are these words, lifted from Armitt Brown's 1878 oration:

In this place
Of Sacrifice
In this vale of Humiliation
In this Valley of the Shadow
Of that Death Out of Which
The Life of America Rose
Regenerate and free[35]

For Patriots, Valley Forge had been the "Valley of the Shadow." For the Religious Society of Friends, their own "Valley of the Shadow" and "vale of Humiliation" had been in Winchester, Virginia, where their leaders had been sent by Patriot leaders in an act of shaming meant as a preventive detention for irksome dissenters viewed by some as dangerously naïve. There, two among them had died as martyrs—a martyrdom that arose out of dearly held principles of protest against war and in favor of the individual and religious liberties that have become dear to many Americans. Henry Armitt Brown died at thirty-three, shortly after this oration, yet his words live on. They serve as a fittingly ironic end to the story of the Quaker exile and a visible manifestation of the reconciliation between former foes.

EPILOGUE

In the introduction, I noted that I had spent my first six years in an eighteenth-century stone house in Edge's Mill in Caln Township, near Downingtown, Chester County, Pennsylvania, attended a Quaker preschool at Downingtown Friends meetinghouse, and napped on hard Quaker benches. To me these seemed salient facts related to my book project, though my wife wondered why. After more than eight years of researching and writing this book, I discovered an uncanny coincidence. My father bought the stone house, a former blacksmith's residence and real fixer-upper, in 1937 and called it Three Corners (it was on a triangular-shaped lot of about one and three-fourths acres). Our house was one of six stone buildings on four different but contiguous land tracts in our rural village. Our property was separated from that of our playmates, Jacob and Tommy Edge, by the peaceful waters of Beaver Creek and a stone bridge built in 1916. I knew that our neighbors the Edges were, or maybe had been, Quakers, or at least I thought so, and that the village was called Edge's Mill. But over time, I learned that it only came to be called that in the 1850s.

In 1747, an Irish immigrant, Robert Valentine (1717–1786), described in records as a shopkeeper, married Rachel Edge, and in 1762 they bought the land on which these six stone buildings had been built along with a mill that came to be referred to as Valentine's Mill. They owned the buildings until 1781, when Valentine sold them to his son of the same name. Robert Valentine the father and his wife were members of the Religious Society of Friends; not only that, they both held esteemed positions, he as a public Friend, and she as an elder in Uwchlan Friends Meeting. After completing the manuscript for *Prisoners of Congress*, I learned that Henry and Elizabeth Drinker not only knew the Valentines but that on April 7, 1778, two days after dining with George and Martha Washington at Valley Forge, Elizabeth Drinker and the women's mission had stayed the night with the Valentines. Moreover, on April 28, after the exiles had been released at Lancaster, the Valentines had hosted both Elizabeth and Henry and as many as twenty other members of the exiles' party.[1] The beloved homestead of creek and woods, swimming hole and tree house of which I had always spoken so fondly had served, over a hundred and sixty years prior to my infant residence there, as a way station for Friends during and after the Quaker exile. The idyllic, rural village of my youth had a place in the eighteenth-century human drama that captured the exceedingly rapt attention of my retirement years and propelled me to research and write this book.

I do not know for certain where inspiration comes from. I now realize that in my first six years, I might have absorbed by osmosis not the story of the Quaker exile—for this I developed only by reading a lot of documents and diaries, a labor of love—but a strong inclination leading to a firm and constant lifelong interest in Quakers along with the determination to uncover the Quaker exile story and the drive to find it all and present it for the first time in a complete way to those fond of reading about history and our nation's messy founding years.

HOMAGE

THOMAS GILPIN JR.

JABEZ MAUD FISHER

FIG. 17 | Thomas Gilpin Jr. (1776–1853), the namesake son of a martyred exile, paper mill entrepreneur, and author, compiled a book of documents of the Quaker exile and published them for subscribers in *Exiles in Virginia* (1848), which became almost a sacred book for nineteenth-century Quakers. Silhouette, Historical Society of Pennsylvania portrait collection [V88]. Reproduced with permission from the Historical Society of Pennsylvania.

FIG. 18 | Jabez Maud Fisher (1750–1779), the youngest Fisher brother and an ardent Loyalist intellectual, naturalist, and diarist, was hurried by his father, Joshua, onto a ship bound for England after Patriots showed him their passionate ire at Jabez's Loyalist sentiments. He died at age 29 in England, never having seen his family again. Pastel portrait by James Sharples, Friends Historical Library of Swarthmore College.

APPENDIX A

Combined Timeline of the Quaker Exile (September 11, 1777–April 30, 1778) amid the Philadelphia Campaign (August 25, 1777–June 18, 1778), Including Governance of the City

DATE	EVENT
Until July 4, 1776	Gov. John Penn, grandson of William Penn, presides over the colonial government apparatus, on top of which Patriots add revolutionary committees.
September 1776	New state apparatus under the Constitution of Pennsylvania adopted, but elections not yet held. Essentially an interregnum.
December 1776	Gen. George Washington gives Gen. Israel Putnam command of the city during emergency threat of a British invasion.
1777	
January	
2	Broadside published by Gen. Putnam warns residents that they might be exiled if they fail to accept the Continental currency created by Congress.
25	Continental soldiers quartered on the disaffected of the city, including the Drinkers.
February	
11	Thomas Wharton Jr. elected president of the Supreme Executive Council (SEC) of Pennsylvania.

| 11 | First laws passed by new Pennsylvania government. English common law reestablished. Treason law enacted. |

March

| 17 | Act to Regulate the Militia of the Commonwealth of Pennsylvania passed in the Assembly. |

May

| 17 | Gen. Philip Schuyler asks for one thousand blankets from Quakers, who decline. |

June

| 13 | Test Act requires oath of allegiance for voting. |

July

| 4 | Quakers refuse to celebrate first anniversary of the Declaration of Independence; Patriots break non-illuminated windows in Quaker homes. |

| 23 | British ships and troops leave New York Harbor, destination unknown. |

| 30 | British realize that navigation up the Delaware River to Philadelphia is blocked by chevaux-de-frise. They sail south to the mouth of the Chesapeake Bay and, on the Bay, head north. |

August

| 25 | British arrival at northern tip of Chesapeake Bay: Head of Elk, Cecil County, Maryland (260 ships, 15,000 troops or more). |

| 28 | Maj.-Gen. John Sullivan sends Congress the Spanktown Papers, assigned to committee on spies; Congress recommends arrest of eleven Philadelphia Quaker leaders (first congressional debate on this issue), suggests Pennsylvania add more names. |

| 31 | SEC president asks for help in forming a "list of persons dangerous to the state, who ought to be arrested." Secret committee culls its list of hostiles, concluding with a list of thirty to add to the eleven, |

for a total of forty-one men to be arrested if they do not sign a house-arrest parole or oath to the state.

September

2–11   Quaker leaders arrested, confined loosely at Freemason's Lodge.

5   Congress debates four hours (second debate) whether to exile the Quaker leaders without a chance to be heard in their defense. Unresolved, it passes responsibility to the SEC, which declines to act.

6   Pennsylvania authorities lob Quaker issue back to Congress.

8   Congress again debates (third debate) fate of Quakers, this time for five hours; resolves to send them away "unheard" as men who "maintained a correspondence and connection highly prejudicial to the public safety."

9   *Pennsylvania Packet* publishes the Spanktown Papers, submitted by Congress, along with Quaker-authored policy statements and records of Quaker "sufferings" Congress believed showed guilt.

10   *Pennsylvania Gazette* publishes Congress's papers against Quakers.

11   Battle of Brandywine. On same day in Philadelphia, twelve Quaker leaders, five other Quakers, two former Quakers, and one non-Quaker forcibly exiled; caravan with militia guard departs Philadelphia to jeers by some and sobs by others.

12–13   Ten prisoners apply to Pennsylvania Supreme Court for writs of habeas corpus; Chief Justice Thomas McKean approves but privately suggests law suspending right of habeas corpus.

14   John Roberts attempts to arrange Quaker exiles' rescue by British troops. Habeas writs arrive, but guards deliberately ignore them.

16   Pennsylvania Assembly passes Banishing Law, ex post facto, seemingly "legalizing" the exile and suspending

the issuance of writs of habeas corpus; law contains sunset provision to January 2, 1778.

18	Quaker Isaac Zane and son Isaac Jr. meet with exiles in Reading; Zanes get exiles' destination changed by John Adams, board of war, from Staunton, Virginia, to Winchester, Virginia.
20	Battle of Paoli ("Paoli Massacre").
23	Continental Congress flees Philadelphia for Lancaster, then York.
	SEC flees for Lancaster.
26	British Army captures Philadelphia, begins occupation.
27	Exiles cross over Mason-Dixon Line into Washington County, Maryland.
28	Battle of Mud Island begins on Delaware River.
	Philadelphia Yearly Meeting (PYM) of Quakers begins in Philadelphia.
	Exiles cross Potomac River into Virginia at Williamsport, Maryland.
29	Quaker exiles reach Winchester, Virginia; angry crowd gathers to protest their arrival.

October

4	Battle of Germantown. PYM annual meeting ends.
6	PYM peace mission of five ministers and one elder visits Gen. Howe.
7	PYM peace mission visits Gen. Washington.
17	Battle of Saratoga (NY) ends in American victory. British surrender 5,791 men; more dead, wounded, captured.
23	British sixty-four-gun Man of War *Augusta* and a thirty-two-gun ship are blown up on Delaware River. Howe secretly sends his resignation to London, awaits answer.

November

15   Battle of Mud Island ends in British victory after seven weeks.

20   Battle of Red Point (Ft. Mercer, NJ); Hessians win battle but at a cost of nine hundred British and Hessian troops. Americans scuttle the remainder of Pennsylvania's small fleet to prevent British from seizing boats.

            British engineers begin to remove the chevaux-de-frise; hundreds of British ships can soon dock at Philadelphia.

December

5–8   Battle of White Marsh. Howe fails again to crush Continental Army.

6   Howe appoints former Quaker party speaker of the Pennsylvania house Joseph Galloway as superintendent of police and the Port of Philadelphia; Howe appoints Quaker Samuel Shoemaker as a magistrate.

8   British Army enters winter quarters in Philadelphia with fresh supplies.

11   Gen. Lord Cornwallis leads foraging and provisioning raid on surrounding western suburbs of Philadelphia, with John Roberts, miller, guiding his light horse troops.

14   Exiled disowned Quaker William Drewet Smith escapes from Winchester to Philadelphia.

16   Philadelphia Quakers appeal to London and Dublin Quakers to send a ship of scarce supplies.

18   Board of war charges that exile Owen Jones Jr. depreciated the currency.

19   Washington's troops enter winter quarters at Valley Forge in tatters.

31   British Major John Crammond quarters himself and staff in Drinker household; other families of exiles already have British officers quartered on them as well.

1778

January

In Jan.
British Ministry, London, decides United States cannot be conquered militarily, but troops should fight on anyway.

2
Banishing Law's life extended, to expire April 24, 1778.

February

In Feb.
Exile Thomas Pike escapes from Winchester.

4
US–French Treaty of Alliance signed in Paris.

March

2
Quaker exile Thomas Gilpin, merchant and scientist, dies at Winchester.

6
Pennsylvania Assembly passes conditional attainder law against traitors but does not charge any of the exiles at this time—exiles Thomas Wharton Sr. and Charles Eddy will later be charged.

16
Congress agrees to release Quaker exiles to Pennsylvania; state authorities in Lancaster drag their feet.

31
Quaker exile John Hunt, merchant and minister, dies at Winchester.

April

4
Women's mission departs Philadelphia; its members lodge at John Roberts's home in Merion township.

5
Women's mission meets with George and Martha Washington at Valley Forge.

6
Washington writes to President Wharton that "Humanity pleads strongly in their behalf."

Women proceed to Lancaster to petition the SEC.

10
Women's petition is read in the Council; in response, the SEC orders exiles' release accelerated with release at Lancaster rather than Shippensburg.

28
SEC gives exiles a limited "discharge" that is not an exoneration. Exiles are released, and some lodge

	overnight at Robert Valentine's home in/near Downingtown.
29	Exiles lodge overnight at John Roberts's home in Merion. Washington authorizes their pass into the enemy-held city.
30	Remaining Quaker exiles return home.

May

1	Battle of Crooked Billet. British burn captured soldiers.
2	News of French alliance reaches Valley Forge, results in celebrations.
8	Gen. Sir Henry Clinton arrives in Philadelphia to replace Howe.
	New British peace commission also arrives in Philadelphia.
18	The Meschianza—lavish gala, parade, and fair—is held in tribute to Howe.
20	Battle of Barren Hill. Howe tries to capture Gen. Lafayette but again fails to gain a strategic advantage.
22	President Wharton dies in Lancaster; SEC Vice President George Bryan assumes lead role.

June

18	British Forces evacuate Philadelphia, depart through New Jersey for New York City.
	Patriots retake Philadelphia immediately.
	Washington gives Gen. Benedict Arnold command of the city.
24	A total eclipse of the sun occurs in Philadelphia. The city goes dark for an hour (a sign of nothing in particular, nevertheless remarkable).

September

26	Quaker Abraham Carlisle, master carpenter, is tried and convicted of treason.

30	Quaker John Roberts, miller, is tried and convicted of treason.
November	
4	Roberts and Carlisle are hanged on the common.
	Chief Justice Thomas McKean's sentencing statement on John Roberts's case is published in newspapers at behest of SEC, reflecting their view of the Quaker exile.
December	
1	Joseph Reed becomes second president of the SEC.
1779	PYM appoints committee of inquiry into the cases of Roberts and Carlisle; committee investigates but does not disclose its report until 1785.
1780	John Drinker, clerk of the Meeting for Sufferings, publishes in the local newspaper a vindication of the actions of the Quakers in 1777.
1784	Pennsylvania Council of Censors declares unconstitutional the 1777 suspension of habeas as to the prisoners.

APPENDIX B

Israel Pemberton et al., [Protest] "To the President and Council of Pennsylvania," September 8, 1777[1]

To the President and Council of Pennsylvania,
The Remonstrance of the Subscribers, Freemen & Inhabitants of the City of Philadelphia, now confined in the Lodge
Sheweth

That it is with pain we find ourselves under the disagreeable necessity of again remonstrating ag[ain]st your extraordinary mode of treating us: when our last remonstrance was del'd to your President he gave Expectation to our Fellow-Citizens who waited on him, that he would lay it before you, and return an Answer—Notwithstanding which we have as yet received no Answer whatsoever to it, but instead thereof a Paper signed by your Secretary was del'd us by William Bradford, the Contents of which we shall have occasion to remark on:

But we must not omit another letter rec'd thro the same Channell by which we are confirmed in the Truth of what we had before heard, that on the very day you were address'd by three of us to *be heard*, and before we were furnished with a Copy of the General Warrant you had resolved to banish us to Stanton [Staunton] in the County of Augusta in Virginia, a Place where you claim no Jurisdiction, & to which we are utter Strangers:—This Resolution form'd against a Body of innocent Freemen while demanding to be heard is we believe the first Instance of the kind to be found in the History of our Country & besides the violent Infringement of the Laws & Constitution which you have engaged to govern by, the Hardship is heightened by the particular Situation of that Country at this time as it is publickly asserted that the Indians have already commenced Hostilitys [*sic*] upon the

Frontiers of Virginia, not very far distant from the Place of our intended Banishment, as tho' you could find no Place of Security without endangering our Lives:

From the Profession you have repeatedly made of your Love of Liberty & Justice, & the manner in which we have demanded our undoubted Rights, we had reason to expect to have heard from you on the Subject of our last remonstrance: but we find we were mistaken, & the Complaints of injured Freemen still remain unanswered.

Whether you imagine we are of too little Consequence to be regarded, or expect that Confinement will reduce us to a tame Acquiescence with your arbitrary proceedings we shall not determine—it will not divert our Attention from the important Object we have in view in behalf of ourselves, & our Country—nor will subtile [sic] Proposals fit only to captivate the unwary decoy us from the sure Ground on which we stand into a measure as illegal and unconstitutional as your General Warrant, & our oppressive Treatment under it.

The Proposition contained in your Resolve of the 5th Instant to discharge us upon taking the Test "required by law," or the new Test framed by yourselves now demands our Notice.

And first we would observe that if you had a Right to make such a Proposition, we think it very improper to be made to men in our Situation— you have first deprived us of our Liberty on one Pretence [sic] which finding you are not able to justify you wave [sic], and require as a Condition of our Enlargement, that we should confess ourselves men of suspicious Characters by doing what ought not to be expected from innocent men. This kind of Procedure is not new in History, for tho' the great Patriots at the Revolution found better Expedients for the Security of their Government than what arises from Oaths of Abjuration, yet the Annals Both of Old & new England are stained with Accounts of men in Circumstances similar to our own, dragged before magistrates, on the bare suspicion of Crimes: of whom Tests, which they conscientiously scrupled to take, have been afterward demanded, as the Condition of their Enlargement:—But such Examples we should hope would not have found Patrons among Men professing to be Reformers upon all the Plans of Civil, & Religious Liberty adopted by the free nations of Europe.

It is strange to us that Men entrusted with *Supreme Executive Powers should* be so regardless of the Laws you have most solemnly engaged to execute as to require us to do more than those very Laws enjoin—By the Test

Act every Inhabitant may take the Test & enjoy all the Rights of Freemen or decline it & submit to a deprivation of some of them which are express'd in that Act, but no power is given to any Officer of Justice whatsoever to render it to any Person except in particular Circumstances, and as the Charge against us is not founded on a Breach of that law, it[']s evident you exceed your Authority in putting it to us:

But if after what has past we could be surprised at anything you do, We should have been astonished at the rapid Progress of your Usurpation in assuming legislative Powers to yourselves while the Assembly was sitting under the same roof, You have overturned the only Security the Constitution has given the People against absolute Despotism by attempting to exercise the Authority of framing a Resolve, operating as a Law & at the same time of executing it. Your Duty as one Branch of the Constitution is to [be] confined to the executing the Laws as you find them, & does not extend to the making new ones to salve your own irregular Conduct—you have undertaken all this by proposing a new Test of your own enacting unknown to the laws & Constitution of the Govermt which you are to execute unsupported by any Authority under which you act, and this an ex post Facto Law made to criminate by a Refusal those who before were innocent. And if we were in your opinion such dangerous Persons as you under the Sanction of the Congress have endeavor'd to represent us, & could not be secured without sending us to so remote & dangerous a part of the country beyond the Limits of your Jurisdiction, how will the public be secured by our taking either of the Tests you have proposed[?]—That men of bad Principles will submit to any Tests to cover their dangerous, & wicked purposes is evident to all who have been conversant in Public Affairs.

The great Lord Halifax, who in the name of the People of England presented the Crown to King William & Queen Mary at the Revolution, has expressed himself on this Subject in the follow'g nervous terms: "As there is no real Security to any State by Oaths, so no private Person, much less Statesmen, would ever order his Affairs as relying on it; for no man would ever sleep with open Doors, or unlocked up Treasure or Plate, should all the Town be sworn not to rob."[2]

Another most extraordinary Proceeding we find in your Secretary's letters; where he says that *you asked & received the Advice of Congress* upon our Remonstrance before you determined upon it—What! Shall unaccused Citizens demand'g their inherent Rights be delayed or refused a Hearing until Congress can be consulted? A Body who have engaged not to interfere in the internal Police of the Government? Perhaps you thought the Authority of a Recommendation from Congress would render your arbitrary Designs effectual, & countenance you in the Eyes of the People—we trust you will be mistaken, & that neither Congress nor the People will approve your measures:

Having thus remarked on your Proposal protesting our Innocence, we again repeat our pressing demand to be informed of the Cause of our Commitment, & to have a Hearing in the Face of our Country before whom we shall either stand acquitted or condemned.

Mason's Lodge
Philad'a Sept'r 8th 1777
/s/ ChaJervis
/s/ Tho's: Pike
/s/ Tho's Gilpin
/s/ Samuel R Fisher
/s/ Thomas Fisher
/s/ Elijah Brown
/s/ Miers Fisher
/s/ Charles Eddy

/s/ Isr: Pemberton
/s/ Jam's Pemberton
/s/ John Hunt
/s/ ThoWharton
/s/ Thomas Coombe[3]
/s/ Edw'd Penington
/s/ John Pemberton
/s/ Henry Drinker
/s/ Phineas Bond
/s/ Thos: Affleck
/s/ Owen Jones Jr
/s/ Wm Drewet Smith
/s/ Sam'l Pleasants
/s/ Wm Smith
Broker

The Women's Petition, April 1778[1]

To the Congress, Board of War, President and Council, and Assembly of Pennsylvania.

We, the afflicted and sorrowful wives, parents and near connexions [*sic*] of the Friends in banishment, at and near Winchester, think ourselves bound by the strongest ties of natural affection, sympathy, and regard, to request you, that you suffer Christian charity and compassion so far to prevail in your minds as to take off the bonds of those innocent and oppressed Friends, and entreat you not let the ruin of such, who have evidenced their strong attachment to their native country, and a benevolent disposition to mankind in general, to lie at the door of a people professing the tender and compassionate religion of Christ, one of whose excellent precepts was, "Whatsoever ye would that men should do to you, do ye even so to them."[2]

[*Verso of petition from Swarthmore copy*][3]

A parcel [i.e., letter] of afflicted & sorrowful Quakers to Congress

[*Body of petition from Swarthmore copy with most notable variations from Gilpin copy*][4]

The melancholy account we have lately received of the Indisposition of our Beloved Husbands and Children and that the awful missinger [*sic*] Death had made an inroad on one of their number [Gilpin version adds: "(Thomas Gilpin)"] to the unspeakable grief & irreparable Loss of an Amiable Wife and children hath deeply affected our minds, & divers of our families are in a distressed situation—We therefore ardently desire you to make the case your own—no doubt many of you have Wives and tender children and must know that in the time of trial and distress none are so proper to alleviate

& bear apart [Gilpin version: "a part"] of the Burthen as their affectionate Husbands.

We firmly believe these our Dear friends are Clear and Innocent of the charges alledged [*sic*] against them which they for themselves and the[ir fri]ends for them have fully answered, and that they are now suffering for a st[eady and firm adher]ance to their Innoffensive & peaceable principles. [*Letters in brackets supplied to match those in the Gilpin copy.*]

This application to you on this interesting subject is Entirely An Act of our Own, we have not Consulted our absent friends on the occation [*sic*] hoping and believing it would not be of disservice and Request you will take no offence at the freedom of Women so deeply interested as we are in this matter—And that divine Benevolence may so influence your Hearts as to Grant our Earnest Request in which we doubt not you will find true peace in the Hour of Retribution, & it will be an Inexpressible satisfaction to you. [Gilpin version: "inexpressible consolation to your suffering and sorrowful friends."]

SUFFERING & SORROWFUL FRIENDS

/s/ Mary Pleasants /s/ Rachel Hunt /s/ Mary Pemberton
/s/ Mary Brown /s/ Esther Fisher /s/ Rebecca Jarvis
/s/ Eliza Smith /s/ Hannah Pemberton /s/ Mary Eddy
/s/ Eliza Jervis /s/ Eliza Drinker /s/ Sarah Penington
/s/ Isabella Afflick /s/ Phoebe Pemberton /s/ Rachel Wharton
/s/ Sarah Fisher /s/ Susanna Jones
/s/ Sarah R. Fisher[5]

N.B. This Address was signed in Philadelphia and sent by Susanna Jones, Phoebe Pemberton, Mary Pleasants, & Eliza Drinker 4 mo 1778.

[*Version in Gilpin's* Exiles in Virginia *(1848):*]

/s/ Hannah Pemberton, /s/ Mary Pemberton,
/s/ Isabella Affleck, /s/ Eliza Drinker,
/s/ Rebecca Jervis, /s/ Sarah Fisher,
/s/ Phebe Pemberton, /s/ Susanna Jones,
/s/ Sarah R. Fisher, /s/ Mary Pleasants,
/s/ Mary Eddy, /s/ Mary Brown,
/s/ Sarah Pennington, /s/ Elizabeth Smith,
/s/ Rachel Wharton, /s/ Eliza Jervis,
/s/ Esther Fisher, /s/ Rachel Hunt.

Philadelphia, 4th month 1st, 1778.

According to Elizabeth Drinker's diary, Mary Pemberton Pleasants (1738–1821)—Samuel Pleasants's wife and Israel Pemberton's daughter—drafted the petition with an addition by her stepmother,· Mary Stanbury Pemberton (1704–1778), Israel's second wife. The petition was signed three times as alterations were made to it after the women learned on April 2 of the death of John Hunt on March 31. The petition, or one version of it, was signed by all the women on March 31, 1778 (all there except Rachel Hunt and Lydia Fisher Gilpin). Another copy was prepared on April 2 to add a reference to the death of Hunt. Then a third copy of the petition was prepared April 4 to again mention the death of Hunt.[6]

As of 2001, when Patricia Law Hatcher published her original article on the women's petition, the original petition presented to the SEC had not been located; nor has it been located since.[7] There are two known copies of the petition. The copy reproduced here is based on the Swarthmore copy, but the handwriting has been attributed to Miers Fisher, who would only have seen the petition after he was released from exile. It is undated, and the signatures on it are not original. The second known copy of the petition is the Gilpin copy reproduced with minor word variations by Thomas Gilpin Jr. in *Exiles in Virginia* (1848). The Swarthmore copy refers only to the death of one exile (Gilpin died on March 2) and therefore was one of those drafted before April 2, when they learned of Hunt's death. The petition was "read & considered" by the SEC on April 10, though the women were not admitted, as they requested, to face the Council. As a result of the petition, the SEC resolved only that the prisoners be brought to Lancaster to be released there rather than, as earlier planned, at Shippensburg, some eighty miles west of Lancaster and less convenient for their relatives. The SEC also added later that the prisoners could have the choice of being released at Potts Grove. These were minor and grudging concessions to the women's petition.

The women's petition addressed a variety of authorities—"the Congress, Board of War, President and Council, and Assembly of Pennsylvania"—but since the women only reached the Council and the men were released as a result, the petition was never presented to the other addressees.

Each of the eighteen women signed for at least one of the remaining men. Lydia Fisher Gilpin, whose husband died March 2, never signed, but Rachel Hunt, whose husband died March 31, did sign one of the versions before she knew of her husband's death. One woman, Mary Pemberton Pleasants, was related to four exiles: her father, Israel; her uncles, the two younger Pemberton brothers; and her husband, Samuel Pleasants. Two female relatives of exile Charles Jervis signed both versions: his wife, Elizabeth, and his sister, Rebecca (who signed Jarvis on the Swarthmore version and Jervis on the other, there being alternative contemporaneous spellings of the name).

NOTES

INTRODUCTION

1. Henry Drinker to Elizabeth Drinker [HD to ED], Mar. 24, 1778, QSC.

2. HD to ED, Feb. 18, 1778, QSC.

3. John Sullivan to John Hancock, Aug. 25, 1777, in Sullivan, *Letters and Papers of Major-General John Sullivan*, 1:443–44.

4. The first to do so was Doyle, *Enemy in Our Hands*.

5. Atkinson, *The British Are Coming*, 562.

6. *JCC*, 8:694.

7. Resolution of Council, Aug. 31, 1777, in *EV*, 128. The term "hostiles list" is my own.

8. Isaacson, *Benjamin Franklin*, 342.

9. Nash, *Unknown American Revolution*, xvi, xviii.

10. Henry and Elizabeth Drinker Letters, 1777–1778, QSC; *DED*. Elizabeth Drinker's original diary, in thirty-four manuscript volumes, was given to and deposited at HSP in 1955 by Henry S. (1880–1965) and Sophie H. (1888–1967) Drinker. As completed, the three volumes published in 1991 comprise nearly twenty-four hundred useful and well-documented pages of historical information. All scholars of the period owe a great debt of gratitude for Elaine Forman Crane's decade of exceedingly thoughtful and painstaking work on Elizabeth Drinker's diary. As Crane did (e.g., "the" for "ye"), I have very slightly modified the spelling of the Drinkers' words for readability.

11. Indeed, George Washington himself may have complained of Parliament's decision to suspend habeas in England, which he knew meant indefinite detention without trial. The veracity of the source, however, is uncertain. Tyler, "Forgotten Core Meaning of the Suspension Clause," 675.

12. APS, HSP, and LCP, *A Rising People*, 125.

13. *EV*; Vining, *Virginia Exiles*. For early books that contain a glimpse at the Quaker exile, see Sharpless, *Two Centuries of Pennsylvania History*; and Jones et al., *Quakers in the American Colonies*. Arthur J. Mekeel elaborated on the subject in his 1940 Harvard PhD thesis, first published in 1979 as *The Relation of the Quakers to the American Revolution* and updated and reprinted in 1996 as *The Quakers and the American Revolution*; see also Marietta, *Reformation of American Quakerism*. William Pencak's edited volume *Pennsylvania's*

Revolution contains only a few lines about the Quaker exile. Several journal articles and books have illuminated parts of the exile. Biographical studies include Anderson, "Thomas Wharton," 425–47; Castro, "'Being Separated from My Dearest Husband,'" 40–63; Godbeer, *World of Trouble*; Radbill, "Ordeal of Elizabeth Drinker," 147–72; and Thayer, *Israel Pemberton*. For works that approach the exile within the context of Loyalism, see Oaks, "Philadelphians in Exile," 298–319, 321–25; and Ousterhout, *A State Divided*. Whidbee's more recent "Quaker Exiles," 28–57, analyzes the rhetoric on both sides and compares it usefully. Aaron Sullivan's *The Disaffected* begins its introduction with a dramatic scene of the day the Quakers were arrested.

14. The school was cofounded by, among others, exile Thomas Fisher.

15. *DED*, 3:1677.

16. The most recent and complete treatment of the Drinkers is Godbeer, *World of Trouble*.

17. Bowen, *Family Portrait*, 5.

18. William Penn to William Markham, 1681, quoted in Wilson, *Philadelphia Quakers*, 9–10, and "Introduction," *EV*, 18.

CHAPTER 1

1. Resolve of Council, Nov. 28, 1776, in *CRP*, 11:18 (emphasis added). There was precedent for this: in 1775 in Massachusetts, the government had requisitioned from local communities four thousand blankets for soldiers at General George Washington's request. [Mass. Bay colony] House of Representatives, Jan. 4, 1776, in Fowler, *Guide to the Sol Feinstone Collection*, 144.

2. DTO, 414. I am grateful to Kacy Dowd Tillman's insightful analysis of the diaries of Loyalist women, including Fisher and other Quakers. See Tillman, *Stripped and Script*.

3. *DED*, 1:225, 225n8.

4. Reynell, "To the Monthly Meeting of Friends in Philadelphia for the Southern District," July 28, 1777, in *EV*, 294.

5. Reynell, "Minutes of the Quarterly Meeting Held in Philadelphia, 3rd month, 4th, 1777"; DTO, 435. The PYM's jurisdiction covered parts of Pennsylvania, Delaware, and New Jersey as well as parts of Virginia and Maryland. The Meeting for Sufferings was the executive and publishing committee of the PYM.

6. Schuyler to Pemberton, May 17, 1777, in *LDC*, 7:89–90. See also DTO, 435. Quakers recognize only lay ministers, unofficial positions held by individuals known as talented speakers.

7. Bell and Greifenstein, "James Pemberton," in *Patriot-Improvers*, 3:156 ("King of the Quakers"). Dawkins, "An Indian Squaw King Wampum spies. [. . .]" ("King Wampum"); Kafer called him such a savvy politician that he was Benjamin Franklin's peer in Pennsylvania (Kafer, *Charles Brockden Brown*, 19). According to Marietta, the Penns considered him "the most turbulent creature that has appeared in the Province" who "prys into . . . all matters [of public business]" and has "no discretion [he] pushes himself into every thing." Marietta, *Reformation of American Quakerism*, 43, 199n25. He was widely respected among Quakers and was eager to do good in the world. He was elected a member of the American Philosophical Society in 1768.

8. Each Pemberton brother had refused to meet the demands of the Patriot authorities earlier, when the government had requested the use of one of their carriages to transport General Roberdeau of the Pennsylvania militia to Lancaster. Schuyler to Pemberton, May 22, 1777, in *LDC*, 7:107.

9. Schuyler to Washington, May 18, 1777, in *LDC*, 7:90.

10. Crabtree, *Holy Nation*, 13.

11. "Declaration . . . Against All Plotters and Fighters in the World," addressed

to King Charles II of England by George Fox and eleven other Friends, Jan. 1660. This belief derives from James 4:1–2 (KJV): "From whence come wars and fightings among you? come they not hence, even of your lusts that war in your members? Ye lust, and have not: ye kill, and desire to have, and cannot obtain: ye fight and war, yet ye have not, because ye ask not."

12. By 1680, William Penn could document that 10,000 Quakers had been imprisoned in England, and 243 Quakers had already died for their faith. Sharpless, *Quaker Experiment*, 19.

13. Fischer, *Albion's Seed*, 459.

14. *EV*, 47. The Quakers had protested taxation without representation in the colonies as early as 1679 in neighboring West Jersey.

15. Bauman, *Reputation of Truth*, 3–4.

16. Calvert, *Quaker Constitutionalism*, 230.

17. Marietta, *Reformation of American Quakerism*, 196.

18. Foner, *Tom Paine and Revolutionary America*, 21. See also Lemon, *The Best Poor Man's Country*.

19. Oaks, "Big Wheels in Philadelphia," 351.

20. Brock, *Pacifism in the United States*, 184.

21. Marietta, *Reformation of American Quakerism*, 220–21, 220n59, citing the epistle to members of the PYM dated Sept. 24, 1774. Although historians now date the beginning of the war to 1754, the Quaker representatives resigned from the Pennsylvania Assembly in 1756.

22. Bockelman and Ireland, "Internal Revolution in Pennsylvania," 125–59, 132, 149.

23. Ibid., 156.

24. Ibid. See also Ireland, "Crux of Politics," 453–75.

25. Bockelman and Ireland, "Internal Revolution in Pennsylvania," 131; Oaks, "Big Wheels in Philadelphia," 357; Ireland, "Crux of Politics," 470–71.

26. Wulf, "Introduction," in La Courreye Blecki and Wulf, *Milcah Martha Moore's Book*, 8, 9.

27. Mekeel, *Quakers and the American Revolution*, appendix 1, 388–89.

28. Knauss, "Christopher Saur the Third," 235–53, passim.

29. Brock, *Pacifism in the United States*, 260, 261, 285–86, 309–10 (quote).

30. Ibid., 180, 271–72 (quote).

31. Ibid., 267–69; Durnbaugh, *Brethren in Colonial America*, 362–65.

32. Bradley, *Ephrata Cloister*, 32; Luthy, "The Ephrata Martyr's Mirror," 21–23.

33. Durnbaugh, *Brethren in Colonial America*, 377–78, 380, 387–88.

34. *DED*, 1:218, 218n12; DTO, 425.

35. Drinker et al., members of a committee reporting to "The Monthly Meeting [Religious Society of Friends] for the Northern District, Philadelphia," in *EV*, 297–98; DTO, 434n66; Marietta, *Reformation of American Quakerism*, 216–17; APS, HSP, and LCP, *A Rising People*, 21.

36. Lansing to Richard Varick, Apr. 10 and May 29, 1777, quoted in Van Buskirk, "They Didn't Join the Band," 312; *DED*, 1:225, 225n9.

37. Joseph Ellis and other historians have described New York as the state with the largest or most active Tory population. Ellis, *Revolutionary Summer*, 34, 41. Nash reminds us that contemporaries believed that the "lower counties" of Pennsylvania, which became the state of Delaware, were perhaps the most Loyalist place on the eastern seaboard. Thomas McKean, a revolutionary leader, believed this area's Kent County was five-eighths Loyalist and Sussex three-fourths Loyalist. Nash, *Warner Mifflin*, 73.

38. Pemberton, "The Ancient Testimony and Principles of the People Called Quakers," Jan. 20, 1776, quoted in Paine, "Epistle to Quakers," an appendix to the third edition of *Common Sense*, in Foner, *Complete Writings of Thomas Paine*, 2:55, also in *EV*, 290–91; Paine, "The Crisis III,"

Apr. 19, 1777, in Foner, *Complete Writings of Thomas Paine*, 1:36.

39. Paine, "The Crisis III," 1:36 (emphasis in original).

40. Paine, *The American Crisis*, 3:37.

41. Phillips, *1775*, 150.

42. Ibid., 38. The exemption from militia service in Pennsylvania was reserved for men under age sixteen or over fifty-three.

43. "An Act to Regulate the Militia of the Commonwealth of Pennsylvania, March 17, 1777," in *SLP*, 9:75–94.

44. Hamburger, "Religious Freedom in Philadelphia," 1606n6.

45. Marietta, *Reformation of American Quakerism*, 230–31.

46. "Laws Enacted in a General Assembly of [. . .] Pennsylvania," 37–39. The Test Act was "An ACT Obliging the White Male Inhabitants of this State to Give Assurances of Allegiance to the Same and for Other purposes Therein Mentioned, June 13, 1777," in *SLP*, 9:110–14.

47. Calvert, *Quaker Constitutionalism*, 266.

48. Ousterhout, *A State Divided*, 150.

49. Burdick, *Revolutionary Delaware*, 42.

50. Ibid., 43.

51. Nash, *Warner Mifflin*, 181.

52. Gerbner, "'We Are Against the Traffik of Men-Body,'" 149–72.

53. Marietta, *Reformation of American Quakerism*, 120.

54. Nash, *Warner Mifflin*, 132, 141. Exile James Pemberton became the Pennsylvania Abolition Society's second president after the 1790 death of its first president, Benjamin Franklin.

55. Ibid.

56. Ibid., 121.

57. Burdick, *Revolutionary Delaware*, 82.

58. Nash, *Warner Mifflin*, 121.

59. Mifflin, "Defense of Warner Mifflin," in Justice, *Life and Ancestry of Warner Mifflin*, 87.

60. David Rittenhouse to Colonel Bedford, Aug. 5, 1776, in *CRP*, 10:669.

61. Council of Safety minutes, Oct. 7, 1775, in *CRP*, 10:358.

62. Gray, *National Waterway*, 2.

63. Ibid., 1–2.

64. DTO, 434.

65. Reynell, "To the Monthly Meeting of Friends in Philadelphia for the Southern District," 295.

66. Mekeel, *Relation of the Quakers to the American Revolution*, 167.

67. *DED*, 1:225n9. In the "Testimony of the People Called Quakers" of Jan. 1775, James Pemberton, clerk, wrote that "we . . . declare against every usurpation of power and authority of [the government in Pennsylvania]," in *EV*, 283–84.

68. Marietta, *Reformation of American Quakerism*, 244.

69. *DED*, 1:225.

70. Brown quoted in Kafer, *Charles Brockden Brown's Revolution*, 182 (emphasis in original). Charles Brockden Brown, Elijah's son, went on to write America's first gothic novels. Peter Kafer traces Brown's literary tastes to this terrifying incident.

71. Laurens to John Lewis Gervais, Aug. 5, 1777, in *LDC*, 7:423–24.

72. Scholars have used different methods to calculate the number of exiles. Some report that twelve men were exiled. See, for example, Bauman, *Reputation of Truth*; and La Courreye Blecki and Wulf, *Milcah Martha Moore's Book*, 50. This number reflects only the twelve most important and most prominent Quaker leaders among the twenty men exiled; it does not include the five Quaker middling merchants and shopkeepers or the two disowned Quakers and one non-Quaker (Brown, Drewet Smith, and Pike, respectively) who were also among the men exiled. Some scholars identify seventeen exiles—those who were Quakers in good standing. Numbers larger than twenty also appear. See Marietta, *Reformation of*

American Quakerism, 240, which names twenty-two exiles; and Sheila Jones, "The Other Side of the American Revolution," which names twenty-one. These numbers include men—clergyman Thomas Coombe Jr. and Phineas Bond, Esq., both Anglicans, who signed the September 8 protest while they were held at the Freemason's Lodge—who were supposed to be exiled but were struck off the roll. At the last minute, the man in charge of organizing the journey into exile, town major Lewis Nicola, advised the SEC that he could not obtain enough wagons to take more than twenty prisoners. A third man, William Smith, D.D. (often referred to as Provost William Smith), Bond's brother-in-law, was also on the hostiles list and ordered to be seized. Benjamin Franklin had recruited the Oxford-educated Smith to serve as the first provost of the Academy and College of Philadelphia (later the University of Pennsylvania), but this anti-Quaker, Anglican minister attracted Patriot ire after giving a eulogy for General Hugh Mercer, killed at the Battle of Princeton, that seemed to lack patriotic ardor. He was arrested and possibly held in the lodge for a night or two but took a parole—only later to reveal military intelligence to a Hessian officer on the eve of the Battle of Germantown (Ewald, *Diary of the American War*, 92). The Patriot methodology for selecting exiles was imperfect, and those whom they chose did not necessarily present a greater threat than some of those whom they paroled.

CHAPTER 2

1. See, for example, HD to ED, Oct. 12, 1777, QSC; and Concord Quarterly Meeting (then known as Chester Quarterly Meeting), Minutes, Feb. 9 and Nov. 4, 1778.

2. Crabtree, *Holy Nation*, 26.

3. According to Samuel Rowland Fisher, the Quakers did not send their

money to Boston with that of others "because we should have looked upon ourselves by that act as parties to everything done there [i.e., Washington's army]." Morris, "Journal of Samuel Rowland Fisher," 193. See also Moses Browne to William Wilson, Jan. 2, 1776.

4. Crabtree, *Holy Nation*, 75.

5. PYM quoted in Mowday, *September 11, 1777*, 206–7n12. Bruce E. Mowday is the only historian who identifies this key letter connecting the PYM to the Birmingham Friends Meeting and its members living where the very pitched Battle of Brandywine took place.

6. See, for example, Cope, "Chester County Friends in the Revolution"; and Concord Quarterly Meeting, Minutes.

7. For example, Goshen Friends Meeting (Chester County, Pennsylvania) had seventy-one such disownments and complaints between 1776 and 1782. "Goshen Friends—Minutes Regarding the War."

8. "Journal of the Exiles," in *EV*, 173.

9. The phrase appears, for example, in DTO, 417, 418.

10. For example, Warner Mifflin "felt restricted from receiving [Continental currency] lest I might thereby, in some sort, defile my hands with one of the engines of war." Mifflin, "Defense of Warner Mifflin," 87.

11. Exiles Edward Penington (sugar trade), Charles Eddy (ironmonger), William Smith, broker (merchant), and Charles Jervis (hatter) most likely also refused the Continental currency.

12. Mekeel, *Relation of the Quakers to the American Revolution*, 185.

13. Baack, "Forging a Nation State," 641; Calomiris, "Institutional Failure," 55.

14. Calomiris, "Institutional Failure," 55.

15. Baack, "Forging a Nation State," 654.

16. The Continental currency was never an issue among Quakers in New

England. Brock, *Pacifism in the United States*, 209.

17. In 1776, John Drinker and Thomas and Samuel Rowland Fisher were published as "enemies to their country"; no one in the colonies was to deal further with them. *Pennsylvania Gazette*, Feb. 14, 1776.

18. Edward Rutledge to Robert Livingston, Oct. 2, 1776, in Burnett, *Letters to Members of the Continental Congress*, 2:13.

19. "Israel Whelen," Pennsylvania State Senate Historical Biographies. Whelen was disowned by his meeting but was received back into the Society of Friends after the war and was buried in their cemetery at Fourth and Arch streets, Philadelphia. Benjamin Jacobs, like Whelen a Chester County Quaker, was, however, permanently "disowned by Friends [Uwchlan Meeting] Oct. 9, 1777, for signing currency for carrying on war." Futhey and Cope, *History of Chester County*, 1:612.

20. Pennsylvania Council of Safety resolution, Nov. 13, 1776, in *CRP*, 11:612.

21. General Israel Putnam, "Proclamation and General Order," Dec. 12, 1776, in Marshall, *Passages from the Diary of Christopher Marshall*, appendix E, xv, xvi (quote).

22. Robert Morris (Philadelphia) to the Commissioners in France (Paris), Dec. 11, 1776, in Commager and Morris, *Spirit of 'Seventy-Six*, 789–90 (emphasis added). When he wrote "internal enemies," "rich," and "speak plainer," this signaled a reference to Quakers, generally known for plain speaking, and perhaps some of the men later exiled.

23. DTO, 420–21.

24. Bell and Greifenstein, *Patriot-Improvers*, 3:372.

25. Boatner, *Encyclopedia of the American Revolution*, 332.

26. Betz and Carnes, *American National Biography*, 13:389–92; *Biographical Directory of the United States Congress*, 1357–58.

27. Scharf and Westcott, *History of Philadelphia*, 1:367.

28. *JHMM*, 3:398.

29. "An Act obliging the White Male Inhabitants of the State to Give Assurances of Allegiances [. . .]," in *SLP*, 9:110.

30. There were in fact many similarities between the plight of Quakers in Philadelphia in 1777 and the plight of Quakers during the English Civil War (1642–51), and the Philadelphia Quakers were well aware of this similarity. Frost, *Quaker Family in Colonial America*, 190–91.

31. Matthew 5:33–37 (KJV).

32. Stern, "William Penn on the Swearing of Oaths," 94–95. Penn's stand on affirmations led to the provision in the United States Constitution permitting affirmation as an alternative to swearing an oath of office (presidential and other). Ibid., 98.

33. Stern, "William Penn on the Swearing of Oaths," 87. Penn had cowritten with Richard Richardson a *Treatise on Oaths* published in 1675. On reading it, Stern claimed, he was "overwhelmed by the erudition which Penn displayed." Ibid. See also Frost, *Quaker Family in Colonial America*, 11.

34. Commager and Morris, introduction to "The Treason of Benedict Arnold," in *Spirit of 'Seventy-Six*, 745–46. George Washington signed his own oath of allegiance on May 12, 1778. Washington, *Writings of George Washington*, 2:frontispiece.

35. Ousterhout, "Controlling the Opposition," 13.

CHAPTER 3

1. Major-General John Sullivan to George Washington, Aug. 24, 1777, in *PGW*, 1:62–63. The officer supposedly defecting was Colonel Leslie Antill. A court of inquiry subsequently determined in 1780 that even in this Sullivan was

wrong and that Colonel Antill had not defected.

2. Rahway held a quarterly (not annual) meeting of Quakers, where delegates from monthly meetings congregated. Henry Drinker traveled there with minister Samuel Emlen on the morning of August 14, 1777, and returned on August 22. *DED*, 1:226.

3. Munn, *Battles and Skirmishes*, 99.

4. The originals of the Spanktown Papers, slightly edited for publication, can be found in *Papers of the Continental Congress, 1774–1789*, no. 53, folios 83–101, National Archives and Records Administration, College Park. This version was published by order of Congress in Philadelphia newspapers on September 9–11, 1777, and handed out as a newspaper supplement for the public to read. The Quaker testimonies include notations that seem to indicate which portions might have been omitted and underlined sections that might suggest the language to which members of Congress objected. They were also published in other states' newspapers.

5. APS, HSP, and LCP, *A Rising People*, 101 (emphasis in original).

6. Peterson, *Robert Smith*, 3, 152–57. Smith's stellar work for the Patriot side in defense of the city has long gone underreported and underappreciated. Smith was never dealt with or disowned by his fellow Quakers for his very important and public cooperation with the American war effort, nor was "this worthy and ingenious man," in the words of a newspaper report, adequately lauded when he was interred in Friends burying ground at his death in February 1777 (well in advance of knowing whether the chevaux-de-frise would be effective), though the act was "attended by many persons of character." Obituary, *Pennsylvania Evening Post*, Feb. 11, 1777.

7. Sullivan, *Letters and Papers of Major-General John Sullivan*, 1:443–44.

8. See also "Observations on [. . .] the Resolves of Congress," in *EV*, 239–58,

particularly 252 (where they called the papers "a *direct falsehood and forgery*") and 253 (where they maintained, probably on Drinker's assurance, that "no paper, or intelligence of any public nature, kind, or tendency whatsoever, was made therein"), et seq. (emphasis in original).

9. Drinker, "A Short Vindication of the Religious Society Called Quakers [. . .]," *Pennsylvania Packet*, Sept. 2, 1780.

10. Isaac Jackson, clerk, "Philadelphia Yearly Meeting Testimony of 4th of the 10th month, 1777," in *EV*, 57–59.

11. Drinker, "A Short Vindication of the Religious Society Called Quakers."

12. The Spanktown Papers were published in *Dunlap's Pennsylvania Packet*, Sept. 9, 1777; *Pennsylvania Gazette*, Sept. 10, 1777; *Boston Independent Chronicle*, Sept. 11, 1777; *Providence* (RI) *Gazette*, Sept. 6, 1777; *Connecticut Journal* (New Haven), Sept. 25, 1777; and *New-York Gazette, and Weekly Mercury*, Sept. 29, 1777.

13. Drinker, "A Short Vindication of the Religious Society Called Quakers."

14. *JCC*, 4:357.

15. Ibid., 5:475.

16. Ibid., 4:357–58; Young, "Treason and Its Punishment," 288, 289, 290n5, 302.

17. Ousterhout, *A State Divided*, 204.

18. *Biographical Directory of United States Congress*, 933; Jones, "Public Career of William Duer." On Duer's zeal, see Roger Sherman to Jonathan Trumbull Sr., May 14, 1777, in *LDC*, 7:82. Duer had been added to the committee for suppressing Toryism on April 22, 1777. *JCC*, 7:291.

19. Mather, *Magnalia Christi Americana*, book 7, chapter 4, 21 (emphasis in original). John Adams's own copy of the *Magnalia Christi Americana* is in the John Adams Library at the Boston Public Library.

20. Adams autobiography, in *AP*, 3:312. See also Pestana, "Quaker Executions as Myth and History," 441–43;

Massachusetts General Court, "A Declaration of the General Court of the Massachusetts [Bay Colony] Holden at Boston, in New-England, October 18, 1659, Concerning the Execution of Two Quakers," and "An Act Made at a General Court Held at Boston, the 20th of October, 1658," in Dreisbach and Hall, *Sacred Rights of Conscience*, 110, 110–13. See also Mekeel, *Relation of the Quakers to the American Revolution*, 99.

21. Bowen, *John Adams and the American Revolution*, 539.

22. Adams diary, Oct. 14, 1774, in *AP*, 2:152.

23. Adams autobiography, in *AP*, 3:312.

24. Adams to James Warren, July 24, 1775, quoted in Bowen, *John Adams and the American Revolution*, 539.

25. *JCC*, 8:694 (Aug. 28, 1777); Kafer, *Charles Brockden Brown*, 3 ("committee on spies").

26. Ibid. (emphasis added).

27. *JCC*, 8:694; "Resolves of Congress, Aug. 28, 1777," in *EV*, 261–63; Adams was much warmer toward the Moravian pacifists, who did not pose an obstacle to independence. Henry Laurens, too, was favorably inclined toward John Ettwein, leader of the Moravians, but not the Quakers. See, for example, "Order to Continental Officers" signed by Adams, Laurens, Hancock, Richard Henry Lee, and other delegates on Sept. 22, 1777, as the delegates rested in Bethlehem on their flight from Philadelphia to Lancaster. *AP*, 5:292–94.

28. Resolve of Congress, Aug. 27, 1777, in Minutes of the Supreme Executive Council of Pennsylvania, Aug. 27, 1777, in *EV*, 260.

29. Ellis, *Revolutionary Summer*, 157.

CHAPTER 4

1. Wilson, *Philadelphia Quakers*, 57. Wilson's fine book also provides many illustrations pertaining to the Quaker exile.

2. *CRP*, 10:572.

3. Coelho, *Timothy Matlack*, 53.

4. See, for example, Marshall, *Passages from the Diary of Christopher Marshall*, 69; and Foner, *Tom Paine and Revolutionary America*, 118–19.

5. "Journal of the Exiles," 65.

6. Ibid., 66–67, 72 (list), 72–74; *CRP*, 11:283. SEC President Thomas Wharton Jr. later claimed to his cousin, exile Thomas Wharton Sr., that he had no part of the exile itself, which may explain why the minutes note that the order was signed by Vice President George Bryan, though in truth Thomas Jr. was far from innocent. Thomas Bradford, William's son and printing partner, was also a member of the arresting party. For members of the arresting party, see *EV*, 91. One legal scholar cites these arrests of men because they were Quakers as the "first example" of (religious) "profiling" in the new republic. Cloud, "Quakers, Slaves and the Founders," 370.

7. Stone, "How the Landing of Tea Was Opposed in Philadelphia by Colonel William Bradford and Others in 1773," 385–93. This article includes images of three intimidating broadsides by the zealous Bradford. On Cannon, see Nash, *Unknown American Revolution*, 186.

8. "Journal of the Exiles," 119.

9. Ibid., 65. The eight were Joshua Fisher (an elderly Quaker merchant, father of the three Fishers and father-in-law of Samuel Pleasants), Drinker's partner, Abel James (because his son was ill), Shoemaker, Jeremiah Warder (a Quaker merchant), Caleb Emlen (another Quaker merchant and Warder's son-in-law), Adam Kuhn (a German immigrant doctor), Thomas Ashelton (a non-Quaker merchant whom the SEC "indulged with liberty of going within the bounds of the city"), and Samuel Murdock (another non-Quaker allowed certain movement).

When the arresting party came for Shoemaker in September 1777, he stated that
he had "given his Promise not to go from
his House, that he has never had anything
to do in the meetings of Sufferings & has
disapproved of the proceedings signed by
Pemberton." He had also promised not to
do anything to the prejudice of the State
of Pennsylvania. Shoemaker later served as
a magistrate of the city under British General Howe, obviously violating his terms.
[Report of the Arresting Party to the
Council], Sept. 3, 1777, in *EV*, 264–66.

10. "Journal of the Exiles," 66.

11. Gilpin [Jr.], "Introduction," in *EV*,
39. Gilpin paraphrased the Resolves of
Congress directed to Pennsylvania.

12. Peale, *Selected Papers of Charles
Willson Peale*, 5:59.

13. John Pemberton, manuscript diary
1777–1778, p. 1, box 1, Pemberton Family
Papers, HSP.

14. Anderson, "Thomas Wharton,"
434.

15. Peale, *Selected Papers of Charles
Willson Peale*, 5:59–60; Sellers, *Charles
Willson Peale*, 1:166–67.

16. Simpson, *Lives of Eminent Philadelphians*, 396.

17. Duché et al. to Supreme Executive
Council of Pennsylvania, Sept. 9, 1777, in
PA, 1st ser., 5:600–601.

18. Supreme Executive Coun-
cil to Episcopal Churches of Philadelphia, Sept. 9, 1777, in ibid., 5:603–4, 603
(quote).

19. Doyle, *Enemy in Our Hands*, 44.

20. SEC quoted in Wilson, *Philadelphia Quakers*, 56; "Journal of the Exiles,"
82. The Freemason's Lodge was a club-
house for Masons constructed by Quaker
architect-builder Robert Smith and
located on Lodge Alley (later Norris Alley)
above Second Street, near Sansom Street,
about three blocks from the Drinker
home.

21. "Journal of the Exiles," 67.

22. *CRP*, 11:290.

23. "Journal of the Exiles," 70, 92–94,
95–99.

24. Israel Pemberton et al., "To the
Congress," Sept. 5, 1777, in *EV*, 82–83.

25. Pennsylvania Constitution of 1776,
Declaration of Rights art. X.

26. Ousterhout, "Controlling the
Opposition," 33–34.

27. Timothy Matlack to William Bradford, Sept. 5, 1777, in *EV*, 85.

28. *CRP*, 11:293.

29. The SEC's request as set forth in
JCC, 8:722–23.

30. Israel Pemberton et al., "Protest to
the President and Council of Pennsylvania," in *EV*, 113 (emphasis in original).

31. "To the President and Coun-
cil of Pennsylvania, Sept. 5, 1777," in *EV*,
116. Signers included Quakers Anthony
Benezet (teacher of Elizabeth and Mary
Drinker, public intellectual, and anti-
slavery activist), William Savery Sr.
(cabinetmaker), and Robert Proud (schoolteacher and historian/author).

32. Israel Pemberton et al., "To the
President and Council," Sept. 8, 1777, in
EV, 107–10, 108 (quote), 110 (quote) (see
frontispiece and a transcription in App. B).
Re: Bond and Coombe, who were not
exiled, see chap. 1, note 72.

33. Duché et al. to Supreme Executive
Council of Pennsylvania, Sept. 9, 1777.

34. Laurens to John Lewis Gervais,
Sept. 5–8 and Sept. 8–9, 1777, in *LDC*,
7:606, 633.

35. Laurens to Gervais, Sep. 5–8, 1777,
7:612 (emphasis in original).

36. Ibid.

37. *JHMM*, 3:76.

38. *JCC*, Sept. 8, 1777, 8:723. This may
have been the first instance in the new
republic that Congress ordered such a
harsh punishment for a group of citizens
(white persons all of one religion and dedicated to nonviolence) whom they had
hastily investigated (if at all), offered no
hearing to defend themselves, and accused
of no crime.

39. Washington to Jonathan Trumbull, Aug. 11, 1776, in *PGW*, 5:671–72; Skemp, *William Franklin*, 212, 216. Both Penn and Chew were Quaker-born, though neither practiced the faith.

40. *CRP*, 11:295 (misnumbered 395); "Journal of the Exiles," 127–28.

41. John Adams to Abigail Adams, Sept. 8, 1777, FO. See also *AP*, 3:311–18. This passage in his autobiography recounts his attacks on the Quakers, likely in retaliation for what he saw as an attack on him in October 1774. No biography of John Adams notes (and supports with citations) so carefully and fully as the present account his antipathy toward Quakers or his role in engineering the exile or connects these actions to his later attempt as president to curb dissent with the 1798 Sedition Act, which was partially responsible for his failure to win election to a second term.

42. Lee to Patrick Henry, Sept. 8, 1777, in *LDC*, 7:637; Gerry to James Warren, Oct. 6, 1777, in ibid., 8:66; Hancock to William Livingston, Aug. 30, 1777, in ibid., 7:572.

43. Nathanael Greene to Catharine Greene, Sept. 13, 1777, in *PNG*, 1:163.

44. New Hampshire delegates to Meshech Weare, Sept. 2, 1777, in *LDC*, 7:596; Lovell quoted in Mekeel, *Relation of the Quakers to the American Revolution*, 176. Within days of the SEC's decision, Washington ordered General Sullivan himself court-martialed for some questionable maneuvers. "They have Censored and Condemned me without Evidence," Sullivan complained ironically. Sullivan to John Adams, Sept. 28, 1777, in *AP*, 5:295. Sullivan was cleared by a court-martial on October 12, 1777. Sullivan, *Letters and Papers of Major-General John Sullivan*, 1:531–32.

45. "Address to the People of Great Britain from the Delegates [. . .] at Philadelphia, the 5th day of September 1774,"
in *JCC*, unnumbered page between 80 and 81. Pennsylvania attorney and Quaker fellow traveler John Dickinson authored this address. Dickinson had been raised a Quaker, married a strict Quaker, and raised his children as strict Quakers, but he apparently never joined himself.

46. Allen, "Diary of James Allen, Esq., of Philadelphia (II)," 293.

47. The New Hampshire Delegates to the President of New Hampshire, Sept. 2, 1777, in *LDC*, 2:471.

48. *CRP*, 11:283.

49. John Adams to Abigail Adams, Sept. 30, 1777, in *AP*, 2:349–50. Quaker Major-General Nathanael Greene described the scene in an equally colorful way: "The inhabitants from the Head of Elk to Philadelphia in general are as much the friends of G. Howe as one Britain [*sic*, Briton] can be to another." Greene to Susanna Livingston, Nov. 11, 1777, in *PNG*, 2:195. Most of the territory between Howe and Philadelphia was part of southern Chester County, with a high proportion of Quaker residents and several Quaker meetinghouses.

50. Galloway himself claimed he had "made Howe's victory possible." Ewald, *Diary of the American War*, 392n36. On Galloway's aid to Howe at the Battle of Brandywine, see Coleman, "Joseph Galloway," 272–300. See also more generally Galloway, *Loyal Traitor*.

CHAPTER 5

1. DTO, 447.

2. Pemberton, *Diary of John Pemberton*, 3.

3. Morton, "Diary of Robert Morton," 4–5.

4. "Journal of the Exiles," 133–56.

5. HD to ED, Sept. 12, 1777, QSC.

6. "Journal of the Exiles," 135.

7. Graham, "The Loyalist," 28.

8. *JHMM*, 3:75.

9. Maxey, *Treason on Trial*, 144. He is referred to as "John Roberts, miller" because there were contemporaries of the same name but without the same taint of treason. Roberts may not have had a personal relationship with any of the exiles, but he would have known several of them by name through business and by their prominence in Quaker circles. Howe declined to lend his troops to rescue the exiles on the grounds that he could not spare them at the time.

10. Adams to County Lieutenant of Frederick County, Virginia, Sept. 13, 1777, in *EV*, 161–62.

11. Thomas Wharton Jr. to John Hancock, Sept. 17, 1777, in *EV*, 161. The template for the exile is described in Washington to Trumbull, Aug. 11, 1776.

12. "Journal of the Exiles," 36–37.

13. "An Act to empower the Supreme Executive Council of this Commonwealth, to provide for the security thereof in special cases [. . .]" (the Banishing Law), in *EV*, 137–39, 138.

14. Tyler, "Forgotten Core Meaning of the Suspension Clause," 1013.

15. "An Act to Empower the Supreme Executive Council of This Commonwealth," 137–38.

16. Ibid., 141. The law also provided that state officials arresting the Quakers would be indemnified by the state if the Quakers later brought suit against the state or the individuals for unlawful arrest or some other wrongful act (they never did).

17. Fisher to McKean, Sept. 18, 1777, in *EV*, 141–43.

18. McKean to Adams, Sept. 19, 1777, FO.

19. Ibid.

20. The Quakers did not know of McKean's perfidy at the time, and no historian has referred to it in the context of the Quaker exile. In Coleman, "Thomas McKean," 117, the author asserts that McKean "granted a writ of habeas corpus to a number of prominent Quakers who were accused of being Loyalists—only to have the Assembly suspend the writ of habeas corpus and take the whole case out of his hands." McKean's letter to Adams reveals that McKean had no reason to be surprised or dismayed that the Assembly had undermined the very writs he had just granted.

21. Morton, "Diary of Robert Morton," 6; Rowe, *Thomas McKean*, 107.

22. HD to ED, Sept. 18, 1777, QSC (emphasis in original).

23. Allen, "Diary of James Allen," 293.

24. Some historians have argued that the exiles were prisoners of war. Lewis N. Barton calls the exiles "prisoners of war" ("Revolutionary Prisoners of War," 30), but my work concludes differently. If the British held them, they would rightfully be called POWs, but since their own countrymen held them, the term "political prisoners"—for persons who have opposed or criticized the government responsible for their imprisonment—is more accurate and is perhaps another dubious first in the history of the new republic.

25. Ousterhout, "Controlling the Opposition," 4, 7. The government of Pennsylvania suspended the writ of habeas corpus for the first and only time in September 1777, and the US federal government has suspended the privilege only twice since 1777. It is a rare day, but the United States Constitution of 1787 allows for the suspension of habeas corpus when in "Cases of Rebellion or Invasion the public Safety may require it." US Constitution, article 1, § 9, clause 2. Habeas was suspended by President Abraham Lincoln in 1861 in Maryland at the very beginning of the Civil War and again by President Ulysses S. Grant in 1871 in South Carolina during Reconstruction.

26. "Journal of the Exiles," 136.

27. See, for example, HD to ED et al., Sept. 13, 1777, QSC.

28. Graydon, *Memoirs of a Life*, 307.

29. "Journal of the Exiles," 155.

30. Ibid.

CHAPTER 6

1. John Smith to John Hancock, Oct. 1, 1777, in *EV*, 162–63, 163 (quotes).

2. Worrall, *Friendly Virginians*, 214.

3. Ibid., 179.

4. HD to ED, Oct. 12, 1777.

5. Ibid.

6. "Journal of the Exiles," 171.

7. HD to ED, Oct. 12, 1777.

8. Ibid.

9. Lee to Henry, Sept. 8, 1777.

10. Worrall, *Friendly Virginians*, 207; Atkinson, *The British Are Coming*, 183; HD to ED, Nov. 20, 1777, QSC; Israel Pemberton et al., "To the Congress," Oct. 1, 1777, in *EV*, 164–66.

11. In 1756, exile Thomas Fisher's father, Joshua, also a Quaker, had published the most accurate chart to date of Delaware Bay. In 1776, a printer in London used Fisher's map to reengrave a version the British navy used, casting enough of a shadow on Joshua Fisher to earn him a place on the hostiles list.

12. "Journal of the Exiles," passim.

13. John Harvie (1742–1807) was a lawyer and officer of the militia. *Biographical Directory of the United States Congress*.

14. HD to ED, Oct. 12, 1777.

15. HD to ED, Oct. 23, 1777, QSC.

16. Joseph Nourse to [Joseph Holmes], n.d., in *EV*, 185–86, 186 (quote).

17. HD to ED, Oct. 12 and Nov. 20, 1777.

18. HD to ED, Oct. 14, 1777, QSC.

19. HD to ED, Oct. 12, 1777, QSC.

20. *DED*, 1:251.

21. HD to ED, Nov. 18, 1777, QSC.

22. Thomas Fisher diary, Nov. 23, 1777.

23. *CRP*, 11:342.

24. "Journal of the Exiles," 136.

25. Moss, "Isaac Zane, Jr.," in *Men and Events of the Revolution*, 71; "Journal of the Exiles," 154; Wayland, *Hopewell Friends History*, 102, 107; John Pemberton to Joseph Pemberton, Dec. 10, 1777, Pemberton Papers, HSP.

26. Isaac Zane Jr. to John Pemberton, Nov. 29, 1777, quoted in Bell and Greifenstein, *Patriot-Improvers*, 1:288. See also Jones, "The Real Isaac Zane"; and National Register of Historic Places Registration Form for Old Forge Farm. In 1774, his former Quaker meeting in Philadelphia disowned Isaac Jr., a thirty-four-year-old iron entrepreneur and member of the American Philosophical Society, for taking an oath and moving to Virginia without a relocation certificate from the meeting. He, like many disowned Quakers, never entirely left his Quaker upbringing behind, though he skirted its discipline and enjoyed the rank of colonel in the Virginia militia.

27. Thomas Fisher diary, Dec. 25, 1777. To illustrate the care the Quakers took of one another, Isaac Zane Sr. left Philadelphia only after "having visited all our Families the day before" so he could give "an account of their . . . situation." Ibid.

28. A list of the names of those active in the Quaker network aiding the exiles could easily be compiled from a page-by-page review of *EV*.

29. *DED*, 1:264; Thomas Fisher diary, Nov. 28, 1777.

30. HD to ED, Dec. 13, 1777, QSC.

31. Ibid. The county lieutenant offered a reward of $100 for the capture of Drewet Smith. Thomas Fisher diary, Dec. 15, 1777.

32. Drewet Smith subsequently evacuated Philadelphia, going to New York City with the British Army in June 1778, and from there he self-exiled to Canada in the 1780s. Later, he filed a petition requesting British authorities to compensate him for his losses as a result of his Loyalism. "William Drewitt [*sic*, Drewet] Smith, druggist," Proclamation (No. 4), Oct. 30, 1778, in *PA*, 3rd ser., 10:540; Commonwealth of Pennsylvania, *Black List*, 15.

33. HD to ED, Dec. 13, 1777. Exile Thomas Pike would not escape exile until the following February.

34. Israel Pemberton et al., "Observations on the Charges Contained in Several Resolves of Congress [. . .]," in *EV*, 239–58.

35. Nourse to [Holmes], Dec. 10, 1777, 185–86, 186 (quote); "Deposition Taken at Yorktown of [Unknown]," in *EV*, 186–87.

36. "Deposition of Jacob Settler of York, dated Dec. 8, 1777," in *EV*, 186–87.

37. Thomas Fisher diary, Dec. 1 and Dec. 17, 1777.

38. HD to ED, Dec. 27, 1777, QSC.

39. HD to ED, Dec. 19, 1777, QSC.

40. *DED*, 268.

41. Ibid., 270, 271; Frost, *Quaker Family in Colonial America*, 193.

42. "Journal of the Exiles," 193.

43. HD to ED, Dec. 19, 1777. As of November 1777, only seventeen of the original fifty-six delegates remained to continue meeting as the Second Continental Congress.

44. Thomas Fisher diary, Dec. 31, 1777; Pemberton et al., "Observations on the Charges Contained in Several Resolves of Congress," 239.

45. HD to ED, Dec. 27, 1777.

CHAPTER 7

1. *CRP*, 11:298–99.

2. *JHMM*, 3:63; DTO, 417. The vials of the wrath of God poured out on the world are set forth in the New Testament. See Revelation 16 (KJV).

3. *DED*, 1:232.

4. ED to HD, Sept. 16, 1777, QSC. On Quaker mutual aid and socialization patterns, see Tomes, "Quaker Connection."

5. Van Buskirk, *Generous Enemies*, 22. It was unclear what the source of the New York fire was. One rumor held that Patriots would set the city on fire to deny city amenities to the British, another that the British would burn the city for its

residents' part in the Declaration of Independence and disrespect to the king.

6. DTO, 448.

7. ED to HD, Sept. 23, 1777, QSC.

8. DTO, 449, 449n95.

9. Ibid., 449.

10. Morton, "Diary of Robert Morton," 7. The two men "taken up" might have been the same ones whom Drinker mentioned, Barnhill and Hysham.

11. Coleman, "Joseph Galloway," 288.

12. DTO, 450. Both Bond and Story were later attainted of treason. Bond: "Phineas Bond, Attorney at Law," Proclamation (No. 7), July 27, 1780, in *PA*, 3rd ser., 10:537; Story: Commonwealth of Pennsylvania, *Black List*, 15.

13. Morton, "Diary of Robert Morton," 7–8.

14. *DED*, 1:235–36.

15. Scharf and Westcott, *History of Philadelphia*, 1:367. Shortly after taking control of the city, the British took a census of the city. Galloway estimated that there were about one thousand Quakers remaining in the city and approximately six thousand able-bodied men who had fled.

16. Fisher, "Social Life in Philadelphia," 241.

17. McGuire, *Philadelphia Campaign*, 1:146. Howe authorized his provost marshal to "execute upon the Spot all Soldiers . . . detected in Plundering or devastation of any kind." General Sir William Howe, "General Orders, August 29, 1777," in Kemble, *Journals of Lieut. Col. Stephen Kemble*, 480–81. Captain John Montrésor, engineer, and Major Charles Stuart of the British Army, among others, complained of the plundering.

18. Morton, "Diary of Robert Morton," 7. Thomas Willing (1731–1821), a colonial Crown Supreme Court justice descended from Quakers (the Shippens), had been elected to the Continental Congress and voted against the Declaration of Independence. He refused to take an oath of

allegiance to the king during the occupation. Balch, "Thomas Willing of Philadelphia," 9.

19. Morton, "Diary of Robert Morton," 11. On October 2, Morton recorded that the British officer gave him a receipt for one hundred pounds of hay from the plantation of his stepfather, James Pemberton, though the family's agent there said it had weighed ten times that much. Thereafter Morton visited occasionally to advocate for fair payment. Ibid.

20. *DED*, 1:236. Drinker regularly misspelled "American," perhaps unintentionally symbolizing her discomfort with the new political landscape. In keeping with my practice to maintain readability, I have silently corrected her spelling here.

21. *DED*, 1:237.

22. Ibid., 1:238.

23. ED to HD, Oct. 4, 1777, QSC.

24. *DED*, 1:238.

25. Ibid., 1:238.

26. Ibid., 1:239–40; DTO, 451.

27. Harris, *Germantown*, passim.

28. McGuire, *Philadelphia Campaign*, 2:127–28, notes 152 Americans killed, 521 wounded, and about 400 captured, for a total loss of a little over 1,000; and 71 British killed, 448 wounded (including 24 Hessians), and 14 missing, for a total of 533 lost. Among those captured by the Americans was Christopher Saur III (1754–1799), who had turned Tory and served as a scout for the British in his native Germantown. Durnbaugh, *Brethren in Colonial America*, 396. Saur and his father were later attainted of treason and their property confiscated. Commonwealth of Pennsylvania, *Black List*, 15.

29. *DED*, 1:239–40.

30. Hutchinson to Pemberton, Oct. 4, 1777, James Hutchinson Papers, APS.

31. HD to ED, Nov. 1–2, 1777, QSC.

32. *DED*, 1:241.

33. DTO, 455.

34. *JHMM*, 3:625.

35. Ibid.

36. Ibid. In June 1778, local authorities assessed the damages done by British troops during the occupation of Philadelphia. No Quaker names appear on the list, which includes both individuals and a handful of denominations. The Quakers may not have wished to reveal the extent to which their buildings were spared, and/or they may have conducted their own assessment. Cuthbert, "Assessment of Damages Done," 323–35; Jones, "Assessment of Damages Done [. . .] (Concluded)," 544–59.

37. Scharf and Westcott, *History of Philadelphia*, 2:1253.

38. Nathanael Greene to Jacob Greene, Oct. 27, 1777, in *PNG*, 2:183–84.

39. *JHMM*, 3:97. Neither the diaries of Elizabeth Drinker, Sarah Logan Fisher, or Robert Morton nor any other source that I have reviewed mentions any such tribute payment.

40. Marietta, *Reformation of American Quakerism*, 240, 241n67.

41. Nathanael Greene to Jacob Greene, Oct. 27, 1777.

42. *DED*, 1:243. For a first-person account of the Battle of Mud Island, see Martin, *Narrative of a Revolutionary Soldier*, 74–83.

43. *DED*, 1:243. A rumor also circulated that Washington planned to requisition household goods from local residents. Allen, "Diary of James Allen," 295–96.

44. Lowell, *The Hessians*, 169.

45. *DED*, 1:245.

46. Ibid., 1:254n62. For a drawing of the chevaux-de-frise, see Baurmeister, "Letters of Major Baurmeister (III)," 167.

47. *DED*, 1:246.

48. Ibid., 1:247.

49. Ibid., 1:252.

50. Ibid., 1:250.

51. Ibid., 1:247.

52. Ibid.

53. Ibid., 1:248.

54. Paine to Franklin, May 16, 1778, FO.

55. McGrath, *Give Me a Fast Ship*, 168.

56. *DED*, 1:248.

57. Lowell, *The Hessians*, 207–8.

58. *DED*, 1:247–48, 248n55.

59. Scharf and Westcott, *History of Philadelphia*, 1:372.

60. Ousterhout, *A State Divided*, 246–47. Prior was a baker from Burlington, New Jersey. *DED*, 3:2201.

61. *DED*, 1:250.

62. Jordan, *Colonial and Revolutionary Families*, 1:841.

63. Ewald, *Diary of the American War*, 387.

64. *JHMM*, 3:94, 97.

CHAPTER 8

1. Marietta, *Reformation of American Quakerism*, 257.

2. Waln (1742–1813) was a successful lawyer before joining the ministry. Malone, *Dictionary of American Biography*, 10:386; McFarland and Herr, *William Lewis*, 4–5. In December 1776, Brown (1705–1780/86), an uncle to Elijah, had publicly prayed for the king in meeting, and as a result he faced cruel treatment by Patriots. DTO, 418; Minutes of Meeting for Sufferings, PYM, 2:174, QSC. Emlen (1730–1799) had the financial means to devote himself primarily to Quaker affairs. Quaker leaders also assigned him to check in with Elizabeth Drinker periodically for spiritual and temporal guidance while her husband was away. Leach, "Old Philadelphia Families: Emlen"; *DED*, 3:2144. Thornton (1727–1794) was a British-born Quaker who traveled a great deal in the ministry. Cadbury Collection, QSC; Davis, *History of Bucks County*, 346; *DED*, 3:2221. Joshua Morris (1713–1802) had resigned from the Assembly in 1755 when Quakers first retreated from government. Nash, *Warner Mifflin*, 64. Mifflin (1745–1798) was a wealthy Delaware farmer and fervent abolitionist. See Nash, *Warner Mifflin*.

3. Isaiah 2:4 (KJV).

4. "Testimony, Philadelphia Yearly Meeting, Oct. 4, 1777," in *EV*, 57.

5. "Journal of the Exiles," 182.

6. Washington had previously made the Stenton mansion his headquarters from August 23 to August 24, 1777. James Logan (1674–1751) was an Irish Quaker who arrived with William Penn and served as his colonial secretary. He became wealthy and made himself a public intellectual and a force for good.

7. Sharpless, *Quaker Experiment*, 12.

8. Nash, *Warner Mifflin*, 8, 66. For part of this characterization of the peace mission, I am indebted to Nash's excavation of Mifflin's correspondence. Nash, however, never really puts together a detailed exposition of the peace mission. He warns, though, about embellishments coming much later from thirdhand sources—European intellectuals who let their romantic imaginations run free with the given facts. They saw the peace mission and the visit to Washington as Mifflin's alone and coming from Delaware Quaker bodies, both erroneous assumptions that created a Mifflin mythology. See ibid., 149–51 and passim.

9. Ibid., 85.

10. Ibid., 64, 167 (seven feet tall). Nash concludes that Mifflin was *the* spokesman. See ibid., 65.

11. Ibid., 29 (Galloway), 57, 144–45 (Thomas Mifflin). Warner Mifflin would have nevertheless embraced Thomas Mifflin (which he later did), though at the same time considering him spiritually "rebellious" and "back-sliding." Ibid., 159.

12. Ibid., 151.

13. Mifflin to Nathanael Greene, Oct. 21, 1783, in *PNG*, 13:156.

14. Warner Mifflin to Archbishop of Canterbury, June 30, 1787, p. 7, autograph collection, HSP. The principal subject of this letter was Mifflin's message that slavery "in my view does threaten the downfall of the British Empire." Ibid., 2.

15. Jordan, *Colonial Families of Philadelphia*, 1:847.

16. "Report [appointed by PYM to visit the generals]," Oct. 1, 1778 [it may be misdated in *EV* as the committee only returned to the city around Oct. 10], in *EV*, 59–61.

17. Nash, *Warner Mifflin*, 66 ("proto-Loyalists"), 57 (intelligence).

18. Mifflin to Greene, Oct. 17, 1783, in *PNG*, 13:156–57. Mifflin pleaded for Greene's soul when he laid before Greene, whom he knew to have been educated in Quaker beliefs, the immorality of slavery. Ibid., 13:157.

19. Brier, *They Passed This Way*; General Orders, Oct. 5, 1777, n1, in Washington, *Papers of George Washington, Digital Edition*.

20. Howe to Washington, Oct. 3, 1777, in *PGW*, 11:384. The inclusion of terms such as "peaceable" and "Sufferings" suggests strongly that Howe's strategist, Quaker sympathizer Joseph Galloway, wrote or contributed to the letter.

21. Washington to Howe, Oct. 6, 1777, in Washington, *Papers of George Washington, Digital Edition*. Washington's practice was to have his men disable Quaker-owned mills because their mills or their milled products were liable to fall into British hands. His men did this by removing the millstone, which disabled the mill but did not destroy the property.

22. George Washington to David Forman, Oct. 6, 1777, in ibid.

23. John Clark Jr. to George Washington, Oct. 6, 1777, in ibid. Jones (1724–1796) was a farmer in Uwchlan Township, northern Chester County. John Clark Jr., an attorney from York, Pennsylvania, served as an aide-de-camp for the Quaker Major-General Nathanael Greene and became General Washington's spymaster between October 1 and December 31, 1777. His letters to Washington are replete with references to Friends (often unnamed)

on whom he believed the general could rely. See, for example, Clark to Washington, Nov. 24, 1777, in *PGW*, 12:510–11; and Valley Forge National Park, "Spy System 1777."

24. "From George Washington to John Gill, 6 October 1777," FO.

25. "Report [of the PYM committee to visit the generals]," 60.

26. Nash, *Warner Mifflin*, 79.

27. See Brock, *Pacifism in the United States*, 254.

28. Armstrong to Wharton, Oct. 8, 1777, quoted in Leach, "Old Philadelphia Families: Emlen."

29. *JHMM*, 3:84 (Oct. 9, 1777).

30. "Report [of the PYM committee to visit the generals]," 61.

31. Ibid., 60. General Wilhelm von Knyphausen (1716–1800) was the German commander in chief of Hessian auxiliaries to the British Army.

32. Ibid., 61.

33. *DED*, 1:242.

34. Philadelphia Yearly Meeting, Meeting for Sufferings and Representative Meeting Records, 2:139, QSC.

35. For eighteenth-century Quaker analogues to this courageous and asymmetrical peace mission, compare the women's mission of 1778 (see chaps. 12 and 13) or the later personal mission in 1798 of Dr. George Logan (1758–1821), a nephew of exile Thomas Fisher and his wife, Sarah Logan Fisher. When the administration of President John Adams was in a quasi-war with France and not talking to its diplomats, Logan, then a member of the Pennsylvania Assembly, traveled to Paris and engaged in serious negotiations with the French government to resolve the crisis—thereby inspiring the Logan Act of 1799, by which Congress and the president sought to ensure that the country had only one foreign policy at a time, making it a crime to do what George Logan had done. See "Certificate for George Logan, 4 June

1798," FO; and Tolles, "Unofficial Ambassador," 3–25.

CHAPTER 9

1. *DED*, 1:251.
2. Ibid., 1:256. Drinker lacked a personal connection to Galloway, yet Abel James was close to Galloway and accommodated her. James, when later attainted of treason, "surrendered [to the court] and [was] discharged." Commonwealth of Pennsylvania, *Black List*, 13.
3. *DED*, 1:258, 259 (quotes).
4. ED to HD, Dec. 3, 1777, QSC.
5. Calvert, *Quaker Constitutionalism*, 192, 239, 264.
6. *DED*, 1:256–57.
7. Morton, "Diary of Robert Morton," 30. Regarding the worst of the Hessians, even Ambrose Serle, secretary of Loyalist affairs, admitted, "It is a misfortune we ever had such a dirty, cowardly set of contemptible miscreants," though there is a wealth of evidence to the contrary, and many settled in America. Serle, *American Journal of Ambrose Serle*, xxii.
8. Morton, "Diary of Robert Morton," 34–35. See also Powers, *Tales of Old Taverns*, 210.
9. "Brigadier General John Cadwalader's Plan for Attacking Philadelphia, 24 November 1777," FO.
10. *PGW*, 12:371–73.
11. *DED*, 1:257.
12. Ibid., 1:260, 261 (quote).
13. Thomas Lightfoot (1728–1793) served as a leading surveyor and member of Uwchlan Monthly Meeting in Chester County and also owned property in the city. He joined the economic boycott by Philadelphia merchants, including nine of the Quaker leaders later exiled, against the Stamp Act in 1765 (Scharf and Westcott, *History of Philadelphia*, 1:273), and he later engaged in many of the same behaviors and faced many of the same harsh and humiliating Patriot punishments as did the exiles. "Thomas Lightfoot, merchant of Philadelphia," attainted of high treason in Proclamation (No. 8), in *PA*, 3rd ser., 10:540. He "surrendered" to the law but was never convicted of any crime. Commonwealth of Pennsylvania, *Black List*, 13.
14. Scharf and Westcott, *History of Philadelphia*, 1:253. See "Edw. Drinker," *Columbian Magazine*, Aug. 1791.
15. *DED*, 1:261, 264.
16. Washington to John Lacey Jr., Apr. 11, 1778, in *PGW*, 14:476–77.
17. Morton, "Diary of Robert Morton," 37.
18. Emlen et al., "Letter of Friends in Philadelphia to Friends in [England and] Ireland," 125–27. London Friends circulated to other Friends in Great Britain and Ireland a printed letter soliciting contributions and reporting that a vessel had already been sent from Bristol to Philadelphia. John Fothergill, David Barclay, et al., to Friends in Great Britain and Ireland, Mar. 6, 1778, PYM Minutes, *U.S., Quaker Meeting Records*, images 324–26.
19. Maxey, *Treason on Trial*, 60, 151 (appendix A, trial notes, testimony of Susanna and Owen Jones Sr.).
20. Serle, *American Journal of Ambrose Serle*, x. Serle was technically the secretary to the British peace commission consisting of the two Howe brothers. In London, Serle had previously been employed in the office of the colonial secretary. In 1776 in New York City, he had been in charge of the political section of a Loyalist newspaper. Serle's diary and his valuable commentary represent the views of "an educated middle-class" English civilian "of considerable ability who had no military or political reputation at stake." Ibid.
21. Ibid., 265.
22. Ibid., 266.
23. Ibid.
24. Ibid.
25. Ibid., 266–67.

26. Ibid., 267.

27. Ibid., 268.

28. Ibid., 267–68.

29. Ibid., 269.

30. Ibid., 271.

31. Washington to Henry Laurens, Dec. 23, 1777, in *PGW*, 12:683–87; Isaacson, *Benjamin Franklin*, 343.

32. According to what "some respectable Quakers" told Major John André, the city under Howe's command presently held about forty-eight thousand people: twenty-three thousand Americans left behind after twelve thousand fled the city, added to which were twenty-five thousand British occupants, of which some sixteen thousand were military. Rosswurm, *Arms, Country, and Class*, 149.

33. On Howe's British troop strength, see Lowell, *The Hessians*, 212. Howe's troop strength as of this date is unchronicled in more recent literature.

34. Ferling, "Joseph Galloway's Military Advice," 173 ("two thirds"), 175 ("dying" and "miscreant troop").

35. Mekeel, *Quakers and the American Revolution*, 208. George Churchman (1730–1814) was a Quaker surveyor in Nottingham Township, southern Chester County, who published a book of sermons and kept a diary for over forty years. The Quaker leaders thought well of him. *DED*, 3:2125; Bauman, *Reputation of Truth*, 236.

CHAPTER 10

1. Israel Pemberton et al., "To the Congress and to the Executive Council of Pennsylvania," in *EV*, 193.

2. HD to ED, Jan. 12, 1778, QSC.

3. "Journal of James Pemberton," in *EV*, 200.

4. HD to ED, Jan. 12, 1778.

5. Thomas Fisher diary, Jan. 17, 1778. McGill was otherwise unidentified, but he appears to have been a local acquaintance who visited the exiles often for a few weeks.

6. Isaac Zane and John Parrish et al., "To Congress Meeting at York Town," undated, box 1, folder 7, Cox-Parrish-Wharton Papers, HSP.

7. HD to ED, Jan. 25, 1778, QSC.

8. *JCC*, 10:85. The other Quakers were Joseph Janney (Jenney), Benjamin Wright, William Jackson, and Joseph Wright. Another account adds William Matthews. Delegates to Congress William Ellery (Rhode Island), John Henry (Maryland), and Abraham Clark (New Jersey), all lawyers, met with the Quakers.

9. HD to ED, Jan. 26 ("grounded on," "dangerous Men") and Jan. 30 ("all Ranks"), 1778, QSC.

10. Jabez Maud Fisher to Dr. Thomas Parke, Jan. 10, 1778, Roberts Collection, QSC.

11. Ibid.

12. Ferling, *Almost a Miracle*, 243.

13. Ibid., 267.

14. Baurmeister, "Letters of Major Baurmeister (III)," 47. There had already been signs, in cannon left on the field at Brandywine by the Americans during their retreat, that France was supporting the American effort sub rosa.

15. Like the Hessians, Anspachers were soldiers sent by a German prince—in this case, the Margrave of Anspach-Bayreuth—who contracted to rent troops. Britain "rented" and sent to America about thirty thousand German mercenaries, most often collectively referred to as Hessians, of which about twelve thousand were killed, died of disease, or stayed behind in America. About 25 percent of the eighteen thousand troops Americans faced during the Philadelphia Campaign were German. Lowell, *The Hessians*, 197, 287.

16. ED to HD, Jan. 8, 1778, QSC.

17. Ibid. Henry was right to fear military influences on his children of an impressionable age; Hessian Major Baurmeister gave a military pin to the son of the Quaker widow with whom he was

staying, a gift the child treasured well into the nineteenth century. Clifford Lewis Jr., "Note" following Baurmeister, "Letters of Major Baurmeister (III)," 182–83.

18. *DED*, 1:272.

19. *DED*, 275.

20. Thayer, *Israel Pemberton*, 229.

21. Elizabeth Allen quoted in Fisher, "Social Life in Philadelphia," 243.

22. Rebecca Franks to Mrs. Paca, in ibid., 246n62.

23. Sarah Logan Fisher, in ibid., 246.

24. *DED*, 1:276.

25. HD to ED, Jan. 25, 1778; *DED*, 1:277. On January 29 and February 5, 1778, the PYM's Meeting for Sufferings met with more than a dozen members present to debrief John James on his long trip and time spent with the exiles at Winchester. Minutes of Meeting for Sufferings, PYM, 2:140.

26. ED to HD, Jan. 25, 1778, QSC.

27. ED to HD, Jan. 28, 1778, QSC.

28. HD to ED, Feb. 7, 1778, QSC.

29. HD to ED, Feb. 7, 1778; "Resolution of Congress, Jan. 29, 1778," in *EV*, 206.

30. Ferling, *Almost a Miracle*, 288.

31. Franklin was not a Quaker, but he did not dissuade the French, many of whom held the sect in high regard, from believing he was, often adopting Quaker dress and behavior. He even wore a beaver skin hat in a portrait of himself painted in Paris in 1777. Miller, "Franklin and Friends," 318.

32. Ferling, *Almost a Miracle*, 261.

33. Ibid.

34. "Treaty of Alliance Between the United States and France, Feb. 6, 1778," in Miller, *Treaties and Other International Acts*, 2:1–40.

CHAPTER 11

1. *DED*, 1:286.

2. HD to ED, Mar. 31, 1778, QSC. Though Pennsylvania also had a board of war, Drinker referred to Congress's board. John Adams had led the board until he left for Paris in the fall of 1777. Now Major-General Horatio Gates chaired the board, consisting of himself and members quartermaster general Thomas Mifflin, adjutant general Timothy Pickering, former commissary general Joseph Trumbull, and Richard Peters, the board's permanent secretary. *JCC*, 9:874, 959–60, 971–72.

3. HD to ED, Mar. 31, 1778.

4. "Resolution of Council," in *EV*, 277. James Morton was a stepson of exile James Pemberton and brother of the young diarist Robert Morton.

5. Committee [of Soldiers] at Camp (Valley Forge) to Henry Laurens, Feb. 25, 1778, in *LDC*, 9:174.

6. Pemberton et al., "To the Congress and to the Executive Council of Pennsylvania," 188–93.

7. *DED*, 1:286.

8. ED to HD, Mar. 23, 1778, QSC.

9. *DED*, 1:290.

10. *DED*, 1:284.

11. Scharf and Westcott, *History of Philadelphia*, 1:377.

12. *CRP*, 11:427. The Quaker delegation also included Joseph Husband, James Jackson, Abraham Gibbons, William Jackson Jr., and Jacob Lindley.

13. Ibid., 11:426–27.

14. HD to ED, Mar. 24, 1778.

15. Israel Pemberton, "An Account of the Illness and Decease of Thomas Gilpin, of Philadelphia, at Winchester, Virginia," in *EV*, 210–11, 210 (quotes).

16. Thomas Fisher to Sarah Fisher, Dec. 13, 1777, in Oaks, "Philadelphians in Exile," 311.

17. HD to ED, Mar. 8, 1778, QSC.

18. Pemberton, "An Account of the Illness and Decease of Thomas Gilpin, of Philadelphia, at Winchester, Virginia," 211.

19. HD to ED, Mar. 8, 1778.

20. Ibid. See also Thomas Fisher diary citing multiple severe trials, Mar. 15–16, 1778.

21. "James Pemberton's Journal of the Exiles," in *EV*, 214; HD to ED, Mar. 8–10, 1778, QSC. Ironically, the leg of John Hunt, an ardent crusader for the peace testimony, had been amputated by a man who had made his living waging war, a former general of the Continental Army. Adam Stephen (1718–1791) had fought at Washington's side on and off since the French and Indian War but had recently been dismissed from the army after appearing at the Battle of Germantown in an inebriated state. He then retired to his home in rural Virginia, from which he was summoned by one of the exiled Quakers to attend to a suspected Tory, John Hunt. Boatner, *Encyclopedia of the American Revolution*, 1055.

22. HD to ED, Mar. 8–10, 1778.

23. HD to ED, Mar. 31, 1778, QSC.

24. "James Pemberton's Journal of the Exiles," 215. Both men were buried in unmarked graves, as was the custom, in Hopewell Friends cemetery north of Winchester. Unlike some other religious groups, Quakers as a society do not officially recognize martyrs, but they kept records of their members' sufferings for their faith, and they called an earlier collection of those tales *The Boston Martyrs*, the name given in Quaker tradition to the three English members of the Society of Friends who were executed in Boston in 1659 and 1661. See Besse, *Collection of the Sufferings of the People Called Quakers*.

25. "James Pemberton's Journal of the Exiles," 215.

26. HD to ED, Mar. 24, 1778.

27. *Pennsylvania Evening Press*, Apr. 3, 1778, in Tracy, *266 Days*, 261. The other obituary was for Loyalist John Allen in February. John was the brother of diarist, lawyer, and Loyalist James Allen, whose father had been former chief justice William Allen (1704–1780), once one of the wealthiest merchants in the colony, on his way at this point into self-exile in England, where he died.

CHAPTER 12

1. *DED*, 1:280.

2. Tillman, *Stripped and Script*, 24, 57; "James Pemberton's Journal of the Exiles," 208.

3. *DED*, 1:281–82.

4. Ibid.

5. Ibid., 1:288–89.

6. Ibid., 1:288.

7. HD to ED, Mar. 31, 1778. General Howe, by contrast, made a "great show of not opening letters from or to high-society women." Van Buskirk, *Generous Enemies*, 189. Judith Van Buskirk maintains that during the occupations of New York and Philadelphia, "upper class women benefited from the gallant behavior and courtly regard owed to a lady by a gentleman" (189).

8. ED to HD, Mar. 23, 1778.

9. Ibid.

10. *DED*, 1:291.

11. Ibid., 1:291–92.

12. Ibid., 1:292–93.

13. Ibid., 1:293.

14. Ibid., 1:293–94. See text of the women's petition in App. C.

15. Ibid., 1:294.

16. Pemberton to Washington, Mar. 31, 1778, in *EV*, 222.

17. Carl Baurmeister to Major-General von Jungkenn, May 10, 1778, in Baurmeister, "Letters of Major Baurmeister (III)," 171. James Thomas Flexner argues that it was "probably to embarrass Washington" that Howe allowed the four women to leave Philadelphia for Valley Forge to beg Washington for the release of "their rich and influential husbands." Flexner, *George Washington in the American Revolution*, 285.

18. *DED*, 1:294–95.

19. Pleasants et al., "To the Congress, Board of War, President and Council, and Assembly of Pennsylvania," in *EV*, 279–80.

20. Ibid., 279; Matthew 7:12 (KJV), "Therefore all things whatsoever ye would that men should do to you, do ye even so to them: for this is the law and the prophets," is commonly referred to as the golden rule.

21. Pleasants et al., "To the Congress, Board of War, President and Council, and Assembly of Pennsylvania," 279–80.

22. Ibid., 280.

23. Ibid.

24. Hatcher, "'Entirely an Act of Our Own,'" 145. Hatcher, the first historian to recognize the significance of this petition, notes that there had been two similar instances in colonial Massachusetts.

25. *DED*, 1:295. The minutes of the PYM's Meeting for Sufferings reported that earlier Israel Morris had been arrested and charged in New Jersey with not taking the oath there and fined the important sum of £75. Minutes of Meeting for Sufferings, PYM, 2:178–79.

26. ED to HD, Apr. 3 and 4, 1778, QSC.

27. *DED*, 1:294. While Rachel Hunt did not travel to Lancaster to confront Thomas Wharton Jr. and the SEC, neither escaped facing responsibility for John Hunt's death. On April 11, Thomas Jr. noted that a pass "and a gentleman to attend her with the necessary servants" would be granted "speedily" to Rachel to attend to details regarding the death of her husband in Winchester. Wharton to Colonel Tench Tilghman (secretary to General Washington), Apr. 11, 1778, Records of Pennsylvania's Revolutionary Government, 27, roll 13, image 1148 of 1386.

28. *DED*, 1:295–96.

CHAPTER 13

1. *DED*, 1:296.

2. Ibid. Riding postilion, in a cramped special seat nearer the horses, was for the purpose of urging them on at a faster pace, a measure of the tensions driving their journey.

3. Ibid., 1:296–97.

4. Washington to John Lacey Jr., Mar. 20, 1778, in Washington, *Writings of George Washington*, 2:114.

5. *DED*, 1:296–97.

6. Ibid.

7. See Pemberton to Washington, Mar. 31, 1778, 223.

8. Ibid., 222.

9. Washington to Wharton, Apr. 5, 1778, in *EV*, 223; Van Buskirk, *Generous Enemies*, 61.

10. *DED*, 1:297.

11. Ibid.

12. Pemberton to [unknown], [Nov.] 13, 1777, in Fowler, *Guide to the Sol Feinstone Collection*, 173, referring to a letter from Pemberton to [unknown], Sol Feinstone Collection, APS.

13. "Journal of the Exiles," 176. John Augustine Washington (1736–1787) was the third of George Washington's five younger siblings (he also had three older half-siblings). During the revolution, John Augustine Washington was elected to the Fifth Virginia (revolutionary) Convention. He served on the Westmoreland County, Virginia, committee of safety as well as that county's 1775 committee in aid of Boston. See George Washington to John Augustine Washington, Oct. 18, 1777, FO. Founders Online records indicate that the brothers exchanged about eighteen letters in 1777 alone.

14. "Journal of the Exiles," 176.

15. George Washington to John Augustine Washington, Oct. 18, 1777.

16. "Journal of the Exiles," 171.

17. Thomas Fisher diary, Dec. 28, 1777, Feb. 26, 1778.

18. Jordan, *Colonial and Revolutionary Families*, 1:422, 608. See also Bedini, "George Gilpin of Alexandria, Part 1"; Bedini, "George Gilpin of Alexandria, Part 2"; and "Pallbearers," *Digital*

Encyclopedia of George Washington. I have not been able to independently corroborate the relationship between Martha Washington and the Peters sisters, though other evidence suggests that she had known Gilpin since at least 1775, when he wrote to her that he awaited her instructions. Thomas Gilpin Jr. (1776–1853) claimed in a document "found among his [Thomas Sr.'s] papers" after his death that "Col. [George] Gilpin was sent by Gen'l Washington to examine the situation of his brother whose release was offered to him, but the party felt themselves bound by a common tie to assert their innocence & effect their justification & release unitedly and to this determination he fell a victim." Gilpin [Jr.], "Memoir of Thomas Gilpin [Sr.]," 327. By "the party," Gilpin presumably meant the collective Quaker exiles at Winchester, who consistently acted as a body. On the ancestral connection between Washington and Gilpin, see Stern et al., *Our Kindred*, 76, 128; and Gilpin, *Genealogy of the Family of Gideon Gilpin*, 5–6. Thanks to Brian S. Miller for this family genealogy citation.

19. Carl Baurmeister to Major-General von Jungkenn, May 10, 1778, 171. This assertion exaggerates Martha's role but suggests she may have influenced her husband to add the sentence, "Humanity pleads strongly in their behalf." See Washington to Thomas Wharton Jr., Apr. 6, 1778, in *EV*, 223.

20. Washington to Thomas Wharton Jr., Apr. 6, 1778.

21. Ibid.

22. Skemp, *William Franklin*, 222–23. Washington to William Franklin, July 25, 1777, in *PGW*, 10:408; Washington to John Hancock, July 25, 1777, in *PGW*, 10:408–9.

23. Thomas Jr. tipped facsimile copies of Washington's two letters to SEC President Wharton into *Exiles in Virginia*, likely in the belief that Washington secured the release of the Quaker

prisoners, though Congress and Wharton had already decided the issue. See also Gilpin, "Introduction," in *EV* (the facsimiles are inserted between pages 64 and 65, and the letters are also included in the text on pages 222 and 223). The way these two sentences appear in the letter (original held by Library of Congress) suggests that Washington may have added these sentences himself, perhaps demonstrating the issue's importance to him.

24. That the commander in chief may have been sympathetic toward the Quaker exiles in this subtle fashion did not come to the attention of Paul F. Boller Jr. for his otherwise fairly comprehensive article, "George Washington and the Quakers," 67.

25. A recently published work claims that the women's mission approached Washington seeking relief for Henry Drinker, who (the author claims) had been accused of selling supplies to the British. The author cites no source for the claim respecting the charge against Drinker. The work claims as well that Washington decided against their plea, which is congruent with his claim that it was not within his jurisdiction. Despite this, Washington's letter to Wharton likely influenced the speed of the release if not the final decision. Fraser, *The Washingtons*, 193.

26. Boller, "George Washington and the Quakers," 83.

27. *DED*, 1:297.

28. PYM Minutes, *U.S., Quaker Meeting Records*, image 270.

29. *DED*, 1:297.

30. "An Act for the Attainder of Divers Traitors [. . .]," in *SLP*, 9:201–15.

31. With one prominent Quaker (Shoemaker) and two associated with the sect (Galloway and Potts) in leadership positions, the British could give the appearance of normalcy to administration of the city.

32. Thomas Wharton Jr. to Congress, Jan. 7, 1778, in *EV*, 277–78. Elizabeth

Drinker's diary reported on February 1 that speaker of the assembly John B. Bayard had successfully moved a resolution to release the banished Friends. *DED*, 1:280.

33. Horatio Gates to Joseph Holmes, Apr. 8, 1778, in *EV*, 217; Thomas Wharton Jr. to Baily and Lang, Apr. 10, 1778, in *EV*, 221.

34. *CRP*, 11:461.

35. Matlack and Drinker had been educated together at Anthony Benezet's school. Gordon, *Letters of Mary Penry*, 8, 223n6. As a militia colonel, Matlack had already fought in battles at Princeton and Trenton. In 1781, he and others formed the Free Quakers, a formal religious group of men and women who rejected the peace testimony but wanted to keep up much of their Quaker practice. *DED*, 1:298. Matlack had been disowned for gambling while neglecting his obligations to his creditors.

36. The three Council members visited were Colonel Joseph Hart (Bucks County), Jason Edgar (York County), and Jonathan Hoague (variant Hoge) (Cumberland County).

37. Indeed, interest in the members of the women's mission seemed to cross the Tory-Patriot divide. While in Lancaster, the women socialized with, among others, Colonel Owen Biddle Jr. and Christopher Marshall Sr., both disowned Friends and committed Patriots who later joined the Free Quakers. *DED*, 1:298–99.

38. *DED*, 1:298, 303.

39. Ibid., 1:297–98; Timothy Matlack to [Francis Y. Baily and Capt. James Lang], Apr. 10, 1778, in *EV*, 224; Matlack to Pemberton, Apr. 10, 1778, in *EV*, 224. The SEC later offered the option of release in Potts Grove, which the exiles and their families declined.

40. Matlack quoted in Van Buskirk, "They Didn't Join the Band," 319.

41. Matlack to Pemberton, Apr. 10, 1778, QSC.

42. HD to ED, Apr. 16, 1778, QSC. Henry referred to Acts 5:41 (KJV). In the biblical reference, the apostles rejoiced that they "were counted worthy to suffer shame" before the council as a witness for Jesus. Hatcher, "'Entirely an Act of Our Own,'" 146.

CHAPTER 14

1. Thomas Fisher diary, Apr. 10, 1778.

2. "James Pemberton's Journal of the Exiles," 225–26.

3. HD to ED, Apr. 14, 1778, QSC.

4. Ibid.

5. HD to ED, Apr. 16, 1778, QSC.

6. *DED*, 1:301.

7. "James Pemberton's Journal of the Exiles," 227–28. The British-born Horatio Gates (1727–1806) was an officer in the British Army before his immigration to Virginia in 1773. When he learned of the outbreak of hostilities in 1775, he soon sought and was offered a commission as major-general in the Continental Army, ranked third (later second) below Washington.

8. *DED*, 1:302.

9. Ibid.

10. Ibid.

11. "To the President and Council of Pennsylvania," in *EV*, 230.

12. William Lewis, Esq. (1752–1819), a Quaker from Chester County, had studied law under former lawyer Nicholas Waln (1742–1813) in Philadelphia. He later attained fame as a defender of Pennsylvanians accused by the state of treason and other crimes. McFarland and Herr, *William Lewis*, 4.

13. *DED*, 1:302–3; Matlack, "Form of a Pass to Each Prisoner," in *EV*, 231 (see figure 16). The exiles received one private semi-apology from an official over the affair. Charles Thomson (1729–1824), the secretary to the Continental Congress (for its duration, 1774–89), wrote to Israel Pemberton on April 8, 1778, in his individual

capacity: "I am sorry for the death & sickness of your friends. Inclination as well as humanity easily lead me to do you any service in my power." In *LDC*, 9:392. Thomson was not a Quaker, but he married one and had taught at the Quaker-run Philadelphia Academy.

14. *DED*, 1:290–91.

15. Thomas Fisher diary, Apr. 28, 1778; "James Pemberton's Journal of the Exiles," 232.

16. *DED*, 1:303; Brown, *Robert Valentine*, 51–52.

17. *DED*, 1:303.

18. *DED*, 1:303; Tench Tilghman (one of Washington's secretaries), "Pass for James Pemberton, John Pemberton and Samuel Pleasants, Apr. 29, 1778," in Boyle, *Writings from the Valley Forge Encampment*, 4:131. Tilghman, a fierce Patriot despite his largely Loyalist family, was in 1781 to be chosen by Washington to ride from Yorktown, Virginia, to Philadelphia with the news of the victory of the American and French forces.

19. *DED*, 1:303–4.

20. Ibid., 1:306.

21. Muenchhausen, *At General Howe's Side*, 52.

22. *DED*, 1:306.

23. Major Carl Baurmeister to Major-General von Jungkenn, June 15, 1778, in Baurmeister, "Letters of Major Baurmeister (III)," 181.

24. *DED*, 1:305n28; McGuire, *Philadelphia Campaign*, 2:175.

25. *DED*, 1:305n28, 304n27.

26. Ewing, "Diary of George Ewing, a Continental Soldier," in Commager and Morris, *Spirit of 'Seventy-Six*, 657.

27. Serle, *American Journal of Ambrose Serle*, 303–4 (June 3, 1778); compare this account of the talk with Gates in "Return Journey to Pennsylvania," in *EV*, 227–28 (April 24).

28. "Return Journey to Pennsylvania," 227–28. This was not the only contact

between British officers and Quaker leaders in the days before the former departed Philadelphia. Serle enjoyed an especially dear parting adieu (suggesting great familiarity) with minister Samuel Emlen, and Emlen, Isaac Zane Sr., and one of the Pembertons attempted to speak with Howe that June. Serle, *American Journal of Ambrose Serle*, 310; *DED*, 1:311.

29. *DED*, 1:309.

30. Pemberton, *Diary of John Pemberton*, 5.

31. Rosswurm, *Arms, Country, and Class*, 167, 335n95; De Reynal to Count Vergennes, Dec. 1778, in Durand, *New Materials for the History of the American Revolution*, 181.

32. *DED*, 1:309.

33. Ibid., 1:311. Story was attainted of treason by the Assembly.

34. Joseph Galloway (1731–1803), one of the first attainted of high treason, years later applied through a lawyer for the right to return, but the government of Pennsylvania steadfastly chose not to act on his application. Galloway, *Loyal Traitor*, 278–79; Commonwealth of Pennsylvania, *Black List*, 11.

35. DTO, 462.

36. *DED*, 1:311; Rappleye, *Robert Morris*, 149.

37. *DED*, 1:311.

38. Ibid.

39. Ibid.

40. Maxey, *Treason on Trial*, 28.

41. Bartlett to William Whipple, Aug. 18, 1778, in Bartlett, *Papers of Josiah Bartlett*, 20.

42. Samuel Adams to Peter Thacher, Aug. 11, 1778, in *LDC*, 10:420.

43. Maxey, *Treason on Trial*, 28.

44. Ibid. Congress resolved that "any inhabitant of these states" who acted as a guide for the enemy or provided them with intelligence or provisions and was captured within thirty miles of enemy lines would be subject to trial by

court-martial, a harsher form of justice. *JCC*, 9:784 (Oct. 8, 1777); Larson, *Trials of Allegiance*, 86.

45. Maxey, *Treason on Trial*, 32.

46. To their great credit, Wilson and Ross represented the Quaker defendants despite having been members in October 1776 of the congressional committee "to prepare an effectual plan for suppressing the internal enemies of America, and preventing a communication of intelligence to our other enemies." *JCC*, 6:915.

47. McFarland and Herr, *William Lewis*, 4, 5. Lewis had also counseled the Quaker women while in Lancaster.

48. Maxey, *Treason on Trial*, 35.

49. Ibid., 79.

50. McKean's sentencing statement, in ibid., 159–62, 160 (quotes).

51. Ibid., 160–61.

52. The *Pennsylvania Packet* published the statement on November 7, 1778. Maxey, *Treason on Trial*, 159.

53. Carlton F. W. Larson, the most recent historian to judge the Quaker exile, determines that "everyone involved believed that a significant mistake had been made . . . the general view was that the whole regrettable incident should be forgotten as quickly as possible" because, in his words, the Quakers "easily regained" their standing in society (though, he does not add, twelve years later). To the contrary, there were many fellow citizens at the time of the incident who may have looked at what other Quakers had done and, like McKean, believed the exile necessary. See Larson, *Trials of Allegiance*, 84. Rufus M. Jones (assisted by Isaac Sharpless and Amelia M. Gummere) comments in his chapter on "The Friends in the Revolution" of the Quaker exiles: "They were finally returned home, with something of an apology and a recognition of their good motives." He cites no proof of this and reveals that he barely read Gilpin's *Exiles in Virginia*. This was

far from a fair reading of the ending of the Quaker exile, and yet Jones was the leading Quaker public intellectual of the first half of the twentieth century. See Jones, *Quakers in the American Colonies*, 567.

54. McKean's sentencing statement, 159–62, 162 (quote); "An Act for the Attainder of Divers Traitors," 9:201–15. The treason trial of Abraham Carlisle took place September 25. The leading evidence in Carlisle's trial had been an incriminating paper in the handwriting of Joseph Galloway officially appointing Carlisle a gatekeeper at the northeastern entryway from Frankford. This paper made him a direct employee of the British Army. In June, Galloway had urged Carlisle to leave with the evacuating British forces, but he declined to do so. Carlisle was easily convicted of treason by a jury of his peers. There was little controversy about Carlisle's guilt, but his friends nevertheless hoped that there might be some clemency or a pardon coming later. Maxey, *Treason on Trial*, 107.

55. Maxey, *Treason on Trial*, 85.

56. *DED*, 1:333. Thornton had been a member of the PYM peace mission in October 1777.

57. Ibid.

58. Maxey, *Treason on Trial*, 91–92.

59. Jones, "The Other Side of the American Revolution," 43.

60. Ibid.

61. Ibid., 44.

62. The only similar story appearing before the exile was the burning of the Quaker meetinghouse in Lancaster city in August 1777. Gordon, "Entangled by the World," 32; Fox, *Sweet Land of Liberty*, 88–90; Friedrich, "Did Mr. Saur Meet George Washington?" 193–200; "Christopher Saur, the elder, Christopher Saur, the younger, printers," attainted in Proclamation (No. 2), May 21, 1778, in *PA*, 3rd ser., 10:522; Commonwealth of Pennsylvania, *Black List*, 15.

63. Six men were appointed: Israel Pemberton (died April 1779), John Reynell, James Thornton, James Pemberton, Henry Drinker, and Nicholas Waln. Maxey, *Treason on Trial*, 105.

64. Ibid., 104.

65. "Report of Philadelphia Yearly Meeting's Meeting for Sufferings Committee of Inquiry," in ibid., 163–64.

66. Ibid., 165.

67. Ibid., 165–66.

68. Ibid., 163–64.

69. HD to ED, Jan. 30, 1778, QSC.

70. Wallace, "The Muhlenbergs and the Revolutionary Underground," 125.

71. Maxey, *Treason on Trial*, 163.

72. *DED*, 1:393.

73. Rawle, *Laurel Hill*, 403.

74. Rawle and Rawle, "A Loyalist's Account of Certain Occurrences," 107.

75. Hamburger, "Beyond Protection," 1917n322. See Pennsylvania Constitution of 1776, section 47. Thayer, *Pennsylvania Politics*, 211–27.

76. Pennsylvania Government, *Report of the Committee of the Council of Censors*. Frederick Muhlenberg (1750–1801), a Lutheran pastor like his father, prelate Henry Melchior Muhlenberg, served as the first president of Pennsylvania's Council of Censors and later became a US congressman from Pennsylvania and the first speaker of the US House of Representatives.

77. Hamburger, "Beyond Protection," 1917n323. The Council of Censors also decided that Timothy Matlack—secretary of the SEC, disowned Quaker, and sometime antagonist to the exiles—was "unworthy of public trust and confidence." Although he suffered years of enforced estrangement from state government, when he was wont to cry that he was persecuted "unheard," the court finally decided that, instead of him owing the state money, the reverse was true. Pennsylvania Government, *Report of*

the Committee of the Council of Censors; Coelho, *Timothy Matlack*, 150–57, 156.

78. Waln, clerk of "The Religious Society Called Quakers, from Their Yearly Meeting for Pennsylvania, New-Jersey, and the Western Parts of Virginia and Maryland," to Washington, undated (delivered circa Oct. 13, 1789), quoted in Washington to the Society of Quakers, Oct. 13, 1789, n1, FO.

79. Ibid.

80. Ibid.

81. Ibid.

82. Ibid. (emphasis in original).

83. Ibid.

84. Verplanck, "The Silhouette and Quaker Identity," 72, 74.

85. Crabtree, *Holy Nation*, 111.

CODA

1. "Return Journey to Pennsylvania," 227–28; Serle, *American Journal of Ambrose Serle*, 303–4.

2. Fisher, "Social Life in Philadelphia," 242; Thayer, *Israel Pemberton*, 231, 232; Serle, *American Journal of Ambrose Serle*, 304; Gummere, *Journal and Essays of John Woolman*, 515; Pemberton Family, "Annals of the Pemberton Family," 48; Pemberton, *Diary of John Pemberton*, 14.

3. Kafer, *Charles Brockden Brown*, 6, 204n14; *DED*, 3:2230; Anderson, "Thomas Wharton," 447; Thomas Wharton Sr. to Thomas Wharton Jr., Jan. 20, 1778, quoted in Anderson, "Thomas Wharton," 440; George Churchman to Thomas Wharton Sr., May 11, 1778, in Anderson, "Thomas Wharton," 443, 446n57. James Donald Anderson maintains incorrectly with respect to the Quaker exiles that "neither the state nor Congress accused them of treasonous behavior again." The cases of Thomas Wharton Sr., Samuel Rowland Fisher, Charles Eddy, and broker William Smith belie that claim. Anderson, "Thomas Wharton," 446. George Churchman to Thomas Wharton Sr., Dec. 8,

1777, in Marietta, *Reformation of American Quakerism*, 253–54.

4. *DED*, 1:316, 3:2141; *CRP*, 12:28–29; Commonwealth of Pennsylvania, *Black List*, 11. Charles's brother Thomas was also attainted. Commonwealth of Pennsylvania, *Black List*, 11. John Wright to Benjamin Franklin, Feb. 7, 1783, in Franklin, *Papers of Benjamin Franklin*, 39:149–50; Siebert, "Loyalists of Pennsylvania," 96; Sabine, *Biographical Sketches*, 1:402; Samuel Shoemaker diary, 372–400, passim.

5. *DED*, 1:264; *DTO*, 434; Siebert, "Loyalists of Pennsylvania," 45; William Drewet Smith Claim from the Public Records Office, London, in Coldham, *American Migrations*; Canada Loyalist Claim Form of William Drewet Smith; *UK, American Loyalist Claims*; Nourse, "Order of the Board of War," Dec. 1777, in *EV*, 185–87.

6. Cobau, "Precarious Life of Thomas Pike," 230–52. For records of Pike's petition, see *British American Loyalist Claims Commission*. As to Laurens, he was later captured and held by the British for fifteen months as a prisoner, "on suspicion of high treason," in the Tower of London. Boatner, Encyclopedia of the American Revolution, 600.

7. *DED*, 3:2169; *EV*, 215.

8. *DED*, 3:21; Pemberton, "An Account of the Illness and Decease of Thomas Gilpin of Philadelphia, at Winchester, Virginia," 210–11; Gray, *National Waterway*, 4–5.

9. Morris, "Journal of Samuel Rowland Fisher," 146.

10. Ibid.

11. Matlack, *Pennsylvania Packet*, Mar. 1779, quoted (but not cited) in Coelho, *Timothy Matlack*, 114–15.

12. Coelho, *Timothy Matlack*, 114.

13. Morris, "Journal of Samuel Rowland Fisher," 145–97, 274–333, 399–457, passim.

14. A Loyalist, Jabez Maud Fisher was also a talented writer and intellectual, with one diary published two centuries posthumously in the United States (1992) and another in the United Kingdom (2014). Kenneth Morgan, "Introduction," in Jabez Maud Fisher and Kenneth Morgan, ed., *An American Quaker*, 4.

15. *DED*, 3:2149; Sabine, *Biographical Sketches*, 1:415.

16. Morris, preface to "Journal of Samuel Rowland Fisher," 145; Joanna Wharton Lippincott, *Biographical Memoranda*; Yates, *Joseph Wharton*.

17. *DED*, 1:358, 3:2197.

18. Kafer, *Charles Brockden Brown*, 6, 204n14; Bell and Greifenstein, *Patriot-Improvers*, 2:292; Leach, "Old Philadelphia Families: Emlen"; Rawle and Rawle, "A Loyalist's Account of Certain Occurrences," 104–5, 106; Jasanoff, *Liberty's Exiles*, 117.

19. Bauman, *Reputation of Truth*, 174; Pemberton, "Memoirs of James Pemberton," 84; Sabine, *Biographical Sketches*, 2:159.

20. *DED*, 3:2196.

21. Van Buskirk, "They Didn't Join the Band," 12; Gouverneur Morris to Alexander Hamilton, Jan. 27, 1784, in Hamilton, *Papers of Alexander Hamilton*, 3:502; *DTO*, 412.

22. Bidwell, *American Paper Mills*, 263; Hancock and Wilkinson, "The Gilpins and Their Endless Papermaking Machine," 391–405.

23. Tobias Lear to George Washington, Nov. 4–5 and Nov. 21, 1790, FO.

24. *DED*, 1:101, 361–62, 548, 691, 2:807, 807n53, 1097n128; *JCC*, 15:1244; Bauman, *Reputation of Truth*, 173–74, citing letters from Henry Drinker to David Barclay, Jan. 12, 1779, and to Samuel Neale, July 1784; Oaks, "Philadelphians in Exile," 324; Bowen, *Family Portrait*, 297; George Washington to Henry Drinker, Apr. 8, 1790, reproduced in Biddle, *Extracts from the Journal of Elizabeth Drinker*, 222n (unnumbered); and in Goodrich, *Wayne County*, 224–25. Commenting on the

letter to Washington, Drinker noted, "So thee see how I am advanced to a correspondence with the King of America." Maxey, "The Union Farm," 614n17. Branson, "Elizabeth Drinker," 471–72. Today, the Museum of the American Revolution in Philadelphia displays in a separate, three-dimensional vitrine facsimiles of the Drinkers' furniture seized for taxes, as an example of the treatment of dissenting Quakers.

25. *DED*, 3:2173; Oaks, "Philadelphians in Exile," 301.

26. *DED*, 1:300, 3:2107; Wilson, *Philadelphia Quakers*; Philadelphia Museum of Art, *Philadelphia: Three Centuries of American Art*, 98–99; Hornor, *Blue Book of Philadelphia Furniture*, 108; Swanson, "50 Years of Decorating the White House."

27. Records of Pennsylvania's Revolutionary Governments, roll 43, reference #3–4; Sabine, *Biographical Sketches*, 2:578; *CRP*, 11:43.

28. *DED*, 3:2171; Mayor's Court Dockets, Philadelphia, PA, *Pennsylvania and New Jersey, U.S., Church and Town Records*, image 3; *1790 United States Federal Census*; *1800 United States Federal Census*; *Pennsylvania Gazette*, Aug. 25, 1784; *Dunlap and Claypoole's American Daily Advertiser*, Mar. 28, 1786; *Pennsylvania Gazette*, July 15, 1789; *Dunlap's Pennsylvania Packet*, May 22, 1790; Philadelphia Monthly Meeting, Minutes 1777–1781, *U.S., Quaker Meeting Records*, image 312; Charles Jervis, Find a Grave; *Pennsylvania Gazette*, Aug. 25, 1784; *Dunlap and Claypoole's American Daily Advertiser*, Mar. 28, 1786; *Pennsylvania Gazette*, July 15, 1789.

29. *DED*, 247 (Oct. 22, arrested), 263 (Dec. 11, returned); Kafer, *Charles Brockden Brown*, 40.

30. Kafer, *Charles Brockden Brown*, 40.

31. Ibid., 45, 46; Resolution of Council, Aug. 31, 1777, in *EV*, 72–73 (man of reputation).

32. *DED*, 3:2120; Kafer, *Charles Brockden Brown's Revolution*, 43, 45; Brockden

Brown, "Address to the Congress of the United States," 4 (emphasis in original).

33. "Death of Henry Armitt Brown," in *New England Historical and Genealogical Register* [. . .] *for the Year 1879*, 33:272.

34. Brown, *Henry Armitt Brown's Oration at Valley Forge*, 8, 36.

35. Ibid. Valley Forge became a National Park in 1976.

EPILOGUE

1. Brown, *Robert Valentine*. My thanks to John Bryer of Caln Friends Meeting and the author Francis G. Brown's family members, whom I met at Meeting for Worship at Downingtown Friends Meeting on May 12, 2022. See also Lendrat, "4002 Edge's Mill Road: An Historical Overview"; and Dugan, "Sarkissian—Blacksmith Shop: 4019 Edge's Mill Road, Caln Township, Chester County, Pennsylvania."

APPENDIX B

1. Israel Pemberton et al., "To the President and Council of Pennsylvania," Sept. 8, 1777, manuscript petition in MC 950–153, QSC (emphasis in original).

2. The reference is to the Glorious Revolution of 1688 in England when, as a result, in 1689 King James II's daughter, Mary II, and her husband, William III, prince of Orange and stadtholder of the United Provinces of the Netherlands, acceded jointly to the throne.

3. Although arrested and held for a time, neither Thomas Coombe nor Phineas Bond were exiled; they were released by parole before the exile began. Bond (1749–1815) later reentered the city with the British Army on September 26, 1777, and left with the British in June 1778 only to return in 1787 as British consul to the city. After the British evacuated the city in 1778, the SEC gave Reverend Thomas Coombe [Jr.] (1747–1822) a pass (and a

push) to go to New York, then a Loyalist haven, from where he self-exiled to Great Britain and never returned. *DED*, 3:2117 (Bond), 3:2130 (Coombe).

APPENDIX C

1. Pleasants et al., "Representation of the Wives of the Prisoners in Virginia" (emphasis in original). See Hatcher, "'Entirely an Act of Our Own.'" We are all indebted to Patricia Law Hatcher for excavating this petition and bringing the public's attention to the courageous, pioneering women who were its creators and proponents. On provenance, including in whose hand the petition was written, see Hatcher, "'Entirely an Act of Our Own,'" 145n2. Thomas Gilpin Jr. published a copy of the petition with slightly different wording and order of signers in *Exiles in Virginia* (279–80).

2. Matthew 7:12 (KJV): "Therefore all things whatsoever ye would that men should do to you, do ye even so to them: for this is the law and the prophets," known popularly as the Golden Rule.

3. Pleasants et al., "Representation of the Wives of the Prisoners in Virginia."

4. For Gilpin copy, see *EV*, 279–80.

5. The following names have spelling variants: Jervis (Jarvis), Penington (Pennington), Susana (Susanna), Phoebe (Phebe), and Affleck (Afflick). Lydia (Mrs. Thomas) Gilpin did not sign the petition. She was in mourning after learning of her husband's death in March. Rachel Hunt signed the petition as she did not know yet of her husband's death on March 31.

6. *DED*, 1:293 [Mar. 31], 295 [Apr. 2], 296 [Apr. 4].

7. Hatcher, "'Entirely an Act of Our Own,'" 148.

BIBLIOGRAPHY

UNPUBLISHED PRIMARY SOURCES

Alinson Collection. QSC.
Anderson, Bart. Battle of Brandywine, Loyalist Records. Accounts from Public Records Office mss. in London. Chester County Historical Society [CCHS]. Mss. copies of claims made by Chester County, Pennsylvania, loyalists transcribed by Bart Anderson, CCHS librarian, during his WWII service in London.
Colonial and Revolutionary Period Manuscripts. Collection 144. HSP.
Concord Quarterly Meeting. Minutes, 1777–1778. Concord Quarterly Meeting Records. Collection 690. Quaker Collection, Megill Library, Haverford College.
Dawkins, H. Indian Squaw Wampum Spies political cartoon, ca. 1764. Historical Society of Pennsylvania large graphics collection. Collection V65. HSP.
Drinker, Elizabeth Sandwith. Diaries. Collection 1760. HSP.
Drinker, Henry. Correspondence, 1777–1778. Drinker Ms. Collection 854. Quaker Collection, Megill Library, Haverford College.

———. Henry Drinker Papers. Collection 1767. HSP.
———. Henry Drinker Papers, 1756–1869. Dr. & Mrs. Henry Drinker Collection of Miscellaneous Family Papers. Collection 3125. HSP.
Drinker, Henry, and Elizabeth Drinker. Letters, 1777–1778. MC 854. QSC.
Feinstone, Sol. The Sol Feinstone Collection of the David Library of the American Revolution, 1088. APS.
Fisher, Thomas. Diary (Nov. 7, 1777–Apr. 29, 1778). Transcribed by James Gergat, in the transcriber's possession. Original in the Fox Family Papers, 1755–1769, Collection 2028. HSP.
Fisher-Warner Family Papers, 1684–1924. RG 5/042. Swarthmore College Library.
Gilpin, Thomas, Jr. Papers. Collection 0696. HSP.
James Hutchinson Papers, 1771–1928. Mss.B.H97p. APS.
John F. Reed Collection. *The Digital Vault.* Valley Forge National Historical Park. http://digitalvault.omeka.net/collections. (1) Testimony of the PYM dated Oct. 4, 1777, Isaac Jackson, clerk, http://digitalvault.omeka

.net/items/show/93. (2) Epistle of
Mar. 24, 1778, Nicholas Waln, clerk,
Quarterly Meeting of Elders and
Ministers. http://digitalvault.omeka
.net/items/show/132.

Jones Family Archive. Collection 1301.
HSP.

Jones, Karen. "The Real Isaac Zane and
His Influence in the American Rev-
olution." Mss. 1205. The Stewart Bell
Jr. Archives in the Handley Regional
Library, Winchester, Virginia.

Logan-Fisher-Fox Collection. Family
Papers, 1960, vol. 33. HSP.

Minutes of Meeting for Sufferings, Philadelphia Yearly Meeting of the Religious Society of Friends, 1756–1834.
QSC.

Pemberton, Israel, John Hunt, and Samuel
Pleasants. ADDRESS TO THE INHAB-
ITANTS of Pennsylvania BY Those
FREEMEN, of the CITY of Philadel-
phia, who are now confined in the
MASON'S LODGE, BY VIRTUE OF A GEN-
ERAL WARRANT. SIGNED IN COUN-
CIL BY THE VICE PRESIDENT OF THE
COUNCIL OF PENNSYLVANIA. Philadel-
phia: John Bell, 1777. https://quod.lib
.umich.edu/e/evans/N12282.0001.001
?rgn=main;view=fulltext.

Pemberton, James. "James Pemberton's
Diary 1777–1778." Pemberton Family
Papers, Collection 6456. HSP.

Philadelphia Yearly Meeting. Meeting for
Sufferings and Representative Meeting Records, 1719–1954. QSC.

Pleasants, Mary [Pemberton], et al. "Representation of the Wives of the Prisoners in Virginia, to the Congress,
Board of War, President and Council,
and Assembly of Pennsylvania, Read
in Council, April 10th 1778." Misc.
Mss., 1778 4 mo. Friends Historical
Library, Swarthmore College.

Quaker Exiles Collection. Archives,
Handley Regional Library, Winchester, Virginia.

Quaker Miscellany. Collection 951. QSC.
Ms. originals of many of the key documents of the Quaker exile incident.

Quakers Exiled in Virginia Collection,
1777–1778. MC 950.153. QSC. This
collection contains dozens of original documents from the Quaker exile
incident.

Questionnaire Regarding Allegiance Pro-
pounded by the Pennsylvania Assembly and Delivered to the Quakers,
c. 1778, and Draft of Their Reply.
Box 317. Moravian Archives, Bethlehem, Pennsylvania.

Records of Pennsylvania's Revolutionary
Governments, 1775–1790. Pennsylvania State Archives, Harrisburg.

Shoemaker, Samuel. Diary, 1783–85. Shoemaker Family Papers. Am. 152. HSP.

Vining, Elizabeth Gray. Papers. QSC.

"Wilmington Monthly Meeting: Minutes of the Committee Appointed by
Wilmington Monthly Meeting in the
8th Month 1777 to Collect and Keep
a Record of All Sufferings for the
Testimony of Truth and to Advise
in Cases of Difficulty." MS. Friends
Historical Collection, Swarthmore
College.

PUBLISHED PRIMARY SOURCES

Adams, John. The Adams Papers. Edited by
Robert J. Taylor et al. 16 vols. Cam-
bridge, MA: Harvard University
Press, 1977–2014.

———. The Adams Papers, Diary and
Autobiography of John Adams. Edited
by L. H. Butterfield. 4 vols. Cambridge, MA: Belknap Press of Harvard University Press, 1963.

Allen, James. "Diary of James Allen, Esq.,
of Philadelphia, Counsellor-at-Law,
1770–1778." (I) PMHB 9, no. 2 (July
1885): 176–96; (II) PMHB 9, no. 3
(Oct. 1885): 278–96; (III) PMHB 9,
no. 4 (Jan. 1886): 424–41.

American Philosophical Society, Historical Society of Pennsylvania, and Library Company of Philadelphia. *A Rising People: The Founding of the United States, 1765–1789.* Philadelphia: APS, HSP, & LCP, 1976.

André, John. *Journal of John André, June 11, 1777–Nov. 15, 1778.* MssHM 626. Huntington Library, San Marino, California. Original manuscript journal in images online: http://hdl.huntington.org/cdm/ref/collection/p15150coll7/id/22547.

Bartlett, Josiah. *The Papers of Josiah Bartlett.* Edited by Frank C. Mevers. Hanover, NH: University Press of New England, 1979.

Baurmeister, Carl. "Letters of Major Baurmeister During the Philadelphia Campaign, 1777–1778." Edited and translated by Bernard A. Uhlendorf and Edna Vosper. (I) *PMHB* 59, no. 4 (Oct. 1935): 392–419; (II) *PMHB* 60, no. 1 (Jan. 1936): 34–52; (III) *PMHB* 60, no. 2 (Apr. 1936): 161–83.

Baxter, Beverly. "Grace Growden Galloway: Survival of a Loyalist, 1778–79." *Frontiers: A Journal of Women's Studies* 3, no. 1 (Spring 1978): 62–67.

Benezet, Anthony. *Observations on the Inslaving, Importing, and Purchasing of Negroes* [. . .]. Philadelphia: Christopher Sower, 1759.

Besse, Joseph. *A COLLECTION of the SUFFERINGS of the PEOPLE called QUAKERS for the Testimony of a Good Conscience, from the TIME of Their Being First Distinguished by That NAME in the Year 1650, to the TIME of the Act, Commonly Called the Act of Toleration* [. . .]. London: Luke Hinde, 1753.

Blackstone, William. *Commentaries on the Laws of England.* 4 vols. Oxford: Clarendon Press, 1765–69. http://avalon.law.yale.edu/18th_century/blackstone_bk1ch1.asp.

Blanchard, Amos Foxe. *Book of Martyrs: Or, A History of the Lives, Sufferings and Triumphant Deaths of the Primitive* [. . .]. London: N. G. Ellis, 1844.

Boudinot, Elias. *Journal or Historical Recollections of American Events During the Revolutionary War by Elias Boudinot.* Philadelphia: Frederick Bourquin, 1894. https://archive.org/details/journalorhistorioboud.

Boyle, Joseph Lee. *Writings from the Valley Forge Encampment of the Continental Army, December 19, 1777–June 18, 1778.* Vol. 4. Westminster, MD: Heritage Books, 2007.

Boyle, Lee. "The Army Hospital at East Nottingham." *Cecil Historical Journal* 2, no. 1 (Winter 2001–2): 3–9.

British American Loyalist Claims Commission. 141 vols. London: Public Records Office of Great Britain, 1776–1835.

Brown, Charles Brockden. "An Address to the Congress of the United States on the Utility and Justice of Restrictions Upon Foreign Commerce [. . .]." Farmington Hills, MI: Gale, 2012.

Browne, Moses. Moses Browne to William Wilson, Jan. 2, 1776. Burn Bridle Press. http://burnbridle.com/?page_id=184.

Burnett, Edmund C., ed. *Letters to Members of the Continental Congress.* Vol. 2. Washington, DC: Carnegie Institution of Washington, 1923.

Canada Loyalist Claim Form of William Drewet Smith, Late of Philadelphia, Dated 1784. American Loyalist Claims, 1776–1835. National Archives of the UK, Kew, England. https://www.nationalarchives.gov.uk/.

Commager, Henry Steel, and Richard B. Morris, eds. *The Spirit of 'Seventy-Six: The Story of the American Revolution as Told by Participants.* New York: Harper & Row, 1958.

Commonwealth of Pennsylvania. *Black List: A List of Those Tories Who Took Part with Great Britain, in the Revolutionary War, and Were Attainted of High Treason, Commonly Called the Black List*. Philadelphia: Commonwealth of Pennsylvania, 1802.

Conrad, David Holmes. "Early History of Winchester." *Winchester, Virginia, Historical Society* 1 (1931): 169.

Continental Congress. *Journals of the Continental Congress, 1774–1789*. Edited by Worthington C. Ford et al. 34 vols. Washington, DC: US Government Printing Press, 1904–37. https://memory.loc.gov/ammem/amlaw/lwjc.html.

"Declaration from the Harmless and Innocent People of God Called Quakers. Against All Plotters and Fighters in the World." FriendsJournal.org. Accessed September 20, 2022. https://www.friendsjournal.org/wp--content/uploads/2020/08/1660PeaceTestimony.pdf.

Drinker, Elizabeth Sandwith. *The Diary of Elizabeth Drinker*. Edited by Elaine Foreman Crane et al. 3 vols. Boston: Northeastern University Press, 1991.

———. *Extracts from Journal of Elizabeth Drinker, from 1759 to 1807, A.D.* Edited by Henry Drinker Biddle. Philadelphia: J. B. Lippincott, 1889.

Dunlap, John, ed. *Acts of the General Assembly of the Commonwealth of Pennsylvania [. . .]* [1776–1779]. Philadelphia: John Dunlap, 1779.

Early Church Records of Chester County, Pennsylvania, in 3 vols. as follows: Vol. 1: Reamy, Martha. *Quaker Records of Bradford Monthly Meeting*. Westminster, MD: Family Line Publications, 1995. Vol. 2: Meldrum, Charlotte, and Martha Reamy. *Quaker Records of Uwchlan, Goshen, & New Garden Monthly Meetings, and East Vincent Reformed.*

Westminster, MD: Family Line Publications, 1997. Vol. 3: Meldrum, Charlotte. *Quaker Records of Kennett, and London Grove Monthly Meetings, and Extracts from St John's Episcopal Church and Great Valley Baptist Church*. Westminster, MD: Family Line Publications, 1998.

Early Church Records of Delaware County, Pennsylvania, in 3 vols. as follows: Vol. 1: Launey, John Pitts, and F. Edward Wright. *Society of Friends. Chester Monthly Meeting 1681–1801. St. Paul's Protestant Episcopal Church, Chester, PA*. Westminster, MD: Family Line Publications, 1997. Vol. 2: Peden, Henry C., Jr., and John Pitts Launey. *Concord Monthly Meeting 1801–1828. Forks of Brandywine Presbyterian Church. Brandywine Baptist Church. Middletown Graveyard*. Westminster, MD: Family Line Publications, 1997. Vol. 3: Launey, John Pitts. *Radnor-Haverford-Merion Monthly Meeting*. Westminster, MD: Family Line Publications, 1997.

"Edw. Drinker." *Columbian Magazine*, Aug. 1791.

1800 United States Federal Census [database online]. Provo, UT: Ancestry.com Operations Inc., 2010. Images reproduced by FamilySearch.

Emlen, Samuel, Jr., John Reynell, Joshua Howell, Owen Jones [Sr.], William Fisher, Hugh Roberts, Abel James, Richard Waln, John Drinker, Nicholas Waln, Joseph Bringhurst, and James Gough. "Letter of Friends in Philadelphia to Friends in [England and] Ireland, Soliciting Aid During the Occupation of Philadelphia by the British." *PMHB* 20, no. 1 (1896): 125–27.

Ewald, Johann. *Diary of the American War: A Hessian Journal*. Edited and translated by Joseph P. Tustin. New Haven: Yale University Press, 1979.

"Exiles in Virginia." *Bulletin of Friends Historical Society* 2, no. 1 (Mar. 1908): 25–27. Letters of Oct. 3 and Dec. 22, 1777, from exiles in Winchester to Robert Pleasants in Virginia.

Fisher, Jabez Maud. *An American Quaker in the British Isles: The Travel Journals of Jabez Maud Fisher, 1775–1779.* Edited by Kenneth Morgan. New York: Oxford University Press, 1992.

———. *A Quaker's Tour of the Colonial Northeast and Canada: The 1773 Travel Journals of Jabez Maud Fisher of Philadelphia.* Edited by Jack Campisi and William A. Starna. Philadelphia: American Philosophical Society, 2014.

Fisher, Samuel Rowland. "Journal of Samuel Rowland Fisher, of Philadelphia, 1779–1781." Edited by Anna Wharton. *PMHB* 41, no. 3 (1917): 145–97, 274–333, 399–457.

Fisher, Sarah Logan. "'A Diary of Trifling Occurrences': Philadelphia, 1776–1778." Edited by Nicholas B. Wainwright. *PMHB* 82, no. 4 (Oct. 1958): 411–65.

Ford, Worthington Chauncey, ed. "Prisoners of War (British and American) 1778." *PMHB* 17, no. 3 (1893): 159–74.

Founders Online. "Correspondence and Other Writings of Seven Major Shapers of the United States." National Archives. https://founders.archives.gov.

Franklin, Benjamin. *The Papers of Benjamin Franklin.* Edited by Leonard W. Labaree et al. 37 vols. New Haven: Yale University Press, 1959–.

———. *The Papers of Benjamin Franklin.* Edited by William B. Willcox. 43 vols. New Haven: Yale University Press, 1982–.

Galloway, Grace Growden. "Diary of Grace Growden Galloway, Kept at Philadelphia from June 17th, 1778 to July 1st, 1779." Edited by Raymond C. Werner. *PMHB* 55, no. 1 (Jan. 1931): 32–94.

———. "Diary of Grace Growden Galloway, Kept in Philadelphia from July 1 to September 30, 1779." Edited by Raymond C. Werner. *PMHB* 58, no. 2 (1934): 152–89.

Gilpin, Joshua. *Memoir on the Rise, Progress and Present State of the Chesapeake and Delaware Canal.* Wilmington, DE: R. Porter, 1821.

Gilpin, Thomas, [Jr.], ed. and comp. *Exiles in Virginia, with Observations on the Conduct of the Society of Friends During the Revolutionary War, Comprising the Official Papers of the Government Relating to That Period, 1777–1778.* Philadelphia: privately published, 1848. https://archive.org/details/exilesinvirginia00gilp.

———. "Memoir of Thomas Gilpin [Sr.]." *PMHB* 49, no. 4 (1925): 289–328.

Gilpin, Thomas, [Jr.], and Hannah Logan Smith. *Memorials and Reminiscences in Private Life.* Philadelphia: privately published, 1840. Collection 0696. HSP.

"Goshen Friends—Minutes Regarding the War." East Coast Genealogy (Post), September 12, 2019. https://eastcoastgenealogy.com/wp/goshen--friends--minutes--regarding--the--war/.

Graydon, Alexander. *Memoirs of His Own Time.* Edited by John Stockton Littell. Philadelphia: Lindsay & Blakiston, 1846.

———. *Memoirs of a Life, Chiefly Passed in Pennsylvania, Within the Last Sixty Years.* Edinburgh: William Blackwood, 1822.

Greene, Nathanael. *The Papers of General Nathanael Greene.* Edited by Richard K. Showman. 13 vols. Chapel Hill: University of North Carolina Press, 1976–2015.

Gwynedd Friends Meeting History Page. "Gwynedd Monthly Meeting for

Discipline, 1776–1778 (Men's Minutes)." Entry for July 28, 1778. https://www.friendsjournal.org/legacy/abington/gwynedd/minutes1776.html.

Hamilton, Alexander. *The Federalist.* Edited by Clinton Rossiter. New York: Penguin, 1961.

———. *The Papers of Alexander Hamilton.* Vol. 3, *1782–1786.* Edited by Harold C. Syrett. New York: Columbia University Press, 1962.

Hazard, Samuel, ed. *Colonial Records of Pennsylvania.* 16 vols. Harrisburg, PA: Theo. Fenn, 1838–53.

Hazard, Samuel, et al., eds. *Pennsylvania Archives.* 118 vols. Harrisburg, PA: Theo. Fenn, 1852–1935.

Historical Society of Pennsylvania. "Letters from Major John Clark, Jr. to Gen. Washington, Written During the Occupation of Philadelphia by the British Army." *Proceedings of the Historical Society of Pennsylvania* 1, no. 10 (Mar. 1847): 1–36.

Justice, Hilda. *Life and Ancestry of Warner Mifflin: Friend, Philanthropist, Patriot.* Philadelphia: Ferris & Leach, 1905.

Kemble, Stephen. *Journals of Lieut. Col. Stephen Kemble, 1773–1789* [. . .]. New York: Gregg Press, 1972.

Lafayette, Le Marquis de. *Lafayette in the Age of the American Revolution: Selected Letters and Papers, 1776–1790.* Vol. 1, *December 7, 1776–March 30, 1778.* Edited by Stanley J. Idzerda et al. Ithaca, NY: Cornell University Press, 1977.

Marshall, Christopher. *Extracts from the Diary of Christopher Marshall Kept in Philadelphia and Lancaster During the American Revolution, 1774–1781.* Edited by William Duane. Albany: Joel Munsell, 1877. https://archive.org/details/extractsfromdiao0duangoog.

———. *Passages from the Diary of Christopher Marshall, Kept in Philadelphia and Lancaster During the American Revolution.* Vol. 1, *1774–1777.* Edited by William Duane. Philadelphia: Hazard & Mitchell, 1839. https://archive.org/details/passagesfromdia00mars.

Martin, Joseph Plumb. *A Narrative of a Revolutionary Soldier.* New York: Signet Classics, 2001.

Mather, Cotton. *Magnalia Christi Americana: or, The Ecclesiastical History of New England* [. . .]. London: Thomas Parkhurst, 1702.

Mitchell, James T., and Henry Flanders, comps. *The Statutes At Large of Pennsylvania from 1682 to 1809.* 14 vols. Harrisburg: State Printer of Pennsylvania, 1896–1915.

Montrésor, John. "Journal of Captain John Montrésor, July 1, 1777, to July 1, 1778, Chief Engineer of the British Army [. . .]." *PMHB* 6, no. 1 (1882): 50.

———. "Journal of Captain John Montrésor, July 1, 1777, to July 1, 1778." *PMHB* 6, no. 2 (1882): 202.

Morris, Anna Wharton, ed. "Journal of Samuel Rowland Fisher, of Philadelphia, 1779–1781." *PMHB* 41, no. 2 (1917): 145–97.

Morton, Robert. "The Diary of Robert Morton, Kept in Philadelphia While That City Was Occupied by the British Army in 1777." *PMHB* 1, no. 1 (1877): 1–39. https://archive.org/details/jstor--20084252.

Muhlenberg, Henry Melchior. *The Journals of Henry Melchior Muhlenberg.* Edited and translated by Theodore G. Tappert and John Doberstein. 3 vols. Philadelphia: Evangelical Ministerium of Pennsylvania and Adjacent States, and the Muhlenberg Press, 1942–58.

New England Historical and Genealogical Register [. . .] *for the Year 1879.* Vol. 33. Boston: David Clapp and Son, 1879.

"Note and Queries" [Miscellaneous Receipts and Letters Relating to the Exiles]. *PMHB* 24, no. 3 (1900): 373–74.

Paine, Thomas. *The American Crisis, III.* Edited by Steve Straub. The Federalist Papers Project 36. https://www.thefederalistpapers.org/wp--content/uploads/2013/08/The--American--Crisis--by--Thomas--Paine--.pdf.

———. "Military Operations Near Philadelphia in the Campaign of 1777–8." *PMHB* 2, no. 3 (1878): 283–96.

Peale, Charles Willson. *The Selected Papers of Charles Willson Peale and His Family.* 5 vols. Edited by Lillian B. Miller et al. New Haven: Yale University Press, 1996–2000.

Pemberton Family. "Annals of the Pemberton Family, with Notes Respecting Some of Their Contemporaries." *Friends' Miscellany* 7, no. 1 (Apr. 1835): 1–96.

Pemberton, Israel. *Address to the Inhabitants of Pennsylvania by Those Freemen of the City of Philadelphia, Who are Now Confined in the Mason's Lodge, by Virtue of a General Warrant, Signed by Council by the Vice President of the Council of Pennsylvania.* Philadelphia: R. Bell, 1777.

Pemberton, James. "Memoirs of James Pemberton." *Friends Miscellany* 7, no. 126 (May 1835), 49–96.

———. "The Testimony of the People Called Quakers, Given Forth by a Meeting of the Representatives of Said People, in Pennsylvania and New Jersey, Held at Philadelphia the 24th day of the 1st Month, 1775." *Pennsylvania Gazette*, September 10, 1777.

Pemberton, John. *The Diary of John Pemberton for the Years 1777 and 1778.* Edited by Eli K. Price. Philadelphia: Henry B. Ashmead, 1867. Amazon.com photo reprint, 2018.

Pennsylvania and New Jersey, U.S., Church and Town Records, 1669–2013 [database online]. Lehi, UT: Ancestry.com Operations, Inc., 2011.

Pennsylvania Government. *Report of the Committee of the Council of Censors on Whether the Constitution Has Been Preserved Inviolate* [. . .]. Philadelphia: Francis Bailey, 1784.

Quincy, Josiah, Jr. *Portrait of a Patriot: The Major Political and Legal Papers of Josiah Quincy Junior.* Vol. 3, *The Southern Journal (1773).* Edited by Daniel R. Coquillette and Neil Longley York. Boston: Colonial Society of Massachusetts, 2007.

Rawle, Anna, and William Brook Rawle. "A Loyalist's Account of Certain Occurrences in Philadelphia After Cornwallis's Surrender at Yorktown." *PMHB* 16, no. 1 (Apr. 1892): 103–7.

Rawle, William Brook. *Laurel Hill: And Some Colonial Dames, Who Once Lived There.* London: Forgotten Books, 2018.

Reynell, John. "Minutes of the Quarterly Meeting Held in Philadelphia, 3rd Month, 4th, 1777." *Pennsylvania Gazette*, September 10, 1777. Accessible Archives CD-ROM edition of the *Pennsylvania Gazette*, 1991, folio 3 (1766–1783).

Serle, Ambrose. *The American Journal of Ambrose Serle, Secretary to Lord Howe, 1776–1778.* Edited by Edward H. Tatum Jr. San Marino, CA: Huntington Library, 1940.

1790 United States Federal Census [database online]. Provo, UT: Ancestry.com Operations Inc, 2010. Images reproduced by FamilySearch.

Smith, Paul H., et al., eds. *Letters of Delegates to Congress, 1774–1789.* 25 vols. Washington, DC: Library of Congress, 1976–2000.

Sullivan, John. *Letters and Papers of Major-General John Sullivan, Continental Army.* Edited by Otis G. Hammond. Concord: New Hampshire Historical Society, 1930.

Townsend, Joseph. *Some Account of the British Army Under the Command of General Howe and of the Battle of Brandywine on the Memorable September 11, 1777, and the Adventures of That Day, Which Came to the Knowledge and Observation of Joseph Townsend.* Philadelphia: Historical Society of Pennsylvania, 1846.

Tracy, Michael W. *266 Days: Eye-Witness Accounts of the British Occupation of Philadelphia.* Minneapolis: Mill City Press, 2015.

UK, American Loyalist Claims, 1776–1835 [also known as *Canada Loyalist Claims, c1776–1835*]. AO 13, Piece 102B. Ancestry.com [database online]. Provo, UT: Ancestry.com. https://www.ancestry.com/search /collections/3712/.

United States Department of the Interior, National Park Service. National Register of Historic Places Registration Form for Old Forge Farm, 2003. https://www.dhr.virginia.gov/VLR _to_transfer/PDFNoms/034--0125 _Old_Forge_Farm_2004_Final _Nomination.pdf.

U.S., Quaker Meeting Records, 1681–1935 [database online]. Lehi, UT: Ancestry .com. https://www.ancestrylibrary .com/search/collections/2189/.

Washington, George. *The Diaries of George Washington.* Edited by Donald Jackson and Dorothy Twohig. 6 vols. Charlottesville: University Press of Virginia, 1976–79.

———. *The Papers of George Washington.* Revolutionary War Series. Edited by Philander D. Chase et al. 23 vols. Charlottesville: University of Virginia Press, 1983–2016.

———. *The Papers of George Washington, Digital Edition.* Charlottesville: University of Virginia Press, 2008–2022. https://rotunda.upress.virginia.edu /founders/GEWN.html.

———. *The Writings of George Washington from the Original Sources, 1745–1799.* Edited by John C. Fitzpatrick. 39 vols. Washington, DC: US Government Printing Office, 1931–44.

Watring, Anna Miller. *Early Quaker Records of Philadelphia, Pennsylvania.* 2 vols. Westminster, MD: Family Line Publications, 1998.

Wister, Sarah. *The Journal and Occasional Writings of Sarah Wister.* Edited by Kathryn Zebelle Derounian. Madison, NJ: Fairleigh Dickinson University Press, 1987.

Wright, F. Edward, ed. *Abstracts of Philadelphia County Wills, 1763–1784.* Westminster, MD: Willow Bend Books, 2000.

SECONDARY SOURCES

Alexander, John K. "The Fort Wilson Incident of 1779: A Case Study of the Revolutionary Crowd." *William and Mary Quarterly*, 3rd ser., 31 (1974): 589–612.

Anderson, James Donald. "Thomas Wharton, Exile in Virginia, 1777–1778." *Virginia Magazine of History and Biography* 89, no. 4 (Oct. 1981): 425–47.

Ashmead, Henry Graham. *History of Delaware County, Pennsylvania.* Philadelphia: L. H. Everts, 1884.

Atkinson, Rick. *The British Are Coming: The War for America, Lexington to Princeton, 1775–1777.* Vol. 1 of *Revolution Trilogy.* New York: Holt, 2019.

Baack, Ben. "Forging a Nation State: The Continental Congress and the Financing of the War of American Independence." *Economic History Review* 54, no. 4 (2001): 639–56.

Baker, William S. "Itinerary of General Washington from June 15, 1775, to December 23, 1783." *PMHB* 14, no. 3 (Oct. 1890): 268.

Balch, Thomas Willing. "Thomas Willing of Philadelphia." *PMHB* 46, no. 1 (Jan. 1922): 9.

Barton, Lewis N. "The Revolutionary Prisoners of War in Winchester
and Frederick County." In *Men and
Events of the Revolution in Winchester
and Frederick County Virginia*, 9:30–
54. Winchester, VA: Winchester-
Frederick County Historical Papers,
1975.

"The Battle at Birmingham Meeting,"
p. 52. Accessed September 16, 2022.
https://pa01000218.schoolwires.net
/cms/lib/PA01000218/Centricity
/Domain/418/The%20Battle%20of
%20Birmingham%20Meeting.pdf.

Bauman, Richard. *For the Reputation of
Truth: Politics, Religion, and Conflict Among the Pennsylvania Quakers,
1750–1800*. Baltimore: Johns Hopkins
University Press, 1971.

Baxter, Beverly. "Grace Growden Galloway: Survival of a Loyalist, 1778–79."
*Frontiers: A Journal of Women's Stud-
ies* 3, no. 1 (Spring 1978): 62–67.

Bedini, Silvio A. "George Gilpin of Alexandria, Virginia, Part 1." *Professional
Surveyor Magazine*, January/February
1998. https://archives.profsurv.com
/magazine/article.aspx?i=239.

———. "George Gilpin of Alexandria,
Virginia, Part 2." *Professional Surveyor Magazine*, March 1998. https://
archives.profsurv.com/magazine
/article.aspx?i=264.

Beeman, Richard R. *Our Lives, Our Fortunes and Our Sacred Honor: The
Forging of American Independence,
1774–1776*. New York: Basic Books,
2013.

Bell, Whitfield J., Jr., and Charles B.
Greifenstein. *Patriot-Improvers:
Biographical Sketches of Members of
the American Philosophical Society*.
3 vols. Philadelphia: American Philosophical Society, 1997–2010.

Berkin, Carol. *Revolutionary Mothers:
Women in the Struggle for American
Independence*. Reprint ed. New York:
Vintage, 2006.

Betz, Paul, and Mark C. Carnes. *American National Biography*. Vol. 13.
New York: Oxford University Press,
2002.

Biddle, Henry Drinker. *The Drinker Fam-
ily in America to and Including the
Eighth Generation*. Philadelphia: J. B.
Lippincott, 1893.

———. *Extracts from the Journal of Elizabeth Drinker*. Philadelphia: J. B. Lippincott, 1889.

Biddle, Henry Drinker, et al. "Owen Biddle." *PMHB* 16, no. 3 (Oct. 1892):
299–329.

Bidwell, John. *American Paper Mills, 1690–
1832*. Hanover, NH: Dartmouth College Press, 2011.

*Biographical Directory of the United States
Congress, 1774–1989*. Washing-
ton, DC: US Government Printing Office, 1989. https://bioguide
.congress.gov/.

Black, Frederick R. "The West Jersey Society, 1768–1784." *PMHB* 97, no. 3
(July 1973): 379–83.

Boatner, Mark M., III. *Encyclopedia of the
American Revolution*. Guilford, CT:
Stackpole Books, 1994.

Bockelman, Wayne L., and Owen S. Ireland. "The Internal Revolution in
Pennsylvania: An Ethnic-Religious
Interpretation." *Pennsylvania History*
44, no. 2 (Apr. 1974): 124–59.

Bodle, Wayne. "This Tory Labyrinth." In
*Friends and Neighbors: Group Life in
America's First Plural Society*, edited
by Michael Zuckerman, 222–250.
Philadelphia: Temple University
Press, 1982.

Bodle, Wayne K., and Jacqueline Thi-
baut. *Valley Forge Historical Research
Report*. Vol. 3, *In the True Rustic
Order*. Valley Forge, PA: US Department of the Interior, 1980.

Boller, Paul F., Jr. "George Washing-
ton and the Quakers." *Bulletin of
Friends Historical Association* 49, no. 2
(Autumn 1960): 67–83.

Bowen, Catherine Drinker. *Family Portrait*. Boston: Little, Brown, 1970.

———. *John Adams and the American Revolution*. Boston: Little, Brown, 1950.

Bradley, John. *Ephrata Cloister: Pennsylvania Trail of History Guide*. Mechanicsburg, PA: Stackpole Books, 2000.

Brandywine Battlefield Preservation Plan. "Revolution in the Peaceful Valley." Chester County (Pennsylvania) Planning Commission and John Milner Associates, Inc. (1) Appendix B, Historic Resources Inventory: Update to the 2010 ABPP Survey, 2012. (2) Map Atlas, Map 1.6, "Quaker Cultural Influences in the Brandywine Valley," 2013. https://www.chescoplanning.org/Historic/bbpp.cfm.

Branson, Susan. "Elizabeth Drinker: Quaker Values and Federalist Support in the 1790s." *Pennsylvania History* 68, no. 4 (Autumn 2001): 465–82.

Brier, Marc A. *They Passed This Way: An Account of the Many Long Forgotten Marches [. . .] in Southeastern Pennsylvania*. Pennsylvania: Valley Forge National Historical Park, September 2002. https://www.nps.gov/vafo/learn/historyculture/upload/theypassedthisway.pdf.

Brinton, Howard. *Friends for 300 Years: The History and Beliefs of Friends Since George Fox Started the Quaker Movement*. New York: Harper, 1952.

Brock, Peter. *Pacifism in the United States: From the Colonial Era to the First World War*. Princeton: Princeton University Press, 1968.

———. *The Quaker Peace Testimony, 1660–1914*. Syracuse: Syracuse University Press, 1991.

Brown, Francis G. *Robert Valentine, 1717–1786: Thy Affectionate Friend*. Downingtown, PA: John Bryer, 2009.

Brown, Henry Armitt. *Henry Armitt Brown's Oration at Valley Forge June 19th, 1878*. Philadelphia: Holmes Press, 1926.

Burdick, Kim Rogers. "I Remain Your Friend: Daniel Byrnes, a Quaker in the Revolutionary Era." MS HB2. Hale Byrnes House, Newark, Delaware, 2011. http://www.halebyrnes.org/history/iremain.pdf.

———. "A Quaker Struggles with the War." *Journal of the American Revolution* (May 26, 2015). https://allthingsliberty.com/2015/05/a-quaker-struggles-with-the-war.

———. *Revolutionary Delaware, Independence in the First State*. Charleston, SC: History Press, 2016.

Calhoon, Robert McCluer. *The Loyalists in the American Revolution, 1760–1781*. New York: Harcourt, 1973.

Calomiris, Charles W. "Institutional Failure, Monetary Scarcity, and the Depreciation of the Continental." *Journal of Economic History* 48, no. 1 (Mar. 1988): 47–68.

Calvert, Jane E. *Quaker Constitutionalism and the Political Thought of John Dickinson*. Cambridge: Cambridge University Press, 2009.

———. "Thomas Paine, Quakerism, and the Limits of Religious Liberty During the American Revolution." In *Selected Writings of Thomas Paine*, edited by Ian Shapiro and Jane E. Calvert, 602–29. New Haven: Yale University Press, 2014.

Carroll, Kenneth L. "American Quakers and Their London Lobby." *Quaker History* 70, no. 1 (Spring 1981): 22–39.

Castro, Wendy Lucas. "'Being Separated from My Dearest Husband, in This Cruel Manner': Elizabeth Drinker and the Seven-Month Exile of Philadelphia Quakers." *Quaker History* 100, no. 1 (Spring 2011): 40–63.

"Charles Jervis." Find a Grave. https://www.findagrave.com/memorial/207654236/charles-jervis.

Claussen, W. Edmunds. *The Revolutionary War Years in Berks, Chester and Montgomery Counties, Pennsylvania*. Boyertown, PA: Gilbert, 1973.

Cloud, Morgan. "Quakers, Slaves and the Founders: Profiling to Save the Union." *Emory Law Journal* 73 (2003): 369–421.

Cobau, Judith. "The Precarious Life of Thomas Pike, a Colonial Dancing Master in Charleston and Philadelphia." *Dance Chronicle* 17, no. 3 (1994): 229–62.

Coelho, Chris. *Timothy Matlack: The Scribe of the Declaration of Independence*. Jefferson, NC: McFarland, 2013.

Coldham, Peter Wilson. *American Migrations, 1765–1799: The Lives, Times, and Families of Colonial Americans Who Remained Loyal to the British Crown Before, During, and After the Revolutionary War, as Related in Their Own Words and Through Their Correspondence*. Baltimore: Genealogical Publishing, 2000.

Coleman, John M. "Joseph Galloway and the British Occupation of Philadelphia." *Pennsylvania History* 30, no. 3 (July 1963): 272–300.

———. "Thomas McKean and the Origin of an Independent Judiciary." *Pennsylvania History* 34, no. 2 (Apr. 1967): 111–130.

———. *Thomas McKean: Forgotten Leader of the Revolution*. Rockaway, NJ: American Faculty Press, 1975. https://archive.org/details/thomasmckeanforgoocole.

Cooper, Karen G. "Isaac Zane's Marlboro Ironworks: A Colonial Iron Plantation, 1763–1795." MA thesis, James Madison University, 1991.

Cope, Gilbert. "Chester County Friends in the Revolution," *Daily Local News* (West Chester, Pa.), Nov. 20 and 27, 1902. Gilbert Cope Papers. Chester County Historical Society, West Chester, PA.

———. *Genealogy of the Baily Family of Bromham, Wiltshire, England* [. . .]. Lancaster, PA: Wickersham, 1912.

Cope, Gilbert, and Henry Graham Ashmead. *Historic Homes and Institutions and Genealogical and Personal Memoirs of Chester and Delaware Counties, Pennsylvania*. 2 vols. New York: Lewis, 1904.

Cope, Gilbert, and Janetta W. Schoonover. *The Brinton Genealogy: A History of William Brinton Who Came from England to Chester County, Pennsylvania in 1684*. Trenton, NJ: Press of MacCrellish & Quigley, 1924.

Crabtree, Sarah. *Holy Nation: The Transatlantic Quaker Ministry in an Age of Revolution*. Chicago: University of Chicago Press, 2015.

Cuthbert, Anthony. "Assessment of Damages Done by the British Troops During the Occupation of Philadelphia, 1777–1778." *PMHB* 25, no. 3 (1901): 323–35.

Daigler, Kenneth A. *Spies, Patriots, and Traitors: American Intelligence in the Revolutionary War*. Washington, DC: Georgetown University Press, 2015.

Davis, W. W. H. *The History of Bucks County, Pennsylvania: From the Discovery of the Delaware to the Present Time*. Doylestown, PA: Democrat Book and Job Office, 1876.

Day, Lance, and Ian McNeil, eds. *Biographical Dictionary of the History of Technology*. New York: Routledge, 1998.

Diffenderffer, Frank Reid. "The Quaker Exiles." *Papers Read Before the Lancaster County Historical Society* 9, no. 4 (1905): 77–117.

Doerflinger, Thomas M. "How to Run an Ironworks." *PMHB* 108, no. 3 (July 1984): 357–66.

———. "Philadelphia Merchants and the Logic of Moderation, 1760–1775."

William and Mary Quarterly, 3rd ser., 40, no. 2 (Apr. 1983): 197–226.

———. *A Vigorous Spirit of Enterprise.* New York: Norton, 1986.

Doyle, Robert C. *The Enemy in Our Hands: America's Treatment of Enemy Prisoners of War from the Revolution to the War on Terror.* Lexington: University Press of Kentucky, 2010.

Dreisbach, Daniel L., and Mark David Hall, eds. *The Sacred Rights of Conscience.* Indianapolis: Liberty Fund, 2009.

Drinker, Cecil K. *Not So Long Ago: A Chronicle of Medicine and Doctors in Colonial Philadelphia.* New York: Oxford University Press, 1937.

Drinker, Henry S. *The Drinker Family in America.* Philadelphia: n.p., 1893.

———. "History of the Drinker Family." Typescript, 1961. HSP.

Dugan, Mary Larkin. "Sarkissian—Blacksmith Shop: 4019 Edge's Mill Road, Caln Township, Chester County, Pennsylvania." Caln Township.org. Accessed July 7, 2022. https://www.calntownship.org/uploads/9/9/7/5/99755464/sarkissian--blacksmith_shop.pdf.

Durand, John. *New Materials for the History of the American Revolution.* London: Forgotten Books, 2017.

Durnbaugh, Donald, ed. *The Brethren in Colonial America: A Source Book on the Transplantation and Development of the Church of the Brethren in the Eighteenth Century.* Elgin, IL: Brethren Press, 1967.

Ekeland, Tor. "Suspending Habeas Corpus: Article I, Section 9, Clause 2 of the United States Constitution and the War on Terror." *Fordham University Law Review* 74 (2005): 1475–519.

Ellis, Joseph. *His Excellency George Washington.* New York: Vintage, 2004.

———. *Revolutionary Summer: The Birth of American Independence.* New York: Vintage, 2014.

Evans, Charles, ed. *American Bibliography.* 14 vols. New York: Peter Smith, 1941–59.

Falk, Robert P. "Thomas Paine and the Attitude of the Quakers to the American Revolution." *PMHB* 63, no. 3 (July 1939): 308.

Ferling, John. *Almost a Miracle: The American Victory in the War of Independence.* New York: Oxford University Press, 2007.

———. *The Ascent of George Washington.* New York: Bloomsbury Press, 2009.

———. "Joseph Galloway's Military Advice: A Loyalist's View of the Revolution." *PMHB* 98, no. 2 (Apr. 1974): 171–88.

———. *The Loyalist Mind: Joseph Galloway and the American Revolution.* University Park: Penn State University Press, 1977.

Fischer, David Hackett. *Albion's Seed: Four British Folkways in America.* New York: Oxford University Press, 1989.

Fisher, Darlene Emmert. "Social Life in Philadelphia During the British Occupation." *Pennsylvania History* 37, no. 3 (1970): 237–60.

Flexner, James Thomas. *George Washington in the American Revolution (1775–1783).* Boston: Little, Brown, 1967.

———. *The Traitor and the Spy: Benedict Arnold and John André.* Syracuse: Syracuse University Press, 1991.

Foner, Eric. *Tom Paine and Revolutionary America.* New York: Oxford University Press, 1976.

Foner, Philip S., ed. *The Complete Writings of Thomas Paine.* New York: Citadel, 1945.

Fothergill, John. "Dr. Fothergill's Advice to Philadelphia Friends." *Bulletin of Friends' Historical Society* 3, no. 3 (Feb. 1910): 3–11.

Fowler, David J. *Guide to the Sol Feinstone Collection of the David Library of the American Revolution.* Washington

Crossing, PA: David Library of the American Revolution, 1994.

Fox, Francis S. "The Prothonotary: Linchpin of Provincial and State Government in Eighteenth-Century Pennsylvania." *Pennsylvania History* 59, no. 1 (Jan. 1992): 41–53.

———. *Sweet Land of Liberty: The Ordeal of the American Revolution in Northampton County, Pennsylvania.* University Park: Penn State University Press, 2000.

Fraser, Flora. *The Washingtons: Join'd by Friendship, Crown'd by Love.* New York: Alfred A. Knopf, 2015.

Friedrich, Gerhard. "Did Mr. Saur Meet George Washington?" *Pennsylvania History* 10, no. 3 (July 1970): 193–200.

Frost, J. William. *The Quaker Family in Colonial America: A Portrait of the Society of Friends.* New York: St. Martin's Press, 1973.

Futhey, J. Smith, and Gilbert Cope. *History of Chester County, Pennsylvania.* Philadelphia: Louis H. Everts, 1881.

Galloway, Patton Gardenier. *The Loyal Traitor: Joseph Galloway and the American Revolution.* Morrisville, NC: Lulu Press, 2010.

Gerbner, Katharine. "'We Are Against the Traffik of Men-Body': The Germantown Quaker Protest of 1688 and the Origins of American Abolitionism." *Pennsylvania History* 74, no. 2 (2007): 149–72.

Gilpin, Joseph Elliott. *Genealogy of the Family of Gideon Gilpin [. . .].* Baltimore, 1897.

Godbeer, Richard. *World of Trouble: A Philadelphia Quaker Family's Journey Through the American Revolution.* New Haven: Yale University Press, 2019.

Goodrich, Charles A. *Lives of the Signers to the Declaration of Independence.* New York: William Reed, 1829.

Goodrich, Phineas G. *Wayne County, Pennsylvania.* Honesdale, PA: Haines

and Beardsley, 1880. Reprinted with introduction, biography, and index by Richard Orvis Eldred. Baltimore: Gateway Press, 1992.

Gordon, Scott Paul. "Entangled by the World: William Henry of Lancaster and 'Mixed' Living in Moravian Town and Country Congregations." *Journal of Moravian History* 8 (Spring 2010): 7–52.

———. *The Letters of Mary Penry: A Single Moravian Woman in Early America.* University Park: Penn State University Press, 2018.

Gough, Robert. "Notes on the Pennsylvania Revolutionaries." *PMHB* 96, no. 1 (Jan. 1972): 89–103.

Graham, Daniel. "George Washington's Valley Forge Landlady, Deborah (Pyewell) Potts Hewes." *Bulletin of Historical Society of Montgomery County* 36, no. 1 (2009): 3–25.

———. "The Loyalist: John Potts, Junior." *Bulletin of the Montgomery County Historical Association* 32, no. 3 (Fall 1999): 19–103.

Gray, Ralph D. *The National Waterway: A History of the Chesapeake and Delaware Canal, 1769–1965.* Champaign: University of Illinois Press, 1967.

Griffenhagen, George B. "Drug Supplies in the American Revolution." *United States National Museum Bulletin* 225. Washington, DC: Smithsonian Institution, 1961.

Gummere, Amelia Mott, ed. *The Journal and Essays of John Woolman.* New York: Macmillan, 1922.

Hamburger, Philip. "Beyond Protection." *Columbia Law Journal* 109, no. 8 (Dec. 2009): 1823–2001.

———. "Religious Freedom in Philadelphia." *Emory Law Journal* 54 (2005): 1603–77.

Hamm, Thomas D. *The Quakers in America.* New York: Columbia University Press, 2003.

Hancock, Harold B. *The Delaware Loyalists*. Wilmington: Historical Society of Delaware, 1940.

———. *The Loyalists of Revolutionary Delaware*. Newark: University of Delaware Press, 1972.

Hancock, Harold B., and Norman B. Wilkinson. "The Gilpins and Their Endless Papermaking Machine." *PMHB* 81, no. 4 (Oct. 1957): 391–405.

Harris, Michael C. *Brandywine: A Military History of the Battle That Lost Philadelphia But Saved America, September 11, 1777*. El Dorado Hills, CA: Savas Beatie, 2014.

Hatcher, Patricia Law. "'Entirely an Act of Our Own': Women's Petition for Quaker Prisoners, 1778." *Pennsylvania Genealogical Magazine* 42 (2001): 145–61.

Hatfield, Stuart. "Faking It: British Counterfeit During the American Revolution." *Journal of the American Revolution* (Oct. 7, 2015). https://allthingsliberty.com/2015/10/faking--it--british--counterfeiting--during--the--american--revolution/.

High, J. Walter, "Thomas Coombe, Loyalist." *Pennsylvania History* 62, no. 3 (July 1995): 276–92.

Hinshaw, William Wade, and Thomas Worth Marshall, eds. *Encyclopedia of American Quaker Genealogy, 1607–1943*. 6 vols. Ann Arbor, MI: Edwards Bros., 1938–50.

Horle, Craig W., et al., eds. *Lawmaking and Legislators in Pennsylvania: A Biographical Directory*. Vol. 3. Harrisburg, PA: House of Representatives, 2005.

Hornor, William MacPherson. *Blue Book of Philadelphia Furniture: William Penn to George Washington*. Washington, DC: Highland House, 1935.

Hunter, Robert J. "The Activities of Members of the American Philosophical Society in the Early History of the Philadelphia Almshouse." *Philadelphia General Hospital* 71, no. 6 (Apr. 1932): 308–19.

Ireland, O. S. "The Crux of Politics: Religion and Party in Pennsylvania, 1778–1789." *William and Mary Quarterly* 3rd ser., 42, no. 4 (Oct. 1985): 453–75.

Isaacson, Walter. *Benjamin Franklin: An American Life*. New York: Simon & Schuster, 2004.

"Israel Whelen." Pennsylvania State Senate Historical Biographies. Accessed September 28, 2022. https://www.legis.state.pa.us/cfdocs/legis/BiosHistory/MemBio.cfm?ID=5037&body=S.

Jacob, Mark, and Stephen H. Case. *Treacherous Beauty: Peggy Shippen, the Woman Behind Benedict Arnold's Plot to Betray America*. Guilford, CT: Lyons Press, 2012.

Jasanoff, Maya. *Liberty's Exiles: American Loyalists in the Revolutionary World*. New York: Vintage, 2011.

Jones, Hugh. "Assessment of Damages Done by the British Troops During the Occupation of Philadelphia, 1777–1778 (Concluded)." *PMHB* 25, no. 4 (1901): 544–59.

Jones, Robert Francis. "The Public Career of William Duer: Rebel, Federalist Politician, Entrepreneur and Speculator 1775–1792." PhD diss., University of Notre Dame, 1967.

Jones, Rufus M., et al. *The Quakers in the American Colonies*. London: Macmillan, 1911.

Jones, Sheila. "The Other Side of the American Revolution: A Look at the Treatment of Philadelphia Quakers During the Revolutionary War." *Proceedings of the Ohio Academy of History* (2004): 31–48. http://www.ohioacademyofhistory.org/wp--content/uploads/2013/04/2004Jones.pdf.

Jordan, John W., ed. *Colonial and Revolutionary Families of Philadelphia*

Pennsylvania; Genealogical and Personal Memoirs. 4 vols. New York: Lewis, 1911. http://www.ancestrypaths.com/books--by--state/pennsylvania/colonial--and--revolutionary--families--of--pennsylvania.

———, ed. *Colonial Families of Philadelphia*. 2 vols. New York: Lewis, 1911. Vol. 1: https://archive.org/details/colonialfamilies01jord. Vol. 2: https://archive.org/details/cu31924092544133.

Justice, Hilda. *Life and Ancestry of Warner Mifflin: Friend, Philanthropist, Patriot*. Philadelphia: Ferris & Leach, 1905.

Kafer, Peter. "Charles Brockden Brown and Revolutionary Philadelphia: An Imagination in Context." *PMHB* 116, no. 4 (Oct. 1992): 467–99.

———. *Charles Brockden Brown's Revolution and the Birth of American Gothic*. Philadelphia: University of Pennsylvania Press, 2004.

Kashatus, William C., III. *Conflict of Conviction: A Reappraisal of Quaker Involvement in the American Revolution*. Lanham, MD: University Press of America, 1990.

Kauffman, Gerald R., and Michael R. Gallagher. *The British Invasion of Delaware, Aug.–Sep. 1777*. Morrisville, NC: Lulu Press, 2013.

Knauss, James O. "Christopher Saur the Third." *Proceedings of the American Antiquarian Society* 41 (Apr. 1931): 235–53.

Knouff, Gregory T. *The Soldiers' Revolution: Pennsylvanians in Arms and the Forging of Early American Identity*. University Park: Penn State University Press, 2004.

Kriebel, Howard W. *The Schwenkfelders in Pennsylvania*. Lancaster, PA: Pennsylvania German Society, 1904.

Labaree, Benjamin Woods. *The Boston Tea Party*. New York: Oxford University Press, 1964.

La Courreye Blecki, Catherine, and Karin A. Wulf, eds. *Milcah Martha Moore's Book: A Commonplace Book from Revolutionary America*. University Park: Penn State University Press, 1997.

Larson, Carlton F. W. "The Revolutionary American Jury: A Case Study of the 1778–1779 Philadelphia Treason Trials." *Southern Methodist University Law Review* 61 (2008): 1441–524.

———. *The Trials of Allegiance: Treason, Juries, and the American Revolution*. New York: Oxford University Press, 2019.

Leach, Frank Willing. "Old Philadelphia Families: Emlen." *Philadelphia North American*, October 25, 1908. https://emlen.us/Emlen--article.html.

Lemon, James T. *The Best Poor Man's Country: A Geographical Study of Early Southeastern Pennsylvania*. New York: Norton, 1972.

Lendrat, Edward G. "4002 Edge's Mill Road: An Historical Overview." CalnTownship.org. Accessed July 9, 2022. https://www.calntownship.org/uploads/9/9/7/5/99755464/4002_edges_mill_rd.pdf.

Levy, Barry. *Quakers and the American Family: British Settlement in the Delaware Valley*. New York: Oxford University Press, 1988.

Lewis, Clifford, Jr. "Note." *PMHB* 60, no. 2 (Apr. 1936): 182–83.

Lippincott, Horace Mather. *Early Philadelphia: Its People, Life and Progress*. Philadelphia: J. B. Lippincott, 1917.

Lippincott, Joanna Wharton. *Biographical Memoranda Concerning Joseph Wharton, 1826–1909*. Philadelphia: privately printed and circulated by J. B. Lippincott, 1909.

Lowell, Edward J. *The Hessians and the Other German Auxiliaries of Great*

Britain in the Revolutionary War. New York: Harper & Brothers, 1884.

Luthy, David. "The Ephrata Martyr's Mirror." *Pennsylvania Mennonite Heritage* 9, no. 1 (Jan. 1986): 2–5.

MacMaster, Richard K. *Land, Piety, and Peoplehood: The Establishment of Mennonite Communities in America, 1683–1790.* Scottdale, PA: Herald Press, 1985.

MacMinn, Edwin. *On the Frontier with Colonel Antes: Or, the Struggle for Supremacy of the Red and White Races in Pennsylvania.* Camden, NJ: S. Chew & Son, 1900.

Malone, Dumas, ed. *Dictionary of American Biography.* Vol. 10. New York: Charles Scribner's, 1935.

Marietta, Jack D. *The Reformation of American Quakerism, 1748–1783.* Philadelphia: University of Pennsylvania Press, 1984.

Massey, Gregory D. *John Laurens and the American Revolution.* Columbia, SC: University of South Carolina Press, 2000.

Maxey, David W. "Of Castles in Stockport and Other Strictures: Samuel Preston's Contentious Agency for Henry Drinker." *PMHB* 110, no. 3 (July 1986): 413–46.

———. "The Honorable Proprietaries V. Samuel Wallis: 'A Matter of Great Consequence' in the Province of Pennsylvania." *Pennsylvania History* 70, no. 4 (Fall 2003): 361–95.

———. *Treason on Trial in Revolutionary Philadelphia: The Case of John Roberts, Miller.* Philadelphia: American Philosophical Society, 2011.

———. "The Union Farm: Henry Drinker's Experiment in Deriving Profit from Virtue." *PMHB* 107, no. 4 (Oct. 1983): 607–29.

McCullough, David. *John Adams.* New York: Simon & Schuster, 2001.

McFarland, Esther Ann, and Mickey Herr. *William Lewis, Esquire: Enlightened Statesman, Profound Lawyer, Useful Citizen.* Darby, PA: Diane, 2012.

McGrath, Tim. *Give Me a Fast Ship: The Continental Navy and America's Revolution at Sea.* New York: NAL Caliber, 2014.

McGuire, Thomas J. *The Philadelphia Campaign.* 2 vols. Mechanicsburg, PA: Stackpole Books, 2006–7.

Mekeel, Arthur J. "A Quaker Loyalist and General Washington." *Bulletin of Friends Historical Association* 27, no. 1 (Spring 1983): 33–34.

———. "Quaker-Loyalist Settlers in New Brunswick and Nova Scotia." *Bulletin of Friends Historical Association* 36, no. 1 (Spring 1947): 26–38.

———. *The Quakers and the American Revolution.* York, UK: Sessions Book Trust, 1996.

———. *The Relation of the Quakers to the American Revolution.* Lanham, MD: University Press of America, 1979.

———. "The Relation of the Quakers to the American Revolution." *Quaker History* 65, no. 1 (Spring 1976): 3–18.

Messer, Peter C. "'A Species of Treason and Not the Least Dangerous Kind': The Treason Trials of Abraham Carlisle and John Roberts." *PMHB* 123, no. 4 (Oct. 1999): 303–32.

Miller, David Hunter, ed. *Treaties and Other International Acts of the United States of America.* Vol. 2. Washington, DC: US Government Printing Office, 1931–48.

Miller, Jacquelyn C. "Franklin and Friends: Benjamin Franklin's Ties to Quakers and Quakerism." *Pennsylvania History* 57, no. 4 (Oct. 1990): 318–36.

Moss, Robert W., Jr. "Isaac Zane, Jr., A 'Quaker for the Times.'" In *Men and Events of the Revolution in Winchester and Frederick County Virginia,* 9:65–80. Winchester, VA:

Winchester-Frederick County Historical Society Papers, 1975.

Mowday, Bruce E. *September 11, 1777: Washington's Defeat at Brandywine Dooms Philadelphia.* Shippensburg, PA: White Mane Books, 2005.

Muenchhausen, Friedrich von. *At General Howe's Side, 1776–1778: The Diary of General William Howe's Aide de Camp, Captain Friedrich von Muenchhausen.* Translated by Ernst Kipping and annotated by Samuel Stelle Smith. Monmouth Beach, NJ: Philip Freneau Press, 1974.

Munier, Margaret B. "Washington's Headquarters at the Battle of the Brandywine: A Reconstruction of the Benjamin Ring Farm." MA thesis, West Chester State College, 1955.

Munn, David C. *Battles and Skirmishes of the American Revolution in New Jersey.* New Jersey: Bureau of Geology and Topography, Dept. of Environmental Protection, 1976.

Myers, James P., Jr. *The Ordeal of Thomas Barton: Anglican Missionary in the Pennsylvania Backcountry, 1755–1780.* Bethlehem: Lehigh University Press, 2010.

Nagy, John. *Spies in the Continental Capital: Espionage Across Pennsylvania During the American Revolution.* Yardley, PA: Westholme, 2011.

Nash, Gary B. *The Unknown American Revolution: The Unruly Birth of Democracy and the Struggle to Create America.* New York: Viking, 2005.

———. *Warner Mifflin: Unflinching Quaker Abolitionist.* Philadelphia: University of Pennsylvania Press, 2017.

Niles, Hezekiah. *Principles and Acts of the Revolution in America: Or, an Attempt to Collect and Preserve Some of the Speeches, Orations, & Proceedings [. . .].* Baltimore: H. Niles, 1822. https://archive.org/stream /principlesactsofoonile#page/n9 /mode/2up.

Oaks, Robert F. "Big Wheels in Philadelphia: Du Simitière's List of Carriage Owners." *PMHB* 95, no. 3 (July 1971): 351–62.

———. "Philadelphia Merchants and the First Continental Congress." *Pennsylvania History* 40, no. 2 (Apr. 1973): 148–66.

———. "Philadelphians in Exile: The Problem of Loyalty During the American Revolution." *PMHB* 96, no. 3 (Jul. 1972): 298–319, 321–25.

O'Shaughnessy, Andrew Jackson. *The Men Who Lost America: British Leadership, the American Revolution, and the Fate of the Empire.* New Haven: Yale University Press, 2012.

Ousterhout, Anne M. "Controlling the Opposition in Pennsylvania During the American Revolution." *PMHB* 105, no. 1 (Jan. 1981): 3–34.

———. *A State Divided: Opposition in Pennsylvania to the American Revolution.* New York: Greenwood Press, 1987.

"Pallbearers." In *The Digital Encyclopedia of George Washington*, edited by James P. Ambuske. Mount Vernon Ladies' Association, 2012–. https:// www.mountvernon.org/library /digitalhistory/digital--encyclopedia /article/pallbearers/.

Palmer, Scott. "Hockessin Friends Meeting House." *Mill Creek Hundred History Blog.* July 28, 2010. http:// mchhistory.blogspot.com/2010/07 /hockessin--friends--meeting--house .html?m=1.

Pencak, William, ed. *Pennsylvania's Revolution.* University Park: Penn State University Press, 2010.

Pestana, Carla Gardina. "The Quaker Executions as Myth and History." *Journal of American History* 80, no. 2 (Sept. 1993): 441.

Peterson, Charles E. *Robert Smith: Architect, Builder, Patriot, 1722–1777.* Philadelphia: The Athenaeum of Philadelphia, 2000.

Philadelphia Museum of Art. *Philadelphia: Three Centuries of American Art.* Philadelphia: Philadelphia Museum of Art, 1976.

Phillips, Kevin. *1775: A Good Year for Revolution.* New York: Penguin Books, 2012.

Pickering, Octavius, and Charles W. Upham. *The Life of Timothy Pickering.* 4 vols. Boston: Little, Brown, 1867–73.

Pleasants, Henry, Jr. "The Battle of Paoli." *PMHB* 72, no. 1 (Jan. 1948): 44–53.

Powers, Fred. Perry. *Tales of Old Taverns: An Address Delivered by Fred. Perry Powers Before the Site and Relic Society of Germantown, March 17, 1911.* Germantown, PA: Site and Relic Society of Germantown, 1912.

Radbill, Kenneth A. "The Ordeal of Elizabeth Drinker." *Pennsylvania History* 47, no. 2 (Apr. 1980): 147–72.

———. "Quaker Patriots: The Leadership of Owen Biddle and John Lacey, Jr." *Pennsylvania History* 45 (1978): 47–54.

Rappleye, Charles. *Robert Morris: Financier of the American Revolution.* New York: Simon & Schuster, 2010.

Reed, William B. *Life and Correspondence of Joseph Reed.* 2 vols. Philadelphia: Lindsay & Blakiston, 1847. https://archive.org/details/lifeand correspo02reedgoog.

Richards, Nancy E. "The City Home of Benjamin Chew, Sr., and His Family: A Case Study of the Textures of Life." Philadelphia: Cliveden of the National Trust, 1996. https://cliveden .org/wp--content/uploads/2021/04 /benjamin--chew--townhouse.pdf.

Rosswurm, Steven J. *Arms, Country, and Class: The Philadelphia Militia and the Lower Sort During the American Revolution.* New Brunswick: Rutgers University Press, 1989.

Rowe, G. S. *Thomas McKean: The Shaping of an American Republicanism.* Boulder, CO: Colorado Associated University Press, 1978.

Russell, Marvin F. "Thomas Barton and Pennsylvania's Colonial Frontier." *Pennsylvania History* 76 (1979): 313–34.

Ryerson, Richard Alan. *John Adams's Republic: The One, the Few, and the Many.* Baltimore: Johns Hopkins University Press, 2016.

———. *The Revolution Is Now Begun: The Radical Committees of Philadelphia, 1765–1776.* Philadelphia: University of Pennsylvania Press, 1978.

Sabine, Lorenzo. *Biographical Sketches of Loyalists of the American Revolution with an Historical Essay.* 2 vols. Boston: Little, Brown, 1864. https://catalog.hathitrust.org/Record /000365313.

Scharf, J. Thomas. *History of Delaware, 1609–1888.* Philadelphia: L. J. Richards, 1888.

Scharf, J. Thomas, and Thompson Westcott. *History of Philadelphia, 1609–1884.* 3 vols. Philadelphia: L. H. Everts, 1884. http://www.phillyh2o .org/backpages/SW_mainpage.htm.

Seed, Geoffrey. "A British Spy in Philadelphia: 1775–1777." *PMHB* 85, no. 1 (Jan. 1961): 3–37.

Sellers, Charles Coleman. *Charles Willson Peale.* Vol. 1, *Early Life, 1741–1790.* Philadelphia: American Philosophical Society, 1947.

Sewell, William. *The History of the Rise, Increase, and Progress of the Christian People Called Quakers.* 2 vols. London: James Phillips, 1755.

Seybolt, Robert Francis. *A Contemporary British Account of General Sir William Howe's Military Operations in 1777.* Worcester, MA: Davis Press, 1931.

Sharpless, Isaac. *A Quaker Experiment in Government: History of Quaker Government in Pennsylvania, 1682–1783.* Philadelphia: Ferris & Leach, 1902. https://archive.org/details/quaker experimentooshar/.

———. *Two Centuries of Pennsylvania History.* Philadelphia: Lippincott, 1900.

Shoemaker, Benjamin H. *Genealogy of the Shoemaker Family of Cheltenham, Pennsylvania.* Philadelphia: privately published, 1903.

Siebert, Wilbur H. "The Loyalists of Pennsylvania." Contributions in History and Political Science 5. *Ohio State University Bulletin* 24, no. 23 (Apr. 1920). https://archive.org/details /pennsyloyalistoosiebrich/mode /2up.

Simpson, Henry. *The Lives of Eminent Philadelphians, Now Deceased.* Philadelphia: W. Brotherhead, 1859.

Skemp, Sheila. *William Franklin: Son of a Patriot, Servant of a King.* Oxford: Oxford University Press, 1990.

Sloan, David. "'A Time of Sifting and Winnowing': The Paxton Riots and Quaker Non-Violence in Pennsylvania." *Quaker History* 66, no. 1 (Spring 1977): 3–22.

Smith, Anna Wharton. *Genealogy of the Fisher Family, 1682 to 1896.* Philadelphia, 1896.

Smith, Horace Wemyss. *Life and Correspondence of the Rev. William Smith, D.D.* 2 vols. Philadelphia: Ferguson Bros., 1880.

Smith, Page. *John Adams.* New York: Doubleday, 1962.

Sparks, Jared, et al. *Report of a Committee Appointed by the Mass. Historical Society on Exchanges of Prisoners During the American Revolutionary War.* Boston: Massachusetts Historical Society, 1861. https://archive.org/details /reportofcommitteo3mass.

Specht, Neva Jean. "'Being a Peaceable Man, I have Suffered Much Persecution': The American Revolution and Its Effects on Quaker Religious Identity." *Quaker History* 99, no. 2 (Fall 2010): 37–48.

Speidel, Judithe D. "The Artistic Spy: A Note on the Talents of Major André." *New York History* 68, no. 4 (Oct. 1987): 394–406.

Spero, Patrick. *Frontier Country: The Politics of War in Early Pennsylvania.* Philadelphia: University of Pennsylvania Press, 2016.

Springer, Paul J. *America's Captives: Treatment of POWs from the Revolutionary War to the War on Terror.* Lawrence: University Press of Kansas, 2010.

Stern, Cyrus, et al. *Our Kindred: The McFarlan and Stern Families, of Chester County, Pa., and New Castle County, Del.* [. . .] West Chester, PA: F. S. Hickman, 1885.

Stern, T. Noel. "William Penn on the Swearing of Oaths: His Ideas in Theory and Practice." *Quaker History* 70, no. 2 (Fall 1981): 84–98.

Stone, Frederick D. "How the Landing of Tea Was Opposed in Philadelphia by Colonel William Bradford and Others in 1773." *PMHB* 15, no. 4 (1891): 385–93.

Stryker, William S. *The Battles of Trenton and Princeton.* Boston: Houghton, Mifflin, 1898.

Sullivan, Aaron. "In But Not of the Revolution: Loyalty, Liberty, and the British Occupation of Philadelphia." PhD diss., Temple University, 2014.

———. *The Disaffected: Britain's Occupation of Philadelphia During the American Revolution.* Philadelphia: University of Pennsylvania Press, 2019.

Swanson, Abbie Fentress. "50 Years of Decorating the White House." WNYC, February 10, 2012.

https://www.wnyc.org/story/185533
--first--ladies/.

Thayer, Theodore. *Israel Pemberton, King of the Quakers*. Philadelphia: Historical Society of Pennsylvania, 1943.

———. *Pennsylvania Politics and the Growth of Democracy*. Harrisburg: Pennsylvania Historical and Museum Commission, 1953.

Thomson, Wilmer W. *Chester County and Its People*. New York: Union History Company, 1898.

Tillman, Kacy Dowd. *Stripped and Script: Loyalist Women Writers of the American Revolution*. Amherst: University of Massachusetts Press, 2019.

Tolles, Frederick. *Meeting House to Counting House: The Quaker Merchants of Colonial Philadelphia*. New York: Norton, 1963.

———. "Unofficial Ambassador: George Logan's Mission to France, 1798." *William and Mary Quarterly* 3d ser., 7, no. 1 (1950): 3–25.

Tomes, Nancy. "The Quaker Connection: Visiting Patterns Among Women in the Philadelphia Society of Friends, 1750–1800." In *Friends and Neighbors: Group Life in America's First Plural Society*, edited by Michel Zuckerman, 174–195. Philadelphia: Temple University Press, 1982.

Trainer, Anne I. *Quaker Patriots of Delaware County in the Revolution*. Pennsylvania: Chester County Historical Society, 1936.

Treese, Lorett. *The Storm Gathering: The Penn Family and the American Revolution*. University Park: Penn State University Press, 1992.

Tyler, Amanda L. "The Forgotten Core Meaning of the Suspension Clause." *Harvard Law Review* 125 (2012): 901–1018.

Valley Forge National Park. "Spy System 1777." USHistory.org. Accessed September 12, 2022. http://www

.ushistory.org/valleyforge/history/spies.html.

Van Buskirk, Judith L. *Generous Enemies: Patriots and Loyalists in Revolutionary New York*. Philadelphia: University of Pennsylvania Press, 2002.

———. "They Didn't Join the Band: Disaffected Women in Revolutionary Philadelphia." *Pennsylvania History* 62, no. 3 (Summer 1995): 306–29.

Van Doren, Carl. *Secret History of the American Revolution*. Garden City, NJ: Garden City Publishing, 1941.

Verplanck, Anne. "The Silhouette and Quaker Identity in Early National Philadelphia." *Winterthur Portfolio* 43, no. 1 (Spring 2009): 41–78.

Vining, Elizabeth Gray. *The Virginia Exiles*. Philadelphia: J. B. Lippincott, 1955.

Von Kotzebue, August. "The Quaker: A Drama in One Act." Translated by Amelia M. Gummere. *PMHB* 29, no. 4 (1905): 439–50.

Wallace, Paul A. "The Muhlenbergs and the Revolutionary Underground." *Proceedings of the American Philosophical Society* 93, no. 2 (May 1949): 119–26.

Warden, Rosemary S. "The Infamous Fitch: The Tory Bandit, James Fitzpatrick of Chester County." *Pennsylvania History* 62, no. 3 (July 1995): 376–87.

Watring, Anne Miller. *Early Quaker Records of Philadelphia*. Vol. 2, *1751–1800*. 3rd ed. Millsboro, DE: Colonial Roots, 2009.

Wayland, John Walter, and Joint Committee of Hopewell Friends. *Hopewell Friends History, 1734–1934, Frederick County, Virginia: Records of Hopewell Monthly Meetings and Meetings Reporting to Hopewell*. Strasburg, VA: Shenandoah, 1936.

Weigley, Russell Frank, et al. *Philadelphia: A 300-Year History*. New York: Norton, 1982.

Westcott, Thomas. *Names of Persons Who Took the Oath of Allegiance to the State of Pennsylvania Between the Years 1777 and 1779 with History of the "Test Laws" of Pennsylvania*. Philadelphia: John Campbell, 1865. https://hdl.handle.net/2027/yale.39002060927283.

Westtown Boarding School. *A Brief History of Westtown Boarding School* [. . .]. 3rd ed. Philadelphia: Sherman, 1884.

Wharton, Anna H. *Genealogy of the Wharton Family of Philadelphia*. Philadelphia: Collins, 1880.

Whidbee, Paige L. "The Quaker Exiles: 'The Cause of Every Inhabitant.'" *Pennsylvania History* 83, no. 1 (Winter 2016): 28–57.

Wilson, Robert H. *Philadelphia Quakers, 1681–1981*. Philadelphia: Philadelphia Yearly Meeting of the Religious Society of Friends, 1981.

Wokeck, Marianne. "Capitalizing on Hope: Transporting German Emigrants Across the Atlantic Before the American Revolution." In "Transatlantic Migration," edited by Hans-Jürgen Grabbe. Special issue, *American Studies* 42, no. 3 (1997): 345–56.

Wolf, Edwin, II. *Philadelphia: Portrait of an American City*. Philadelphia: Camino Books, 1990.

Woodman, Henry. *The History of Valley Forge*. Oaks, PA: John U. Francis Sr., 1922.

Worrall, Jay. *The Friendly Virginians: America's First Quakers*. Athens, GA: Iberian, 1994.

Wulf, Karin A. "Introduction." In *Milcah Martha Moore's Book: A Commonplace Book from Revolutionary America*, edited by Catherine La Courreye Blecki and Karin A. Wulf, 1–57. University Park: Penn State University Press, 1997.

Yates, W. Ross. *Joseph Wharton: Quaker Industrial Pioneer*. Bethlehem: Lehigh University Press, 1987.

Young, Henry J. "Treason and Its Punishment in Revolutionary Pennsylvania." *PMHB* 90, no. 3 (July 1966): 287–313.

INDEX

Figures and maps are denoted by "*f*" following the page numbers.

Bartlett, Josiah (New Hampshire delegate), 145
Barton, Lewis N., Anglican cleric refusing to take oath, 195n24
Battle of Brandywine (September 11, 1777), 6, 12, 22, 57, 80, 84, 189n5, 194n50, 202n14
Battle of Fort Mercer (October 22–November 16, 1777), 87–88
Battle of Germantown (October 4, 1777), 84, 112, 189n72, 198n28, 204n21
Battle of Princeton (January 3, 1777), 66, 84, 112, 189n72
Battle of Saratoga (October 1777), 7, 83–84, 86, 109, 129, 138
Battle of Trenton (December 26, 1776), 66, 84, 112
Battle of White Marsh (December 5–8, 1777), 102
Battle of Yorktown (September 28–October 19, 1781), 150
Baurmeister, Carl (Hessian officer)
  on American motivation to continue fighting, 110
  on Martha Washington's influence on her husband George, 206n19
  military pin gifted to son of Quaker widow with whom he was staying, 202–3n17
  on Quaker worries about British withdrawal from city, 142
Bayard, James (son of John), arrested by British for spying, 83
Bayard, John B. (speaker of assembly), 21, 207n32
Benezet, Anthony, 193n31
Benezet, Joyce, informing Rachel Hunt of her husband's death, 126
Bethlehem
  Moravian Brethren arrested and dragged through streets of, 149
  Moravian facilities used as hospitals at, 22
Biddle, Clement (disowned Quaker in Continental Army), 138
bills of attainder, 6, 132
Birmingham Friends Meeting (Chester County), 32, 189n5

board of war (Continental Congress)
  appeal by exiles of relocation to Staunton, consideration of, 107, 108
  on exiled Quakers' correspondence, 72–73
  jurisdiction over exiles, 65, 134
  Marlboro Iron Works (owned by Zane, Jr.) and, 74
  members of (1778), 203n2
  order to deliver exiled men for trial, 113–15
  order to exile Quakers to Winchester, 5
  order to release exiled men from Virginia to Pennsylvania authorities, 134
  punishing exiles for Continental currency depreciation, 77
Bockelman, Wayne L., 21
Boller, Paul F., Jr., 206n24
Bond, Phineas
  as British consul to Philadelphia (1787), 212n4
  with British soldiers entering Philadelphia (September 26, 1777), 82, 212n4
  on hostiles list but not exiled, 82, 189n72
  treason charge, 197n12, 212n4
Boston
  The Boston Martyrs, 204n24
  civil liberties demanded by, 56
  Quakers refusal to contribute to relief money for, 32, 189n1
Boston Massacre, Adams as defense attorney for British soldiers in, 54
Boudinot, Elias (American commissary of prisoners), 122
Bowen, Catherine Drinker (1897–1973)
  as biographer, 161
  descendant of Henry Drinker (1734–1809), 13
  A Family Portrait, 13
Bradford, Thomas, in arresting party, 192n6
Bradford, William
  arrested Quakers asking for arrest warrant from, 52
  broadsides published during Tea Act crisis (fall 1773), 48, 192n7
  conversion of forebears from Quakerism to Anglicanism, 48

Delaney, Sharp, 48
Delaware River
    Americans building battery on New
        Jersey side across from Philadel-
        phia, 83
    fighting between British and rebel
        troops keeping British ships from
        Philadelphia, 85–87
    preparations for British invasion, 6, 41
    See also Fort Mercer
diaries
    British occupation of Philadelphia
        detailed in Elizabeth Drinker's diary,
        81–84, 97–99
    Thomas Fisher as diarist of exile, 69, 70
    of Loyalist women, 120
    Morton recording British occupation of
        Philadelphia, 99
    James Pemberton's diary of exile, 69,
        118, 120
    Quaker diaries, communal sharing of,
        120
    See also Drinker, Elizabeth Sandwith
Dickinson, John (of Quaker descent)
    on Continental currency, 37
    in Delaware militia, 98
    in First Continental Congress, 194n45
    refusing to sign Declaration of Indepen-
        dence, 98
Dickinson, Philemon, 37
disenfranchisement for failure to comply
    with Test Act, 27, 106, 148
disownment
    for aiding Patriots, 33
    for lax behavior, 20
    in Philadelphia area, 33, 189n7
    for violating peace testimony tenet of
        pacifism, 19
    See also specific Quakers by name
Downingtown, Pennsylvania, as stopping
    place for returning exiles, 140–41
Downingtown Friends Meeting (Chester
    County), 12, 165
Drewet Smith, William. *See* Smith, Wil-
    liam Drewet
Drinker, Daniel (Henry's brother), 87
Drinker, Elizabeth Sandwith (ca.
    1735–1807)
    on Battle of Fort Mercer, 88, 97

on British arrival in and occupation of
    Philadelphia, 81–84, 97–99
Elijah Brown's family receiving finan-
    cial assistance from, 162
central to story of exile, 7–8
Crammond quartering with, 103–4,
    110, 161
currency transfer to exiled husband by,
    76, 99–100
death of, 161
despair over congressional refusal to
    release exiled men, 111, 115
diary of (*The Diary of Elizabeth
    Drinker*), 8, 97–99, 126, 161, 185n10
drunken British officer intruding into
    house of, 98
Emlen and, 199n2
financial advice from her uncle John
    Jervis, 162
on hanging of convicted traitors, 147–48
at Lancaster meeting with released
    exiles, 139
letters exchanged with husband Henry
    (1777–78), 13, 77, 122
Matlack and, 135, 137, 138, 207n35
on Meschianza celebration by the Brit-
    ish (May 18, 1778), 142
misspelling of "American" by, 198n20
on mob violence against Quakers for
    not celebrating Yorktown victory,
    150
on peace mission's return to Philadel-
    phia, 96
on Pennsylvania Assembly lobbying for
    release of exiled men, 115
personality of, 68
post-exile life of, 160–61
pro-British sentiments of, 83
PYM attendance during battles outside
    of Philadelphia, 84, 85
on Quakers socializing during British
    occupation of Philadelphia, 80, 111
on quiet in Philadelphia due to sus-
    pended shipping while British invad-
    ing the city, 80
refusal to allow Hessian's horse in her
    stable, 97–98
refusal to donate blankets to soldiers,
    16, 97

women's correspondence, decision
  not to open, 204n7
women's mission granted permission by to leave Philadelphia,
  204n17
See also British occupation of
  Philadelphia
Hunt, John (1712–1778)
  arrest of, 49–50
  burial in Hopewell Friends cemetery,
    204n24
  commitment to faith, 2
  death while in exile, 2, 9, 118–19, 124,
    126, 128, 157, 183, 205n27
  as exiled Quaker, 1–2, 25, 29
  illness and surgery in exile, 1–2, 117–18,
    123, 204n21
  as minister of exiled Quakers, 69
Hunt, Rachel (wife of John), 123, 125–26,
  157, 183, 205n27, 213n5
Hutchinson, James, 85
hypocrisy
  Patriots denying civil liberties to Quak-
    ers while demanding civil liberties
    from British, 2–5, 11, 30, 45, 47, 51–53,
    56, 58, 61, 62, 64, 106
  Presbyterians criticizing Quakers for,
    20

illegitimacy of Patriot-established
  government
  Continental currency refused due to,
    33
  Samuel Rowland Fisher's refusal to
    acknowledge state government as
    legitimate, 158
  founded in "Spirit of War and Fight-
    ings," 33
  John Pemberton on, 58, 188n67
  some Quakers' refusal to acknowl-
    edge Assembly's legitimacy, 6, 24, 29,
    31–32, 116, 150
  some Quakers' refusal to take oath
    to new state of Pennsylvania, 38–
    39
Independence Day, Quakers' refusal to
  celebrate, 29
Independence Hall, Philadelphia Museum
  located in, 153
Ireland, Owen S., 21

Jackson, William (Quaker minister),
  refusing to transport currency to
  Henry Drinker, 100
Jacobs, Benjamin, permanently disowned
  by Quakers, 190n19
Jacobs, John (Quaker Speaker of the
  Pennsylvania House), resignation
  of, 21
James, Abel (1725–1790)
  on Battle of Fort Mercer, 88
  James Bayard, extricating from British
    arrest, 83
  female relatives of exiles meeting with
    to review their petition, 123
  Galloway and, 201n2
  interceding for Elizabeth Drinker's
    refusal to allow Hessian's horse into
    her stable, 97–98
  as letter writer to London Friends for
    provisions requested by PYM, 101
  opposed to Patriot cause, 24
  signing parole to avoid arrest, 192n9
  singled out for arrest, 46
  Stamp Act (1765) opposed by, 20
  treason charge, 201n2
  See also James and Drinker (firm)
James, Chalkley (son of Abel), 98
James, John (dates uncertain)
  imprisoned in Lancaster, 111
  incarceration of, 74
  Matlack's attack on, 158
  singled out for arrest, but not arrested,
    46, 73
  spreading false rumor of exiles' removal
    to Staunton, 111
  visiting and offering support to exiles in
    Winchester, 73, 75
James and Drinker (firm), 20, 24, 48, 160
Japanese-American internment during
  World War II, 11
Jervis, Charles (1731–1806)
  as attorney and realtor, 162
  Continental currency refusal and, 162,
    189n11
  death and burial of, 162
  as exiled Quaker, 30
  as hatter, 161
  on hostiles list, 162
  letter to his father John Jervis, 100
  marriage out of meeting, 161

Lee, Richard Henry
  Continental currency refusal alleged
    against, 37
  letter to cousin Patrick Henry (governor
    of Virginia) urging no leniency for
    exiled Quakers, 69
  on Quakers' exile, 56, 68–69
  on Spanktown Papers committee,
    43–44, 68
legal rights of exiled Quakers. *See* habeas
  corpus rights
Lewis, William (1752–1819)
  as attorney for imprisoned Quakers, 51
  as attorney for Roberts, 145
  background of, 207n12
  consulting with women's mission on
    obtaining full reinstatement of civil
    rights for exiles, 139
Library Company of Philadelphia, 7, 9
Lightfoot, Susannah, lobbying Pennsylvania Assembly for release of exiled
  men, 115, 140
Lightfoot, Thomas
  background of, 201n13
  Pennsylvania Assembly lobbied by for
    release of exiled men, 115, 140
  treason charge, 201n13
  visiting and carrying cash for exile
    Henry Drinker, 76, 100
Lincoln, Abraham, habeas corpus sus-
  pended by, 195n25
Lititz, Pennsylvania
  Moravian facilities used as hospitals
    at, 22
  Moravians jailed for pacifist views in,
    149
Loague, William (Quaker farmer), 100
Logan, Charles (Thomas Fisher's brother-
  in-law), encounter with women's mis-
  sion at Valley Forge, 132
Logan, George (nephew of Thomas Fisher
  and Sarah Logan Fisher), 200n35
Logan, George (Thomas Fisher's brother-
  in-law), 123
Logan, James (Quaker who immigrated
  with William Penn), 91, 199n6
Logan, Sarah. *See* Fisher, Sarah Logan
Logan, William (Quaker), refusing to cel-
  ebrate Independence Day, 29
Logan Act (1799), 200n35

London Friends, PYM seeking provisions
    from, 101, 201n18
  arrival of ship, 144
Loring, Betsy (General Howe's mistress),
    110
Lovell, James, 56
Loyalists
  in British Army, 89, 105
  in British-occupied Philadelphia (*see*
    British occupation of Philadelphia)
  forfeit of estates ordered by law, 48–49
  hostiles list giving names of (*see* hos-
    tiles lists)
  New York as state with largest popula-
    tion of, 187n37
  Quakers' actions considered as help-
    ing British, 4, 5–6, 19, 24, 31, 33, 86,
    187n37, 209n53
  renegade exiles (William Drewet Smith
    and Thomas Pike), 72, 76
  Serle's role (*see* Serle, Ambrose)
  See also British American Loyalist
    Claims Commission; Carlisle, Abra-
    ham; Galloway, Joseph; treason; *other
    specific individuals*
Lutherans in Pennsylvania Assembly, 21

Magna Carta (1215), 8, 61
maps
  caravan route to exile, 59f
  Winchester area homes where exiled
    men lodged, 114f
Marietta, Jack D., 186n7
Marlboro Iron Works owned by Zane,
    Jr., 74
Marshall, Christopher (disowned Quaker
    and Patriot diarist), 48, 156
martyrdom of exiles, 64–65, 164
Massachusetts, anti-Quaker law of, 44
Mather, Cotton, 44
Matlack, Billy (son of Timothy), 158
Matlack, Nelly (wife of Timothy), 135
Matlack, Timothy (secretary, SEC,
    1736–1829)
  attack on John James and Thomas
    Fisher for encouraging Matlack's son
    to rejoin Quakers, 158, 160
  background of, 207n35
  British capture of Philadelphia, broad-
    side warning of, 79

Morris, Israel
    accompanying women's mission, 126,
        127
    fined in New Jersey for refusing to take
        oath of allegiance, 205n25
    receiving passes from Valley Forge for
        exiles to return to Philadelphia, 141
    telling Elizabeth Drinker of Edward
        Penington's illness, 137
Morris, Joshua
    background of, 199n2
    in peace mission to army command-
        ers, 90
Morris, Robert, 36, 144–45, 190n22
Morton, James (James Pemberton's step-
    son), 115, 203n4
Morton, Robert
    diary record of British burning Quaker
        homes, 99
    on exiled Quakers, 58
    fearing Patriots' violence in Philadel-
        phia in advance of British occupa-
        tion, 82
    McKean praised by, 63
    on Philadelphians welcoming British
        occupation, 82
    on scarcity and hardship in occupied
        Philadelphia, 101
    trade with British, 198n19
Mowday, Bruce E., 189n5
Mud Island Battery (now Fort Mifflin,
    outside of Philadelphia), 85–87
Muenchhausen, Friedrich von (Hessian
    aide-de-camp to Howe), 142
Muhlenberg, Frederick (1750–1801, son of
    Henry Melchior), 210n76
Muhlenberg, Henry Melchior
    anti-Quaker animus of, 54, 95
    on British invasion of Philadelphia,
        79–80
    on Continental currency controversy, 37
    on Pennsylvania no longer governed
        by British, but by American govern-
        ment, 150
    on Philadelphia churches used for garri-
        sons and hospitals by British, 85–86
    on Philadelphia meetinghouses spared
        by British, 86
    on Quaker peace mission meeting with
        Washington, 95

on Quaker recruits joining British
    Army, 89
on rescue expected by Quakers from
    caravan en route to exile, 60
Murdock, Samuel (non-Quaker), on hos-
    tiles list, 192n9
Musser, John, 77

Nash, Gary B., 7, 187n37, 199n8, 199n10
national security threat
    civil liberties in conflict with (see habeas
        corpus rights)
    concept developed from founding of
        United States, 45
    exile to quell, 7, 11, 33, 142, 147
    Quakers's tenet of pacifism and non-
        recognition (1777–78) of Ameri-
        can government authority as, 3–4,
        11, 13–14, 44–45, 57, 69, 96, 145, 147,
        192n27, 194n41
    straddlers as, 54–55
Native Americans
    Henry Drinker's support for treaty talks
        with, 160
    Israel Pemberton and, 16, 17f
    Quakers criticizing colonists' killing
        of, 19
Nesbitt, Alexander, 58
New York City, British occupation of, 23
    fire during, 80, 197n5
Nicola, Lewis (town major)
    Bryan letter to, ordering arrests of hos-
        tiles, 61
    on inadequate supply of wagons to
        transport all hostiles, 189n72
    in militia executing arrests of Quakers,
        48–49, 51
North, Lord (British prime minister), 109

oath of allegiance requirement
    affirmation as alternative to swearing of
        oath, 38, 190n32
    Anglican cleric's refusal to take oath,
        195n24
    arresting party offering parole instead
        of arrest to Quakers, 49, 50, 52,
        192n9
    Banishing Law (Pennsylvania, 1777)
        requiring oath for release of putative
        offender, 62

oath of allegiance requirement (*continued*)
  disenfranchisement for failure to com-
    ply, 27, 106, 148
  exile justified on refusal to sign oath,
    56, 111–12
  fidelity to new state of Pennsylvania and
    disavowal of king, 26
  hearing denied based on refusal to sign
    oath, 54
  Mennonites' refusal to swear, 149
  offered to exiles in 1778 as condition for
    release, 111–12
  Penn's stand on, 38, 190n32
  Quakers' refusal to swear or affirm, 6,
    21, 38–39, 49
  usefulness of Quakers who took oath,
    73
  See also Test Act
Ousterhout, Anne M., 52, 64
Overseer of the Poor, Charles Jervis as, 162

pacifism
  American Revolution and, 2
  conscientious scruples and, 153
  disownment of Quakers for violating
    tenet of, 19
  forced military recruitment of Quakers
    ended by Washington, 66
  of German sectarians, 22–23, 149
  Patriots targeting religious sects for,
    149
  PYM letter to President Washington
    stating Quaker commitment to, 152
  Quaker faith tenet, 5, 18–19, 24, 31
    (*see also* aid and support to military;
    refusal to bear arms)
  shaming Quakers and other pacifist
    sects, 9, 23
Paine, Thomas
  accusations against John Pemberton,
    25–26, 159
  The American Crisis, 25–26
  on Battle of Fort Mercer, 88
  bias against Quakers, 13, 24–26
  Common Sense, 24
  in Patriot inner circle, 48
  punishment of Quakers, advocating for,
    25–26
Paoli Massacre (September 20–21, 1777),
  84

Parke, Thomas (physician, son-in-law of
    James Pemberton)
  arrest for visiting exiles without permis-
    sion, 115
  correspondence with Jabez Maud
    Fisher, 109
  medical treatment of Henry Drinker,
    116
Parrish, John (1728–1807)
  imprisoned in Lancaster, 111
  oath of allegiance taken by, 73
  petition from exiled men (January 23,
    1778) joined by, 108
  Roberts's death penalty, petitioning
    SEC members to show mercy for, 147
  silhouette of, 74f
  on softening of exiles' opponents, 122
  visiting and offering support to exiles in
    Winchester, 73–75
Paschall, Benjamin, 51
Paxton Boys, 20
peace mission sent by PYM to army com-
    manders, 89, 90–96
  dangers involved in, 91, 93
  Elizabeth Drinker on Emlen's report
    about, 96
  Howe and, 89, 91–93, 95–96
  legacy of, 96, 200n35
  Mifflin's recollection of, 92–93
  Nash on, 199n8, 199n10
  PYM instructions to, 90–91
  PYM members appointed to delega-
    tion, 90
  report on Howe meeting, 93
  report on Washington meeting, 94
  Washington and, 89, 93–96
Peale, Charles Willson
  in militia executing arrests of Quakers,
    48, 50–51
  Philadelphia Museum of, 153
  as portrait painter, 49
  on SEC committee to compile list of
    suspects for arrest, 48
  written account of Quaker arrests by, 50
Pemberton, Hannah Zane (John's wife),
  73, 74, 100
Pemberton, Israel (1715–1779)
  arrest of, 50
  called "King Wampum" or "King of the
    Quakers," 16, 17, 155, 186n7

Quaker archive as source on American Revolution period, 7

Quaker faith
adherence during caravan to exile, 64–65
adherence during confinement in Winchester, 2, 69, 117
affirmation form used in, 38
belief of inward light in all human beings, 18
disownment of lax members, 20
duties to God on higher plane than to government, 20, 31
English treatment of (late 1600s), 19, 38, 187n12
founding during English Civil War, 38
Fox as founder of, 18
governmental authority and, 19
lay ministers in, 186n6
Mather's condemnation of, 44
named for reaction to words of God, 18
pacifism in, 5, 18–19, 24, 31
Penn setting up colony for in America, 13, 19, 154
political dogma of, 31
public shaming of Quakers for pacifism, 9, 23

Quaker rebellion, 15–30
comparison of Quakers with other pacifist sects, 21–23
hostiles lists kept by Patriots, 28–29
hypocrisy of Quakers alleged by Presbyterians, 20
refusal to celebrate fast date declared by Patriots, 29
refusal to celebrate Independence Day, 29
refusal to donate blankets (see aid and support to military)
See also refusal to bear arms; substitute tax or fine in lieu of military service

Quaker refusals
Boston, refusal to contribute to relief money for, 32
Continental currency, 33–37 (see also Continental currency, refusal to accept)
government jobs or voluntary public service, refusal to participate in, 32

Meeting for Sufferings (PYM) letter to Birmingham Friends Meeting (Chester County) on unacceptable behaviors, 32–33
new state's authority, refusal to recognize, 31–32 (see also illegitimacy of Patriot-established government; oath of allegiance requirement)
See also aid and support to military; oath of allegiance requirement; refusal to bear arms; substitute tax or fine in lieu of military service

Quakers. See arrests; caravan journey to exile; hostiles lists; Pennsylvania Quakers; release of exiles; Virginia exile; women's mission; other headings starting with "Quaker"
quartering of British soldiers. See British occupation of Philadelphia

Rahway, New Jersey, 42, 191n2
See also Spanktown Annual Meeting
Rawle, Anna (Loyalist Quaker), 150
Reading, Pennsylvania
on caravan route to exile, 60, 65
Zane, Sr., visiting exiled Quakers at, 74
Red Scare of late 1940s and early 1950s, 11
Reed, Joseph (Patriot lawyer, second president of SEC)
Elizabeth Drinker consulting with, 137
as prosecutor in Roberts' treason trial, 146
refusal to bear arms
forced military recruitment of Quakers ended by George Washington, 66
German Baptist Brethren, 22
Mennonites, 21
Mifflin punished for, 28
militia exemption based on age, 188n42
Moravians, 22
pacifism required of Quakers, 5, 13, 18–19, 24, 31
Patriots' toleration of Quaker position, 18
Quakers in French and Indian War (1754–63), 5, 19, 20
Schwenkfelder sect, 22
release of exiles
arrival of exiles in Lancaster, 138–39
arrival of exiles in Philadelphia, 141

Smith, William, D.D. (Provost)
    anti-Quaker animus of, 189n72
    as Loyalist, evidence of, 189n72
    recruited by Franklin to be first provost
        of Academy and College of Philadel-
        phia, 189n72
Smith, William (broker, before 1742–after
    1805)
    charged and released second time for
        alleged inimical behavior, 161
    Continental currency refusal and,
        189n11
    as exiled Quaker, 30
    friendships with Jervis and Drinker
        families, 161
    payment for room and board in exile,
        67
    post-exile life of, 161
    seldom mentioned in exile records,
        71
Smith, William Drewet
    British POWs treated by, 72
    disowned by Quakers, 30, 156
    escape from exile and joining Brit-
        ish Army, 72, 76, 141, 156–57,
        196n32
    exiled with Quakers, 30, 188n72
    as outsider among exiled men, 72,
        76
    payment for room and board in exile,
        67
    post-war in London, 156
    reward for capture of, 196n31
    self-exile to Canada, 157
Spain
    alliance with America during Revolu-
        tionary War, 112
    as U.S. funding source in Revolution-
        ary War, 34
Spanktown, New Jersey, battles at, 40
Spanktown Papers
    committee appointed to review, 43–45,
        49
    committee's conclusory report to Con-
        gress, 45
    congressional reaction to, 42–43
    false on their face, 41–42, 46, 191n8
    Sarah Logan Fisher engaged in discur-
        sive rebuttal of, 120
    newspaper publication of, 41–42, 191n4

originals of, 191n4
    peace mission objective to rebut charges
        based on, 90, 94
    Philadelphia Quakers refuting authen-
        ticity of, 41–42, 120
    as pretext for arrests, 4, 45–46
    release of exiles without absolving them
        of implicit charges from, 138
    Sullivan reporting to Continental Con-
        gress, 2, 40–42, 45, 120
Spanktown Yearly Meeting (Rahway, New
    Jersey), 40, 42
Stamp Act (1765), 20
    boycott against, 201n13
Stansbury, Joseph, 37
Staunton, Virginia
    move of exiles from Winchester to,
        under consideration, 77, 107–9, 111
    original place designated for exile, 60,
        74
Stedman, Margaret (wife of William
    Drewet Smith), 156
Stenton mansion (former home of James
    Logan)
    as Howe's headquarters, 89, 91
    as Washington's headquarters, 199n6
Stephen, Adam (Winchester physician),
    117–18, 204n21
Stern, T. Noel, 190n33
Story, Enoch (assistant commissioner to
    Galloway)
    attempting to protect wives of exiles
        from quartering British officers, 103,
        104
    with British soldiers entering Philadel-
        phia (September 26, 1777), 82
    departure from Philadelphia, 144
    in London after war, 156
    treason charge, 197n12
straddlers (neither Patriots nor Loyalists),
    4, 54–55
substitute tax or fine in lieu of military
    service
    German Baptist Brethren paying, 22
    Mennonites paying, 21
    Moravians paying, 22
    Pennsylvania Assembly (1776) demand-
        ing from Quakers, 26
    Quakers expected to pay, 105
    Quakers refusing to pay, 26

Wharton, Thomas, Jr. (1735–1778, SEC
    President)
  abstaining from SEC arrest order, 192n6
  blamed by cousin Thomas, Sr., for exile,
    71, 156
  British capture of Philadelphia, broad-
    side warning of, 79
  death of, 147
  John Hunt's death, responsibility for,
    205n27
  as nemesis of Quaker exiles, 24, 71
  ordering exiles to be released, 134
  on Philadelphia preparation for British
    invasion, 23–24, 40
  seeking renewed state jurisdiction over
    exiles, 133
  George Washington's letter on behalf of
    women's mission to, 128, 131
  on Winchester as location for exile, 60
  women's mission's audience with, 134,
    138
Wharton School of the University of
    Pennsylvania, 158
Whelen, Israel (former Quaker as Conti-
    nental currency commissioner), 35,
    190n19
Whidbee, Paige L.: "Quaker Exiles,"
    186n13
White, Alexander (attorney)
  futility of dealing with Congress
    reported by, 111
  hired by exiled Quakers to seek
    relief from Congress and SEC, 77,
    107
  petition to Congress for release of exiled
    men, 115
  report of discord among congressio-
    nal delegates over continuation of
    exile, 108
Williams, Moses (Black silhouette art-
    ist), 153
Willing, Thomas (1731–1821, of Quaker
    descent)
  advising Philadelphia residents during
    British occupation, 82
  voting against Declaration of Indepen-
    dence and refusing to take oath of
    allegiance, 197–98n18
Wilson, James (lawyer), 146, 209n46

Wilson, Robert H., 192n1
Winchester, Virginia
  British prisoners of war housed in, 66,
    67
  Bush's inn as first quarters of exiled
    men in, 67, 113
  description of (1777), 66–67
  dispersal of exiled men to homes of
    individual Quakers in area, 113, 114f
  hostility toward Quakers in, 66
  as location of exile, 1, 5, 60, 66–67, 74
    (see also Virginia exile)
  See also Virginia exile
women's mission, 8, 120–36, 200n35
  conditions for exoneration, objecting
    to, 137–42
  consideration of idea put forth by Suky
    Jones, 120–23
  departure of women's caravan, 127
  encounter with Isaac Penington and
    Charles Logan at Valley Forge, 132
  first collective political action by
    women (possibly) in new republic
    and/or in state of Pennsylvania, 126
  Howe granting permission to leave Phil-
    adelphia, 124, 204n17
  learning of release and continuing to
    seek release details, 132, 137
  letter of introduction to George Wash-
    ington, 124, 128
  Matlack and, 135, 138
  Israel Morris accompanying, 126, 127
  participants in, 122–28, 135
  permission needed from George Wash-
    ington to return to occupied Phila-
    delphia, 139
  petition drafted and signed by women
    (April 1778), 123–25, 181–84
  reunion with exiled men in Lancaster
    (see release of exiles)
  SEC refusing to meet with, 135, 183
  selection of women to carry petition to
    government officials, 124
  similar petitions in colonial Massachu-
    setts, 205n24
  socializing in Lancaster with disowned
    Quakers and Patriots, 207n37
  traveling to Lancaster to petition SEC,
    8, 124, 127, 131–35